THE VOICE OF A CHILD IN FAMILY LAW DISPUTES

The Voice of a Child in Family Law Disputes

PATRICK PARKINSON
JUDY CASHMORE
Faculty of Law, University of Sydney, Australia

OXFORD
UNIVERSITY PRESS

OXFORD

UNIVERSITY PRESS

Great Clarendon Street, Oxford OX2 6DP

Oxford University Press is a department of the University of Oxford.
It furthers the University's objective of excellence in research, scholarship,
and education by publishing worldwide in

Oxford New York

Auckland Cape Town Dar es Salaam Hong Kong Karachi
Kuala Lumpur Madrid Melbourne Mexico City Nairobi
New Delhi Shanghai Taipei Toronto

With offices in

Argentina Austria Brazil Chile Czech Republic France Greece
Guatemala Hungary Italy Japan Poland Portugal Singapore
South Korea Switzerland Thailand Turkey Ukraine Vietnam

Oxford is a registered trade mark of Oxford University Press
in the UK and in certain other countries

Published in the United States
by Oxford University Press Inc., New York

© P. Parkinson and J. Cashmore, 2008

The moral rights of the authors have been asserted

Crown copyright material is reproduced under Class Licence
Number C01P0000148 with the permission of OPSI
and the Queen's Printer for Scotland

Database right Oxford University Press (maker)

First published 2008

British Library Cataloguing in Publication Data

Data available

Library of Congress Cataloging in Publication Data

Data available

Typeset by Newgen Imaging Systems (P) Ltd., Chennai, India
Printed in Great Britain on acid-free paper by
the MPG Books Group, Bodmin and King's Lynn

ISBN 978–0–19–923779–1

3 5 7 9 10 8 6 4 2

Preface

This book is on children's voices concerning their experiences and involvement in the decisions that are made about them after their parents separate. Without the children's willingness to participate in our study, and that of their parents, and of other parents, this book would not have been possible. We acknowledge and appreciate their contribution and have done our best to ensure that our representation of their views is faithful to what they have told us.

This book also explores the perspectives of the professionals involved in such matters – the mediators, counsellors, lawyers and judges. We also acknowledge and appreciate their cooperation and thoughtfulness concerning the issues.

We also acknowledge the sterling contribution of Judi Single, our research associate, who travelled to the children's and parents' homes to conduct most of the interviews and follow-up interviews, kept in contact with the families in between, and also conducted most of the interviews with the counsellors and mediators. She also provided a great deal of other research and administrative support to the project.

We are grateful also to Richard Crallan, who conducted most of the lawyers' interviews. Tharini Mudaliar and Karen Bevan also conducted some interviews with the lawyers and mediators respectively. Tharini Mudaliar also did some research for the project on children's participation in other jurisdictions. We appreciate their contributions. We recruited all the parents and children through writing to lawyers asking them to forward information about the project to their clients. The support of family lawyers for this project was considerable and we are very appreciative of their assistance.

Other colleagues have also contributed in various ways via their work and writings, through discussions, or comments on draft chapters: Richard Chisholm, Carol Smart, Bren Neale, Jacqueline Goodnow; Nicola Taylor and Anne Smith (from the Children's Issues Centre at the University of Otago); Anne Graham and Robyn Fitzgerald (the Centre for Children and Young People at Southern Cross University, Lismore); and Gillian Douglas and her colleagues at Cardiff University. The interviews were transcribed by a small army of transcribers, to whom we also express our gratitude.

We also wish to acknowledge the important contribution, early in the project, of Dr Clare Wilson. She was originally a chief investigator on the project, and was instrumental in developing the computer-assisted interview program for children. Her departure to take up a position in Britain meant that she could no longer remain involved with the project. We are grateful for her collaboration in the conceptualisation of the project and in its very early stages.

Finally, the research on which this book was based was funded by the Australian Research Council under its Discovery Projects funding scheme (project number DP0210133). We are grateful to the Council and to the Australian Government for the funding that made this research possible.

Patrick Parkinson
Judy Cashmore
October 2008

Contents

1

The Debate About Children's Voices

This book is about a dilemma: how to protect children from the conflict between their parents when there are major disputes about post-separation parenting, while also giving children an opportunity to express their views about those arrangements.

Children are at risk of significant psychological harm when parents separate. For most, that risk does not lead to long-term adverse consequences. Children weather the storm. They adjust to the post-separation circumstances. However, parental separation leaves its imprint, and changes the course of children's lives.[1] Children may feel a profound sense of loss that lasts for years, but 'poor outcomes are far from inevitable'.[2]

A minority of children will be deeply affected by their parents' separation and will suffer long-term adverse consequences.[3] The consistent message of research has been that it is the parental conflict—both before and after the separation— that is most harmful to children.[4] When parents are involved in litigation over

---

[1] Hetherington, M E, 'Should we Stay Together for the Sake of the Children?' in M E Hetherington (ed), *Coping with Divorce, Single Parenting and Remarriage: A Risk and Resiliency Perspective* (Lawrence Erlbaum, 1999) pp 93–116; Amato, P, 'The Consequences of Divorce for Adults and Children' (2000) 62 *Journal of Marriage and Family* 1269–1287; Amato, P, 'Children of Divorce in the 1990s: An Update of the Amato and Keith (1991) Meta-Analysis' (2001) 15 *Journal of Family Psychology* 355–370; Pryor, J and B Rodgers, *Children in Changing Families: Life after Parental Separation* (Blackwell, 2001); Schick, A, 'Behavioral and Emotional Differences between Children of Divorce and Children from Intact Families: Clinical Significance and Mediating Processes' (2002) 61 *Swiss Journal of Psychology* 5–14; Kelly, J B and R E Emery, 'Children's Adjustment Following Divorce: Risk and Resilience Perspectives' (2003) 52 *Family Relations* 352–362; Ruschena, E, M Prior, A Sanson, and D Smart, 'A Longitudinal Study of Adolescent Adjustment Following Family Transitions' (2005) 46 *Journal of Child Psychology and Psychiatry* 353–363.

[2] Rodgers, B and J Pryor, *Divorce and Separation: The Outcomes for Children* (Joseph Rowntree Foundation, 1998) pp 4–5; Laumann-Billings, L and R Emery, 'Distress among Young Adults from Divorced Families' (2000) 14 *Journal of Family Psychology* 671–687; also Amato, P R and J M Sobolewski, 'The Effects of Divorce and Marital Discord on Adult Children's Psychological Well-Being' (2001) 66 *American Sociological Review* 900–921.

[3] Hetherington, M E and J Kelly, *For Better or for Worse: Divorce Reconsidered* (W W Norton & Company, 2002).

[4] Simons, R L, L B Whitbeck, J Beaman, and R D Conger, 'The Impact of Mother's Parenting, Involvement by Nonresidential Fathers, and Parental Conflict on the Adjustment of Adolescent Children' (1994) 56 *Journal of Marriage and Family* 356–374; Lamb, M E, R Sternberg, and R A Thompson, 'The Effects of Divorce and Custody Arrangements on Children's Behavior,

their children, there is likely to be intense conflict, and the more so, the further the matter progresses in the litigation process. While in jurisdictions around the Western world, the focus of the court is on the best interests of the child, it is frequently the case that parenting disputes are prosecuted through allegation and counter-allegation, with an emphasis on the deficiencies of the other parent. Even if the matter settles without the need for a trial, written evidence may have been prepared, witnesses lined up, and adversarial positions taken.

1.1 The Protective Approach to Children

What place is there in this process for the children? Should they be given seats to the boxing match, or invited into the ring? Or rather should they be excluded from the venue? In the past, the most common response to this issue around the world has been that the courts should seek to protect the children from the conflict as far as possible. While practices differ between jurisdictions, it is generally very unusual for children to be called to give evidence in parenting proceedings, in contrast to the situation in criminal trials when the prosecution alleges that the child has been a victim of a crime or a witness to one.

This protective stance towards children does not, of course, mean that their voices cannot be heard in the process of decision-making nor that their wishes are unimportant. Children's wishes have typically been one of the factors that courts have been required to consider in many jurisdictions in making determinations about children's welfare. The protective approach does, however, mean that children are shielded as far as possible from being drawn into the conflict.[5]

The development of Family Courts and the involvement of social-science trained professionals in custody evaluation, conciliation and other such roles as part of the process of court-based dispute resolution has made it more possible for children to be shielded from direct involvement. One change that occurred in many jurisdictions, for example, was in relation to the practice of judges interviewing older children in chambers to find out what they wanted in relation to custody disputes. This was an accepted practice in common law countries for many years.[6] While in some jurisdictions, that continues to be a common

Development, and Adjustment' (1997) 35 *Family and Conciliation Courts Review* 393–404; McIntosh, J, 'Enduring Conflict in Parental Separation: Pathways of Impact on Child Development' (2003) 9 *Journal of Family Studies* 63–80.

[5] The cautious, protective approach towards the involvement of children in decision-making is illustrated by the Family Law Act 1975 in Australia. This provides that while any views expressed by a child are to be taken into account, neither the Court nor any other person is permitted to require the child to express his or her views in relation to the matter: Family Law Act 1975, s 60CE.

[6] Jones, J C, 'Judicial Questioning of Children in Custody and Visitation Proceedings' (1984) 18 *Family Law Quarterly* 43–91; Scott, E S, N D Reppucci, and M Aber, 'Children's Preferences in Adjudicated Custody Decisions' (1988) 22 *Georgia Law Review* 1035–1078; Raitt, F E, 'Judicial Discretion and Methods of Ascertaining the Views of a Child' (2004) 16 *Child and Family Law*

practice,[7] the accepted view in most modern common law jurisdictions became that it was better to rely on the work of trained experts to interview children and to interpret their wishes and feelings to the court.

The appointment of a separate legal representative for children has been another way in which children's voices can potentially be heard without direct involvement. However, whether they are in fact heard through their lawyer may depend on whether the lawyer sees it as his or her role to talk directly with the child.

1.2 Views on the Capacities of Children

A protective approach to children is not the only reason why children's voices have either not been heard at all in parenting proceedings, or have been heard indirectly through a custody evaluator or other report writer. Another issue which has prevented children's views being given significant weight in parenting disputes has been a belief that children, especially prior to their adolescence, do not have the capacity to make reasoned choices about important matters. This is, of course, another reason for the protective stance taken towards their involvement. As Pryor and Emery put it: 'The received view is that children are not able to say anything sensible until about the age of twelve.'[8]

The law has typically treated issues of children's capacity as a matter involving a binary choice.[9] Either the child has the capacity to give sworn evidence or he or she does not.[10] Either the child understood the wrongfulness of his or her criminal conduct with the consequence that he or she should be held criminally responsible for his or her actions, or he or she did not.[11] Either the child has the

---

Quarterly 151–164; Hale, B, 'Children's Participation in Family Law Decision-Making: Lessons from Abroad' (2006) 20 *Australian Journal of Family Law* 119–126.

[7] Atwood, B, 'The Child's Voice in Custody Litigation: An Empirical Survey and Suggestions for Reform' (2003) 45 *Arizona Law Review* 629–690; Starnes, C, 'Swords in the Hands of Babes: Rethinking Custody Interviews after Troxel' (2003) *Wisconsin Law Review* 115–169; Davies, C, 'Access to Justice for Children: The Voice of the Child in Custody and Access' (2004) 22 *Canadian Family Law Quarterly* 153–175.

[8] Pryor, J and R Emery, 'Children of Divorce' in P Pufall and R Unsworth (eds), *Rethinking Childhood* (Rutgers University Press, 2004) p 171.

[9] King, M and C Piper, *How the Law Thinks about Children* (Ashgate, 1995).

[10] For a review of the traditional position at common law, see Spencer, J R and R H Flin, *The Evidence of Children: The Law and the Psychology* (Blackstone Press, 1990).

[11] At common law, a child over the age of criminal responsibility, but under a certain age, typically 14 years, was presumed to be not capable of understanding the wrongfulness of his actions with the consequence that the prosecution had to prove that understanding in order to succeed in a criminal prosecution. This is known as the presumption of *doli incapax*. In England, it was abolished by the Crime and Disorder Act 1998. The provisions on capacity vary from one country to another. For a comparison of Sweden and South Africa, see Johansson, K and T Palm, 'Children in Trouble with the Law: Child Justice in Sweden and South Africa' (2003) 17 *International Journal of Law, Policy and the Family* 308–337.

capacity to make a medical decision or he or she does not.[12] If he or she has the capacity, then it is his or her decision. If he or she does not, then it is the parents' decision. A similar approach was taken in civil law countries. In Denmark, for example, children had a right to be heard in parenting proceedings once they reached the age of 12 years. An age threshold had to be crossed before children attained a status that gave them participation rights. This right has in recent years been extended to younger children.[13]

This binary view of children's capacities is at odds with the understanding that developmental psychologists have of how children's capacities develop over time. As theory and research have developed, the earlier age- and stage-related constructs of development and 'incompetence' are now considered to be out of date.[14] As developmental psychologist Lawrence points out, development now needs to be seen in terms of 'the multiple levels of change that is the normal human experience, the multiple functions affected by developmental change, and the multiple contributors to developmental change and their interactions'.[15] Children's development is dynamic, interactional and profoundly affected by their experiences and relationships with those who are significant in their lives, and by their perceptions of and reactions to those experiences and relationships. Children are also now seen to be more competent earlier than previously thought,[16] though adults still tend to underestimate children's capacities. Their capacities are affected by the context and depend on the support they receive in developing that capacity and the extent to which they are allowed to participate in making decisions. As Smith, Taylor and Tapp point out, 'children who are involved in activities before they are fully competent actually acquire more competence in the process'.[17]

1.3 Children as Participants

These notions about children in the legal arena have begun to change in the last few years. The new rhetoric is about the importance of children's participation, and family law jurisdictions in different parts of the world are now exploring how children's voices can better be heard in the legal process. In France, for example,

---

[12] *Gillick v West Norfolk & Wisbech Area Health Authority* [1986] AC 112.

[13] Kronborg, A and I L Svendsen, 'Children's Right to be Heard: The Interplay between Human Rights and National Law' in P Lødrup and E Modvar (eds), *Family Life and Human Rights* (Gyldendal Akademisk, 2004) pp 405–416.

[14] Greene, S, 'Child Development: Old Themes, New Directions' in M Woodhead, D Faulkner and K Littleton (eds), *Making Sense of Social Development* (Routledge and Open University Press, 1999) pp 250–268; Lawrence, J, 'The Developing Child and the Law' in G Monahan and L Young (eds), *Children and the Law in Australia* (Lexis Nexis, 2008) pp 83–104.

[15] Lawrence, n 14 above, p 90.

[16] Lawrence, n 14 above, p 90.

[17] Smith, A B, N Taylor, and P Tapp, 'Rethinking Children's Involvement in Decision-Making after Parental Separation' (2003) 10 *Childhood* 203–218.

legislation was passed in 2007 which gives children the right to be heard by the judge if they so choose.[18] This is intended to be the normal way in which a child will be heard, with an interview by another professional such as a child psychologist being utilized only if it is in the best interests of the child to be heard this way. The judge must also examine whether a refusal by the child to be heard is well founded.[19]

In Britain, a government minister has called for greater participation by children in family law decision-making[20] and two of the country's most senior judges have encouraged the idea that judges should talk directly with children more frequently in determining parenting cases.[21] In Australia, a variety of approaches have been trialed to make decision-making in family law disputes more child-inclusive.[22] In particular, there has been great interest in the practice of child-inclusive mediation, in which the views of the children, interviewed separately, are fed back to the parents.[23] This has shown distinct benefits for both parents and children in comparison with forms of mediation that do not involve hearing from the children.[24]

Why has this change occurred now? Debate about the role of children's wishes in making decisions about their custody and access—as it was called at that

---

[18] Loi n° 2007-293 of 5 March 2007. Available at: http://www.legifrance.gouv.fr/WAspad/UnTexteDeJorf?numjo=SANX0600056L.

[19] Article 388-1 of the Civil Code now provides following these amendments: 'In all proceedings relating to him, a minor capable of discernment may, without prejudice to the provisions as to his intervention or consent, be heard by the judge or, where his welfare requires, by the person appointed by the judge for that purpose.

This hearing is by way of right where the minor so requests. Where the minor refuses to be heard, the judge must determine whether such refusal is well founded. He may be heard alone, with a lawyer or a person of his choice. Where that choice does not appear to be consonant with the welfare of the child, the judge may appoint another person.'

[20] Harman, H, 'Listening to Children: In Open and Accountable Family Courts' speech at *Care and Health/CAFCASS Conference 'Opening Up the Family Courts: An Open or Closed Case?'* (Millenium Mayfair Hotel, London, 30 October 2006). Available at: http://www.dca.gov.uk/speeches/2006/sp061030b.htm. For a review of the British literature concerning listening to children in family law disputes, see O'Quigley, A, *Listening to Children's Views: The Findings and Recommendations of Recent Research* (Joseph Rowntree Foundation, 2000).

[21] Hale, n 6 above; Potter, M, 'The Family in the 21st Century' paper given at *17th World Congress of the International Association of Youth and Family Judges and Magistrates* (Belfast, 28 August 2006). Available at: http://www.judiciary.gov.uk/publications_media/speeches/2006/sp280806.htm.

[22] Moloney, L and J McIntosh, 'Child-Responsive Practices in Australian Family Law: Past Problems and Future Directions' (2004) 10 *Journal of Family Studies* 71–86; Bryant, D, 'The Role of the Family Court in Promoting Child-Centred Practice' (2006) 20 *Australian Journal of Family Law* 127–144.

[23] McIntosh, J, 'Child-Inclusive Divorce Mediation: Report on a Qualitative Research Study' (2000) 18 *Mediation Quarterly* 55–69; Grimes, A and J McIntosh, 'Emerging Practice in Child-Inclusive Divorce Mediation' (2004) 10 *Journal of Family Studies* 113–120.

[24] McIntosh, J and C Long, *Children Beyond Dispute: A Prospective Study Of Outcomes from Child Focused and Child Inclusive Post-Separation Family Dispute Resolution* (Final Report to the Attorney-General's Department, 2006). Available at: http://www.ag.gov.au/www/agd/agd.nsf/Page/Publications_ChildrenBeyondDispute-October2006.

time—is not new. In the 1960s and 1970s, there was a lively debate between those who advocated for children's wishes being determinative and those who took a much more protective stance, arguing that they should not be given too much weight or even any weight at all. In one of the earliest law articles, Foster and Freed argued that:[25]

At least where the pertinent factors are evenly balanced, the child's wishes should be decisive unless the person chosen by the child is obviously unfit or the child's choice is the result of coercion or bribery.

Citing the American Orthopsychiatric Association's 1967 *Position Statement on Child Custody*, Jenkins, a professor of child psychiatry in the US, advocated trusting children's preferences in his advice to expert witnesses on children's cases:[26]

Respect the preceptiveness [sic] of the children in recognizing which parent really cares more about them, and which parent is more dependable. Even in infancy and early childhood it is possible to note the response of confidence and security or fear to the parent persons. While older children often have some apprehension or fear about expressing a preference between their parents, and some insist on walking a tight-rope and expressing no preference, yet in a private interview, after the establishment of some rapport, a few simple questions directed to the child alone usually clarifies this question...Children are less experienced than adults in judging people, but in general, children study their parents more intently and intensively than parents study their children.

Similarly, Lempp, a medical practitioner, argued that an attempt should be made to establish the child's wishes or 'inclinations' in every case, believing the child's welfare to be 'at risk whenever the child is reduced to an object and whenever decisions are made against his will for no compelling reason'.[27]

On the other hand, some lawyers and child psychologists and psychiatrists argued that the wishes of children under certain ages (variously 10, 12 or 14 years) should be given little weight or that they should not be ascertained or considered.[28]

Despite the vigorous debate that occurred during the 1960s and 1970s, the issues associated with children's competence to be involved in decision-making,

[25] Foster, H H and D J Freed, 'Child Custody (Part One)' (1964) 39 *New York University Law Review* 423–443.

[26] Jenkins, R L, 'Maxims in Child Custody Cases' (1977) 26 *The Family Coordinator* 385–389, at 386.

[27] Lempp, R, 'Child Welfare and the Law: A Medical and Psychiatric Viewpoint' in F Bates (ed), *The Child and the Law: The Proceedings of the First World Conference of the International Society on Family Law, Berlin, 1975* (Dobbs Ferry, 1976) vol 1, cited by Lutzyk, A, 'Investigation of Children's Custodial Wishes' (1979) 14 *Australian Journal of Social Issues* 218–229, at 219.

[28] Blaine, G B, 'The Effect of Divorce Upon the Personality Development of Children and Youth' in E A Grollman (ed), *Explaining Divorce to Children* (Beacon, 1969); Allen, J, 'Child Custody—Some Aspects of the Problem' in P E Nygh (ed), *Seminar on the Problems of Child Custody* (Sydney University Law Graduates Association Family Law Committee, 1972); Littner, N, 'The Effects on a Child of Family Disruption and Separation from One or Both Parents' (1973) 11 *Reports of Family Law* 1–15.

especially in family law, received relatively little attention in the literature until the 1990s. There are two related reasons for the more recent interest in children's participation: a shift in developmental views of children and a shift in thinking about children's rights and citizenship.

1.3.1 Understanding children as social actors

There has been a distinct shift over the last few decades in thinking about children in both psychology and sociology and in the new area of developmental science.[29] Children are no longer seen as the passive recipients of parental influence, the targets of socialization within and outside the family nor as 'objects of concern'[30] in relation to outside intervention. They are now seen as social actors who are shaping their own lives, and influencing the lives of those around them, particularly their parents and siblings. This change has occurred as it has become increasingly apparent that children's development is profoundly affected by their interaction with other people and that their learning benefits from their participation.

This new paradigm in the emergent sociology of childhood represents a break away from the earlier construction of children and childhood in sociology.[31] At the same time, the construction of children's agency in developmental psychology[32] has also changed (building on the earlier transactional models,[33] bidirectional models of parent-child relationships and the importance of the broader social context in children's development).[34] As Kuczynski pointed out, there is 'a long tradition within developmental psychology of exploring both behavioral

---

[29] Lawrence, n 14 above.

[30] Smart, C, A Wade, and B Neale, 'Objects of Concern'?—Children and Divorce' (1999) 11 *Child and Family Law Quarterly* 365–376.

[31] Durkheim, E, *Durkheim: Essays on Morals and Education* (Routledge and Kegan Paul, 1979); James, A and A Prout (eds), *Constructing and Reconstructing Childhood: Contemporary Issues in the Sociological Study of Childhood* (The Falmer Press, 1997; 2nd ed); Morrow, V, 'Perspectives on Children's Agency Within Families' in L Kuczynski (ed), *Handbook of Dynamics in Parent-Child Relations* (Sage Publications, 2003) pp 109–129.

[32] Cummings, E M and A C Schermerhorn, 'A Developmental Perspective on Children as Agents in the Family' in L Kuczynski (ed), *Handbook of Dynamics in Parent-Child Relations* (Sage Publications, 2003) pp 91–108; Kuczynski, L, 'Beyond Bidirectionality: Bilateral Conceptual Frameworks for Understanding Dynamics in Parent-Child Relations' in L Kuczynski (ed), *Handbook of Dynamics in Parent-Child Relations* (Sage Publications, 2003) pp 3–24.

[33] Sameroff, A, 'Transactional Models in Early Social Relations' (1975) 18 *Human Development* 65–79; Sameroff, A, 'The Social Context of Development' in M Woodhead, R Carr and P Light (eds), *Becoming a Person: Child Development in Social Context* (Taylor & Francis/Routledge, 1991) vol 1, pp 167–189.

[34] Bronfenbrenner, U, *The Ecology of Human Development: Experiments by Nature and Design* (Harvard University Press, 1979); Goodnow, J J, 'Parenting and the "Transmission" and "Internalization" of Values: From Social-Cultural Perspectives to Within-Family Analyses' in J E Grusec and L Kuczynski (eds), *Handbook of Parenting and the Transmission of Values* (Wiley, 1997) pp 333–361.

and cognitive aspects of children's agency in socialization, moral development, and parent-child relations'.[35]

Earlier assumptions about children's capacities and presumed incompetence are being challenged as it is recognized that children's competence depends not so much on their age as on the context, the support they receive, and the way activities are structured.[36] What children can and cannot do depends on the structure and support—the 'scaffolding'—provided by those with more skills and understanding. The onus is therefore on adults to guide and assist rather than presume that any incompetence is necessarily the child's alone.[37] Kaltenborn put it succinctly: 'the competence of the child is not just the skill of the child but "a way of relating" and requires to be considered in context'.[38] He went on to expand on this:[39]

Children's agency is not just an age-related skill but a complex one constituted by personal characteristics of the child on the one hand, and by structural conditions such as family characteristics, the availability of social support and the practice of the family justice system on the other, all of which are embedded and influenced by societal macro-systems, especially the legal, cultural, political and economic system.

The way we see children and construe their competence has considerable implications for the way society, the law and other institutions treat them. Along with the increasing recognition of children as social actors, there is now a greater understanding that in resolving disputes about parenting, it is important to work with children in the decision-making process. There seems to be increasing acceptance in some quarters that decisions that people seek to make about children's futures, even those presumed to be made on the basis of 'their best interests', cannot be made without an awareness of how the children themselves will respond to those decisions. That is, the decision-maker needs to weigh up the possible effects of different decisions on the children themselves, for the children are the ones who have to live with those decisions. In addition, children's reactions to the decision may in turn determine whether it was in fact in their best interests. American law professor Mnookin, in a classic article in 1975, explained this feedback problem in the nature of best interests decision-making with respect to the reactions of the parents:[40]

---

[35] Kuczynski, n 32 above, p xii.

[36] Kaltenborn, K-F, 'Individualization, Family Transitions and Children's Agency' (2001) 8 *Childhood* 463–498, at 488; Taylor, N, 'What do We Know about Involving Children and Young People in Family Law Decision Making? A Research Update' (2006) 20 *Australian Journal of Family Law* 154–178, at 160.

[37] Bruner, J S and V Sherwood, 'Peekaboo and the Learning of Rule Structures' in J S Bruner and K Sylva (eds), *Play: Its Role in Development and Evolution* (Penguin Books, 1975); Vygotsky, L S, *Thought and Language* (MIT Press, 1986; 7th printing ed).

[38] Kaltenborn, n 36 above, at 486.

[39] Kaltenborn, n 36 above, at 488.

[40] Mnookin, R H, 'Child-Custody Adjudication: Judicial Functions in the Face of Indeterminacy' (1975) 39 *Law & Contemporary Problems* 226–293, at 252.

The best-interests principle requires a prediction of what will happen in the future, which, of course, depends in part on the future behavior of the parties. Because these parties will often interact in the future, this probable interaction must be taken into account in deciding what the outcome is to be.

The feedback issue is also very significant in relation to children's reactions to different possible orders. An awareness of the importance of hearing the voice of the child has emerged from a recognition that for a decision to 'work' it needs to be one which children are able to accept, even if it was not their preferred option. Kaltenborn's research supports this. In following up children for whom reports had been written for the courts in Germany some years before, Kaltenborn found that ignoring children's preferences and attachments often led to 'a difficult situation for the child . . . trajectories of suffering . . . and/or later changes of the living situation'.[41]

The need to consider the workability of arrangements from children's viewpoints has become particularly important as shared parenting has become more commonplace and has been encouraged by legislatures.[42] Shared parenting usually involves more interaction between the parents than is the case in more traditional custody and access arrangements where the non-resident parent is not involved in the day-to-day lives of the children. It also involves more movement for the children between households. Since children respond in quite varied ways to shared parenting arrangements, it can be particularly important to listen to their views about it and to keep on listening as they grow older.

1.3.2 Understanding children as citizens

The movement towards greater participation by children has also emerged because of a conviction that children *ought* to be able to participate. Notions of children's rights in general have been combined with a new focus on children's social citizenship. This helps to build a moral case for the inclusion of children's views and perspectives in all aspects of adult decision-making that affect them.[43] In many different areas of life there has been a movement to encourage such participation in democratic processes by children. As other groups in society are consulted on various problems, policy initiatives or their experience of services, so advocates

---

[41] Kaltenborn, K-F, 'Children's and Young People's Experiences in Various Residential Arrangements: A Longitudinal Study to Evaluate Criteria for Custody and Residence Decision-Making' (2001) 31 *British Journal of Social Work* 81–117; Kaltenborn, n 36 above.

[42] Rhoades, H, 'The Rise and Rise of Shared Parenting Laws' (2002) 19 *Canadian Journal of Family Law* 75–113; Parkinson, P, 'Family Law and the Indissolubility of Parenthood' (2006) 40 *Family Law Quarterly* 237–280.

[43] Roche, J, 'Children: Rights, Participation and Citizenship' (1999) 6 *Childhood* 475; Jans, M, 'Children as Citizens: Towards a Contemporary Notion of Child Participation' (2004) 11 *Childhood* 27–44; Woodhouse, B, 'Re-Visioning Rights for Children' in P Pufall and R Unsworth (eds), *Rethinking Childhood* (Rutgers University Press, 2004) pp 229–243; Lister, R, 'Why Citizenship: Where, When and How Children?' (2007) 8 *Theoretical Inquiries in Law* 693–718.

for children have argued that children too should be included in this citizenship. These ideas have been extended to a focus on children's citizenship in relation to parenting disputes, reflecting also the changing status of children and the greater democratization of relationships within the family.[44]

Children's right to participate is embedded in the United Nations Convention on the Rights of the Child.[45] Article 12(1) of the Convention provides that states should 'assure to the child who is capable of forming his or her own views the right to express those views freely in all matters affecting the child, the views of the child being given due weight in accordance with the age and maturity of the child'. Article 12(2) specifically concerns court proceedings. It provides that the 'child shall in particular be provided an opportunity to be heard in any judicial and administrative proceedings affecting the child, either directly or through a representative or an appropriate body'. This has been identified as one of four general principles which underpin the more specific rights provided by the Convention.[46]

Article 12 does not specify *how* it is that children's voices should be heard in proceedings that affect them. It does not dictate that children should give evidence, nor that they be separately represented—although those are possible ways in which Article 12 may be given effect. There is nothing inconsistent with Article 12 that the child's voice should be heard through an appropriate social-science trained professional, preparing a report for the court. Nonetheless, Article 12, together with other human rights provisions,[47] has acted as a stimulus to evaluate practices in those jurisdictions that have not hitherto given proper voice to children in parenting disputes as a matter of routine procedure. It has also acted as a rallying cry for children's rights advocates who have been promoting children's

[44] Day Sclater, S and C Piper, 'Social Exclusion and the Welfare of the Child' (2001) 28 *Journal of Law and Society* 409–429; Smart, C, 'Children's Voices' plenary address given at the *25th Anniversary Conference, Justice, Courts & Community: The Continuing Challenge, Family Courts of Australia* (Sydney, Australia, Thursday 26–Sunday 29 July 2001); Neale, B, 'Dialogues with Children: Children, Divorce and Citizenship' (2002) 9 *Childhood* 455–475; Van Krieken, R, 'The "Best Interests of the Child" and Parental Separation: On the "Civilizing of Parents"' (2005) 68 *The Modern Law Review* 25–48.

[45] The United Nations Convention on the Rights of the Child (CRC) is the most highly ratified human rights instrument in international law. The Australian government ratified the Convention in December 1990, the UK and Canada in 1991, and New Zealand in 1993. The US has signed but still not ratified the Convention; apart from Somalia, it is the only country that is party to the UN not to have ratified the Convention.

[46] These four principles are the 'child's right to equal enjoyment of their rights (Art 2), the requirement that the best interests of the child be a primary consideration in all matters concerning the child (Art 3), the guarantee of the child's right to life, survival and development (Art 6) and the duty to facilitate the child's expression of his/her views giving them due weight in accordance with the child's age and maturity in all matters concerning him/her (Art 12)' (Kilkelly, U, 'Operationalising Children's Rights: Lessons from Research' (2006) 1 *Journal of Children's Services* 35–45, at 40–41).

[47] There are a number of such provisions in European law. For an overview, see Moylan, A, 'Children's Participation in Proceedings—The View from Europe' in M Thorpe and J Cadbury (eds), *Hearing the Children* (Family Law, 2004) pp 171–185.

participation in various fori in any event, and who have been able to use this provision of international law to build a bridge to the lawmakers, judges and policy experts. The Convention represents a shared international understanding of children's rights to which appeal may be made.

There is considerable variation, however, between different countries and jurisdictions in the extent to which they have incorporated the various articles of the Convention in their own legislation and in guidelines for practice and how they have met their obligations under this international treaty. New Zealand, for example, has been quite explicit in enacting these principles in its Care of Children Act 2004; section 6 specifies the right of children of any age in family proceedings to have reasonable opportunities to express their views on matters affecting them, and any views they do express (either directly or through a representative) must be taken into account.[48]

Article 12 has been taken a step further towards implementation by the European Convention on the Exercise of Children's Rights (ECECR).[49] This Convention applies to family proceedings, and in particular to those proceedings involving the exercise of parental responsibilities such as residence and access to children. Article 3 of this Convention provides that a child of sufficient understanding shall be granted the right to receive all relevant information, to be consulted, to express his or her views and to be informed of the possible consequences of compliance with these views and the possible consequences of any decision.[50] Article 4 provides that the child shall have the right to apply for a special representative where internal law precludes the holders of parental responsibilities from representing the child as a result of a conflict of interest with the latter. Article 5 requires parties to the Convention to 'consider granting' children additional procedural rights including the right to apply to be assisted by an appropriate person of their choice in order to help them express their views; the right to apply themselves, or through other persons or bodies, for the appointment of a separate representative, in appropriate cases a lawyer; the right to appoint their own representative; and the right to exercise some or all of the rights of parties to such proceedings. Other provisions of the Convention concern the roles of judges and separate representatives for children.

---

[48] Boshier, P, 'Involving Children in Decision-Making: Lessons from New Zealand' (2006) 20 *Australian Journal of Family Law* 145–153.

[49] ETS 160. The Convention was made at Strasbourg on 25 January 1996. It is in force in Cyprus, the Czech Republic, France, Germany, Greece, Italy, Latvia, Macedonia, Poland, Slovenia, Turkey and the Ukraine (as at 19 March 2008). Available at: http://conventions.coe.int/Treaty/Commun/ChercheSig.asp?NT=160&CM=1&DF=3/19/2008&CL=ENG.

[50] Sawyer, C, 'One Step Forward, Two Steps Back—The European Convention on the Exercise of Children's Rights' (1999) 11 *Child and Family Law Quarterly* 151–170 argues that rather than being a step forward towards implementation of Article 12, the ECECR back-pedals on Article 12 because the rights are only secured to those who are considered by internal law to have sufficient understanding. This could be set at a very high age. See also Fortin, J, *Children's Rights and the Developing Law* (Lexis Nexis, 2003; 2nd ed) pp 200–202.

This Convention has been ratified by 11 European states.[51] Ratification is no empty gesture. It requires the state to identify three categories of family cases to which it will apply prior to ratification.[52]

The UN Convention has played a part in bringing about an important change in thinking in the area of family law. The concept that it is the child who has rights, with the parents having responsibilities, is becoming more widespread across jurisdictions.[53] Whether or not this is translating in practice to 'rights for children' or becoming a vehicle for parental rights is a contentious issue. Guggenheim, a practising lawyer and legal academic in the US, argues that children's rights, particularly in relation to divorce and post-separation disputes between the parents, are mere rhetoric which disguises the fact that these disputes 'serve adults' interests' but that this is 'nothing new'.[54] It is also clear that children's 'right to contact' is rarely enforced against a parent who is negligent in maintaining contact or in keeping promises and appointments. On the other hand, others argue that the notion that children have rights is not merely rhetorical, that as a way of thinking, it has profound implications for the resolution of the most difficult cases judges are called upon to decide. For example, children's right to contact may sometimes be used to deny contact. If contact is a right of the child, then there is a strong argument for saying that it should not be imposed on children against their wishes, even where a parent has a justifiable claim to contact.[55]

The notion of children's rights in relation to post-separation parenting arrangements has translated into an acceptance that children must also have rights in relation to the process. The concept that children have a right to be heard is the natural corollary of saying that they have substantive rights in relation to the outcome of parenting disputes, for an awareness of children's perceptions, wishes and beliefs may well be significant in providing an understanding of how a court should give effect to their rights. The possibility that taking children's views into account might lead to better and more informed outcomes

---

[51] See http://conventions.coe.int/Treaty/Commun/ChercheSig.asp?NT=160&CM=8&DF=5/22/2007&CL=ENG.

[52] Article 1(4). The Explanatory Report (para 17) provides examples of the categories of family cases. These include custody; residence; access; questions of parentage; legitimacy (declaration, contestation); adoption; legal guardianship; administration of property of children; care procedures; removal or restriction of parental responsibilities; protection from cruel and degrading treatment, and medical treatment. Available at: http://conventions.coe.int/Treaty/en/Reports/Html/160.htm.

[53] See, for example, the Children Act 1989 in England and the Family Law Reform Act 1995 in Australia. The principles for determining parenting disputes from that time have included the notions that 'children have the right to know and be cared for by both parents and that children have a right to contact, on a regular basis, with both their parents and with other people significant to their care, welfare and development'.

[54] Guggenheim, M, *What's Wrong with Children's Rights?* (Harvard University Press, 2005) p 143.

[55] See, for example, *B v B* [1971] 3 All ER 682 (Eng CA); *Litchfield and Litchfield* (1987) 88 FLR 155 (Fam Ct Aus).

that have a greater chance of being acceptable to and workable for children is of course one of the main arguments for doing so.[56] As academic and clinical psychologist Warshak pointed out, 'children have something important to tell us that may change the decisions we make on their behalf and the way in which we make them'.[57]

1.4 The Pitfalls of Listening to Children

It is clear that the notion of involving children in decision-making about parenting after separation is a movement which has considerable momentum. As in other areas of social policy, however, it is necessary to temper the enthusiasm for acting on new insights with a reminder of the reasons why a quite different view has hitherto been taken. Furthermore, there is reason for caution about images of children in the sociology of childhood literature that over-paint abstract and idealized views of children as rational autonomous agents. Day Sclater and Piper, for example, warn against 'notions of children as active human agents...currently enjoying some popularity in sociology' that 'perhaps go too far in that they assume and idealize a rational subjectivity, and fail to take adequate account of the ambiguities and ambivalences in human experience that derive from emotional life'.[58]

Some caution is particularly important in relation to children's position in disputes about post-separation parenting. The issues involved in encouraging children's participation in this area are unlike any other. Listening to children's voices in the public sphere concerning issues such as the governance of their schools, the design of playgrounds or on issues of town planning, all carry obvious benefits with few risks. There may be various objections to the idea of listening to children in formulating policies, such as the time and cost in so doing or the problems of representativeness. These are pitfalls, but they are unlikely to endanger children's well-being. They do not entail the sort of emotional and relational issues involved in decisions about post-separation arrangements. Even when children are involved in decision-making about medical matters, the final decisions on treatment are likely to rest with their doctors and the parents.

---

[56] Lansdown, G, *Taking Part: Children's Participation in Decision-Making* (Institute of Public Policy Research, London, 1995); Chisholm, R, 'Children's Participation in Family Court Litigation' (1999) 13 *Australian Journal of Family Law* 197–218; Warshak, R A, 'Payoffs and Pitfalls of Listening to Children' (2003) 52 *Family Relations* 373–384.

[57] Warshak, n 56 above, at 374.

[58] Day Sclater and Piper, n 44 above, at 427. Michael King also calls for some re-thinking about the applicability and value of the new sociology of childhood's communication with other fields such as law about the competence and abilities of children. King, M, 'The Sociology of Childhood as Scientific Communication: Observations from a Social Systems Perspective' (2007) 14 *Childhood* 193–213.

Involving children in decision-making about post-separation parenting is different because the very process of so doing may be detrimental. What then are the risks in allowing children to participate in decision-making?

1.4.1 Children may be placed in the middle of their parents' conflicts

Since a consistent finding of research on the outcomes for children following relationship breakdown is that exposure to ongoing parental conflict is harmful, the issue arises whether it is right to place children more in the middle of their parents' conflicts in the context of litigation. When children are asked to take sides in their parents' battles, this can be very damaging.

Hearing children's voices in family law litigation can have a number of adverse consequences for children. One is that children are caught in a 'tug of love' between warring parents, being urged by each parent to express a view that supports his or her case and feeling the need to decide between them.

Another adverse consequence is that children may feel the responsibility for the decision if asked to express a view on the issues before the court. The Grand Chamber of the European Court of Human Rights has affirmed that this is a valid reason why, in certain circumstances, a young child should not be asked directly about his or her views. In *Sahin v Germany*,[59] the issue concerned access by a father to his young daughter in circumstances where there was strong resistance by the mother to such contact. An expert held several meetings with the father, the mother and the child when the child was three and explored the child's attitude towards the father without engaging in direct questioning of the child about whether she wanted to see her father. The court denied access to the father. In the course of an appeal, the expert was asked whether the child should be heard directly by the court. She advised against questioning the child about whether she wished to see her father because the child might have the impression that her statements would be decisive in resolving this conflict between her parents. This could provoke serious feelings of guilt.

The Chamber of the Court decided by a majority that this failure to question the child directly had breached the *father's* rights, not the child's rights. This aspect of its decision was overturned by the Grand Chamber, which held that:[60]

It would be going too far to say that domestic courts are always required to hear a child in court on the issue of access to a parent not having custody, but this issue depends on the specific circumstances of each case, having due regard to the age and maturity of the child concerned.

In this case, the German court's decision was deemed reasonable.

---

[59] Application no. 30943/96, 8 July 2003.
[60] At para 73.

1.4.2 The risk of undue influence

When children's views are given such weight that they may in practice be determinative, this may lead to a tug of war as their parents compete for the child's preferences. Warshak explains:[61]

> The more weight accorded children's stated preferences, the greater the risk of children being manipulated or pressured by parents. Through a variety of tactics such as selective attention, repetition, intimidation, overindulgence, and suggestion, a parent can corrupt a child's view of the other parent... Rather than participating meaningfully in developing an optimal parenting plan or being empowered, the child is stripped of a genuine voice; the child's voice is dubbed with the words of the parent who exercises the most influence over him or her.

Listening to children's voices is thus complex. It involves seeking to identify when children are expressing their own preferences, views and perceptions, and distinguishing these from views that merely parrot the opinions of a parent. Empowering children by placing a great deal of weight on their views increases the likelihood that they will be subject to attempts by one or both parents to persuade them to the parent's view. That may well involve denigration of the other parent in a way that undermines the parent-child relationship.

1.4.3 Children may be given the decision-making authority that the parents need to exercise

A body of research indicates that children benefit from authoritative parenting.[62] The term *authoritative parenting* coined by Baumrind refers to a style of parenting which is neither authoritarian nor permissive, and that combines warmth, acceptance and involvement, with discipline and demands for appropriate behaviour.[63] Intrinsic to the notion of authoritative parenting is that the parents exercise their authority in a way that is responsive to the child without being overbearing.

While parents have the responsibility to make decisions in relation to their children, this is more difficult where there is conflict between them. Many times in the work of parenting in intact families, differences of opinion need to be sorted out.[64] This can involve working through significant conflicts. However, it

---

[61] Warshak, n 56 above, at 375.

[62] Baumrind, D, 'Authoritarian v Authoritative Control' (1968) 3 *Adolescence* 255–272; Hetherington and Kelly, n 3 above, pp 127–130.

[63] Baumrind, D, 'Child Care Practices Anteceding Three Patterns of Preschool Behavior' (1967) 75 *Genetic Psychology Monographs* 43–88; Baumrind, D, 'Effective Parenting During the Early Adolescent Transition' in P A Cowan and E M Hetherington (eds), *Advances in Family Research* (Erlbaum, 1991) vol 2, pp 111–163.

[64] For British research on how children are involved in decision-making in families, see Butler, I, L Scanlan, M Robinson, G Douglas and M Murch, *Divorcing Children: Children's Experience of their Parents' Divorce* (Jessica Kingsley, 2003).

is unlikely that responsible parents would see it as the role of a child to resolve the conflict by making the decision instead.[65] They may consult the child, of course, and take into account his or her views, but often the issue is whether the child should be allowed to do what he or she wants—to go to a sleepover, to attend a party where there may be alcohol or drugs, to stay up late to watch a movie, or the hundred and one other issues that can arise when children seek to push the boundaries that parents have imposed. When such decisions have to be made, to default to the child's choices may be the least responsible parenting decision of all. However difficult it may be for the parents to reach agreement on the appropriate boundaries, the role both of decision-making and of conflict resolution rests with the parents in these situations.

Of course, there is a major difference between listening to children and making them the de facto decision-maker. However, in the context of post-separation parenting disputes, that distinction may become blurred. One of the pitfalls of placing too great an emphasis on children's voices in such proceedings is that the more weight that is perceived to be placed upon children's views by the courts, the more likely it is that the child will become the de facto decision-maker. This is because any parent who is engaged in litigation must weigh up the costs and difficulty of litigating a matter through to trial with a realistic assessment of the chances of success. If it is perceived that a court will be likely to go with the solution that most accords with the expressed wishes of a child, whatever may be the influences upon those wishes, then the parent who seeks a different outcome may decide it is too difficult to contest the case.

When children are placed in the position of de facto decision-maker, this reverses the roles that operate in healthy parenting environments. Children may be given a level of power and authority that they are not equipped to bear. That power can undermine parental authority. The fear that children will express a choice for living with the other parent may affect parents' decisions about whether to punish them for wrongdoing, at least while the case is before the courts. Parents may also become indulgent, allowing the child to have control over what they do each day at a stage when this is inappropriate, for fear of the consequences of confrontation. Even after the parenting dispute has been resolved and court orders made, parents may still live with the fear that the decisions will be reopened based upon the child's preferences once he or she is a little older.

1.4.4 Children's voices may provide an excuse for adults to avoid hard decisions

Too great an emphasis on children's voices may lead to poor decision-making if adults rely upon children's wishes as a reason to avoid making difficult

---

[65] Marquard, E, *Between Two Worlds: The Inner Lives of Children of Divorce* (Three Rivers Press, 2005) p 24.

recommendations or decisions. Emery characterizes the message to children of wanting to hear their voices in this way:[66]

Your parents are at war about where you should live. Your Mom and Dad, and their lawyers, only want you to say what they want to hear. The custody evaluator feels strongly both ways. The mediator wants to remain neutral. The guardian *ad litem* is not sure what to do. The judge would rather not have to decide. Why don't you, child, tell us adults what to do?

Emery's characterization is perhaps not a worst case scenario for allowing a child to decide. In a situation where the decision is a finely balanced one, where there are arguments for and against each proposal, and the child may be as well served (or poorly served) by any of the options before the court, then a decision that accords with the child's wishes may be as good as any other, and perhaps better. It is at least a more child-centred approach than leaving the judge to apply his or her general understandings and beliefs about what is good for children to the circumstances of the case.

However, there is a more troubling scenario than that offered by Emery. The parents are at war, the mediator has been unable to help them reach agreement, the case has been set down for a three-day trial, the judge has a very long docket of cases waiting in the queue to be heard, and the judge sees the opportunity to broker a settlement without all the effort of conducting a trial and then having to write a judgment. In such circumstances, a clear wish of even quite a young child, whatever its aetiology and its basis in reasoned thought, may provide the judge with the easy answer to the case. A judge only has to indicate that he or she is likely to place great weight on the wishes of the child in order to make it clear to the parties and their lawyers that there is not much point in going through the stress and expense of a full blown trial. Reliance on children's voices may therefore be a way of reaching a decision which avoids the hard issues rather than tackling them.

1.4.5 The risk that children's voices will be used to facilitate irresponsible adult decisions

A further risk of inappropriate reliance on children's voices is that it can facilitate irresponsible decisions by the parents because the child is not presented with all the choices. This can be the situation, for example, in relocation cases, which are some of the most difficult cases for judges to decide.[67] Let us suppose that two children, aged ten and eight, live primarily with their mother but also spend

---

[66] Emery, R E, 'Children's Voices: Listening—and Deciding—is an Adult Responsibility' (2003) 45 *Arizona Law Review* 621–627, at 623.

[67] Carmody, T, 'Child Relocation: An Intractable International Family Law Problem' (2007) 45 *Family Court Review* 214–246; Duggan, D, 'Rock-Paper-Scissors: Playing the Odds with the Law of Child Relocation' (2007) 45 *Family Court Review* 193–213.

significant time each week with their father, and divide their time during the school holidays equally between their parents. The children have a close relationship with both parents and the shared parenting arrangement appears to be working well. The mother falls in love with a man who lives many hundreds of miles away and wants to live with him. He could move to the same location as the mother. However, it is inconvenient for him to do so because it means changing jobs.[68]

In such a case, the mother may seek a court order allowing her to relocate with the children in order to live with her new partner. The choice may be presented to the children that they will either have to stay where they are and live with their father (with the consequence that they will see their mother much less frequently), or relocate with their mother (with the consequence that they will see their father much less frequently). This kind of binary choice simplifies the options and the issues in such a case.

There are other options. The new lover could be persuaded that if he wishes to pursue his relationship with the mother then he must move, because the children have an important relationship with their father that must be preserved. Alternatively the mother could place the interests of the children in having a close relationship with their father ahead of her own interests in pursuing her new romantic interest. Another option is that the decision about relocation could be postponed for a couple of years, allowing the mother and her new partner time to see whether their relationship is likely to be an enduring one. Another alternative is that the father could relocate to be in the same vicinity as the mother and her new partner.

Presenting to children a binary choice between living with their mother or with their father hundreds of miles apart from the other parent assumes that the relocation by the mother is a foregone conclusion, when it may be that it is in the best interests of the children for the mother not to relocate at all, or not for the time being, or for the problem to be solved in some other way that preserves the shared parenting relationship between the parents. The way in which children are asked about the issues is therefore very important. If they are asked only about the first two choices (living with the father in the present location or with the mother in the new location), then the options will be artificially narrowed and the adults may be relieved from considering the other alternatives. If, by way of contrast, children are asked open-ended questions about their preferences which are not limited to the options being proposed by a parent, they may well say that they want to live close to both parents. Taking this seriously will require the adults concerned to look at the available options for achieving this.

---

[68] For a review of recent Australian decisions on relocation, see Parkinson, P, 'The Realities of Relocation: Messages from Judicial Decisions' (2008) 22 *Australian Journal of Family Law* 35–55.

1.5 Different Levels and Forms of Participation

Participation may be at many different levels, and it may take different forms at different times. It is not a one-off 'event', but is more usefully seen as a process that occurs over time. At the simplest level, it may just mean informing children about what is happening about the separation rather than leaving them to imagine what it means when, for example, one parent 'has gone away for a while'. There are benefits to telling children what is happening in a manner that is appropriate to their understanding. Otherwise they can feel apprehensive and uncertain, and what they imagine may well be worse than the reality.

Once children are aware that their parents are separating or have done so, they may want to talk with someone in trying to come to terms with what it all means for them.[69] Being listened to is therefore another form of participation. But who they talk to is another choice, and not surprisingly, it is clear from a number of studies that children prefer to talk with someone they know and trust, and if possible, someone within their family or network rather than 'outside' professionals.[70]

Children may also be consulted about their views or they may give them of their own accord in relation to the various changes in their lives after the separation. This could involve indicating a preference for how they split their time between their parents' homes rather than which parent they live with, and how often they see the other parent. It might also involve expressing a preference or their views about particular aspects of their lives, such as how much it matters to them to stay at the same school, to be able to maintain their friendships, continue playing for the same sports team or carry on with other recreational activities. Taking these matters into account may be important in making the arrangements more acceptable and workable for children.

In addition, children may also suggest options for consideration during discussion or bargaining processes. In one case, described by Chisholm, two children, aged 11 and 9, suggested a solution that they had discussed between themselves that was then put to the parents during mediation after the parents had not been able to agree on the arrangements for residence.[71] The children said 'they knew each parent was sad when they were not with the children, and that they too missed that parent. The children said that they did not need to be together all the time. And so they suggested a regime in which for some periods one child would be alone with each parent and at other times the children would be together. This

---

[69] Chisholm, n 56 above.
[70] Smart, C and B Neale, ' "It's My Life Too"—Children's Perspectives on Post-Divorce Parenting' (2000) 30 *Family Law* 163–169; Butler et al, n 66 above; Cashmore, J and P Parkinson, 'Children's and Parents' Perceptions of Children's Participation in Decision-Making after Parental Separation and Divorce' (2008) 46 *Family Court Review* 91–104.
[71] Chisholm, n 56 above.

proposal was greeted with relief and high emotion, and formed the basis of the eventual solution finalised by the parents'.[72] As Chisholm points out, 'perhaps the fact that the proposal came from the children made it easier for each parent to accept it without loss of face'.[73]

At another level, children and adolescents may be involved or may involve themselves directly in the decision-making process. Their parents may, for example, invite their direct influence on the way their time is split between the parents, taking account of their school activities and recreational choices. In practice, this might involve offering a restricted choice between particular options depending on competing demands and priorities—what Ackers refers to as a 'children's menu'.[74] Children, and particularly adolescents may also take direct action and may 'vote with their feet' by moving to or refusing to return to a parent's home, with their decisions acceded to by their parents or by the court.

Only the last of these forms of participation involves children having some control over the decision. In the other forms, parents and other decision-makers may well take children's reactions or views into account in making their decisions but the children do not control the decision and they are not *responsible* for it.

A number of studies indicate that children generally do not want to make the decision but they do want their views to be heard and taken seriously.[75] This is quite consistent with procedural justice findings and with the distinction between 'voice' (control of the process) and 'choice' (control over the decision). Being heard and having one's views taken into account (voice) is one of the main determinants of the perception that the decision-making process is fair, even if the outcome is not the one that is wanted.[76] While having some control over the decision may be more important for adults dealing with disputes outside the family, personal respect and trust are thought to be more important in decision-making processes where there is an ongoing relationship with those making the decisions, as,

---

[72] Chisholm, n 56 above, at 218.

[73] Chisholm, n 56 above, at 218.

[74] Ackers, L, 'From 'Best Interests' to Participatory Rights: Children's Involvement in Family Migration Decisions' (Working Paper 18, Centre for Research on Family, Kinship and Childhood, University of Leeds, 2000) p 18.

[75] Smart et al, n 30 above; Gollop, M, A B Smith and N J Taylor, 'Children's Involvement in Custody and Access Arrangements after Parental Separation' (2000) 12 *Child and Family Law Quarterly* 383–399; Smart and Neale, n 72 above; Butler et al, n 64 above; Smith et al, n 17 above; Douglas, G, M Murch, C Miles and L Scanlan, *Research into the Operation of Rule 9.5 of the Family Proceedings Rules 1991* (Report to the Department of Constitutional Affairs, 2006); Taylor, n 36 above.

[76] Thibaut, J and L Walker, *Procedural Justice: A Psychological Analysis* (Erlbaum, 1975); Lind, E and T Tyler, *The Social Psychology of Procedural Justice* (Plenum Press, 1988). This applies across a range of decision-making areas and in diverse contexts (legal, health care, employment and within the family). It includes formal processes such as judicial and jury decision-making, conciliation and mediation and informal processes within families and other groups. See also Fondacaro, M R, E M Brank, J Stuart, S Villanueva-Abraham, J Luescher and P S McNatt, 'Identity Orientation, Voice, and Judgments of Procedural Justice During Late Adolescence' (2006) 35 *Journal of Youth and Adolescence* 987–997.

for example, in families.[77] Unfortunately there is little research relating to children's and adolescents' views of procedural justice, especially within the family.[78] One study with older adolescents (whose average age was 19) found, however, that the level of conflict and cohesion within families was more closely associated with their assessments of personal respect and trust than the extent to which they thought they had some control over the decision or over the process.[79]

This conceptual framework provides some fertile ground for exploring children's views about participation, and providing a more nuanced understanding of their preferences for different forms of participation in different contexts. In addition, it may be helpful to draw a distinction between the degree of influence that children actually have over the decisions concerning them; the extent to which they believe that they have any influence; and whether or not they want to have any influence on the way that decisions are made. As Morrow has argued:[80]

A more nuanced approach to participation, rights and citizenship is needed, which is less based upon a categorical distinction between adults and children. We should also be aware that children may not welcome 'participation' in the adult sense of the word, and we need a broader definition of citizenship, based on relationships between people, because functionalist definitions are too limited and fail to account for what happens in practice when adults consult with children.

These distinctions, the different ways in which children can be heard in relation to decisions concerning them after their parents separate, and the particular preconditions for children's participation will be outlined further in Chapters 3 and 4.

1.6 The Purpose of this Book

This book explores the issue of children's participation in family law disputes through the voices of Australian children, parents, mediators, counsellors, lawyers and judges, drawing also upon the worldwide literature on children's participation in family law decision-making.

The importance of this research lies less in its quantitative findings concerning majority and minority views (which may be specific to the jurisdiction of

---

[77] Kitzmann, K M and R E Emery, 'Procedural Justice and Parents' Satisfaction in a Field Study of Child Custody Dispute Resolution' (1993) 17 *Law and Human Behavior* 554–567; Tyler, T R and P Degoey, 'Community, Family, and the Social Good: The Psychological Dynamics of Procedural Justice and Social Identification' in G B Melton (ed), *The Individual, the Family, and Social Good: Personal Fulfillment in Times of Change* (University of Nebraska Press, 1995) vol 42, pp 115–191.

[78] Hicks, A J and J A Lawrence, 'Children's Criteria for Procedural Justice: Developing a Young People's Procedural Justice Scale' (1993) 6 *Social Justice Research* 163–182; Fondacaro, M R, S L Jackson and J Luescher, 'Toward the Assessment of Procedural and Distributive Justice in Resolving Family Disputes' (2002) 15 *Social Justice Research* 341–371.

[79] Fondacaro et al, n 78 above.

[80] Morrow, V, 'Dilemmas in Children's Participation in England' in A Invernizzi and J Williams (eds), *Children and Citizenship* (Sage Publications) pp 120–130, at p. 128.

research), but rather in the issues that emerge from the lived experience of parents and children who have been through parenting disputes and in the practical wisdom of those who are involved professionally in seeking to resolve such disputes. Hearing the voices of children as well as parents, mediators, counsellors, judges and lawyers provides a useful backdrop to understanding the issues, what children say they want, how and under what circumstances they want to be involved, and how those around them may or may not provide the opportunities for them to be heard.

Cutting across all chapters in the book are the multiple viewpoints of those involved. We have turned to multiple sources of information and viewpoint, and the background to who was involved in the study—the children, parents, mediators, counsellors, lawyers and judges—is outlined in Chapter 2. Chapter 3 outlines the different ways in which children's voices might be heard in the family justice system, and explains how they are heard within the Australian system as a background to the research presented in this book. In Chapter 4, we explore how children and parents involved in both contested and non-contested matters viewed their own experiences of children's participation, how much say children actually had, how much they wanted, to what extent their parents wanted them to be involved and what both saw as the benefits and risks. The following chapter, Chapter 5, compares the views of the professionals involved in family law disputes: the mediators, counsellors, lawyers and judges. These professionals play an important role as advisers, gatekeepers and adjudicators. The advice of counsellors and lawyers may play an important role in how parents see the views of children and the participation of children. Counsellors in the courts who write family reports and lawyers who represent children in the most highly contested disputes also provide two of the more influential means of presenting children's views to the court, or not, depending on the role they play. In Chapter 6 therefore, we explore how these counsellors and child representatives go about this, and we present children's and parents' accounts of their experiences of the family report process, and for those who had children's lawyers, how effective they found them to be. Chapter 7 focuses specifically on the issue of judicial interviews with children in the course of determining parenting cases. It takes into account the views of children and parents, as well, of course, as those of the judges. In our final chapter, Chapter 8, we bring the various findings together and draw out the implications for a more nuanced view of children's participation in terms of protecting children *in* participation rather than protecting them *from* participation.

The voices in this book speak with Australian accents, but the message of the book is international, as of course are the complex issues with which this book seeks to grapple.

2

The Research

This chapter outlines our overall approach to the exploration of children's participation in family law disputes, and the way in which this research was conducted. It also explores some of the practical and ethical issues about doing research in this area, particularly with children. There are three main elements to our approach: it is interdisciplinary, it is mixed method (using both quantitative and qualitative data), and it draws upon the multiple perspectives of children, parents, mediators, lawyers and judges.

First, our interdisciplinary approach draws on the literature and research methods from law, developmental psychology and the sociology of childhood. One of the authors is a lawyer, and the other a developmental psychologist, and both are familiar with the literature on the sociology of childhood. While the earlier writings in the sociology of childhood positioned this area in opposition to developmental perspectives concerning children, we are keen not to lose the developmental perspective in trying to understand children's lived experience and their participation in the development of post-separation arrangements for them. The focus on children's 'perspectives, experiences and their agency' in the sociology of childhood literature has driven a greater understanding of children's lived experiences and the importance of their views in shaping their world and their interactions with those around them. At the same time, developmental psychology has embraced transactional concepts and the importance of relational contexts in understanding children's development and experience, and their role in influencing the way they are treated and themselves influenced by others.[1] As Neale and Flowerdew point out, these changes in thinking are important to 'a more holistic understanding of children and young people as simultaneously *being* and *becoming*', whose current lived experiences are important in their own right but

---

[1] Vygotsky, L S, 'Mastery of Memory and Thinking' in M Cole, V John-Steiner, S Scribner and E Souberman (eds), *Mind in Society: The Development of Higher Psychological Processes* (Harvard University Press, 1978) pp 38–51; Bronfenbrenner, U, *The Ecology of Human Development: Experiments by Nature and Design* (Harvard University Press, 1979); van der Veer, R and J Valsiner, *Understanding Vygotsky: A Quest for Synthesis* (Blackwell Publishers, 1991); Goodnow, J J, 'Parenting and the "Transmission" and "Internalization" of Values: From Social-Cultural Perspectives to Within-Family Analyses' in J E Grusec and L Kuczynski (eds), *Handbook of Parenting and the Transmission of Values* (Wiley, 1997) pp 333–361; Greene, S and D Hogan (eds), *Researching Children's Experience: Approaches and Methods* (Sage, 2005).

different from those of adults by virtue of differences in their developmental level and understanding and their social power.[2] As Hogan says:[3]

The goal of understanding processes of change in individual functioning is not intrinsic-ally incompatible with the perspective on children as active agents in their own worlds. Accepting a role for chronological age [or developmental level or maturity] as one of many factors potentially shaping human experience does not necessarily pose a threat to a valid exploration of children's experiences.

Secondly, it is mixed method, drawing upon both qualitative and quantitative methodologies. While there has been a continuing debate about the different underlying epistemologies in quantitative and qualitative methods, there seems now to be growing acceptance that these need not be mutually exclusive. As several commentators have pointed out, the issue is how best to match and integrate methods to address the research questions.[4] As Fretchling and Sharp noted in their 'user-friendly handbook for mixed method evaluations', ' "mixed method" designs can yield richer, more valid, and more reliable findings' than those 'based on either the qualitative or quantitative method alone'.[5]

Thirdly, and perhaps most importantly, it draws upon the multiple perspectives of children, parents, mediators, lawyers and judges. Children and parents are the ones most affected by the arrangements, but children generally are likely to have less influence than their parents. The reasons for our focus on the multiple perspectives of the children, parents and the professionals are outlined in the following section.

2.1 The Importance of Multiple Perspectives

In approaching the question of how children can participate more in decision-making about post-separation parenting arrangements, the perspectives of parents, children and legal and counselling practitioners are all important. While each set of perspectives is important in its own right, together they provide an

---

[2] Neale, B and J Flowerdew, 'Time, Texture and Childhood: The Contours of Longitudinal Qualitative Research' (2003) 6 *International Journal of Social Research Methodology* 189–199; Neale, B and J Flowerdew, 'New Structures, New Agency: The Dynamics of Child-Parent Relationships after Divorce' (2007) 15 *International Journal of Children's Rights* 25–42 at p 28.

[3] Hogan, D, 'Researching "The Child" in Developmental Psychology' in S Greene and D Hogan (eds), *Researching Children's Experience: Approaches and Methods* (Sage, 2005; 2nd ed) pp 22–41, at p 37.

[4] Fretchling, J, L Sharp and Westat Inc (eds), *User Friendly Handbook for Mixed Method Evaluations* (Directorate for Education and Human Resources, August 1997); Frankel, S, 'Researching Children's Morality: Developing Research Methods that Allow Children's Involvement in Discourses Relevant to their Everyday Lives' (2007) 1(1) *Childhoods Today* (July 27).

[5] Fretchling, Sharp and Westat Inc, n 4 above, Ch 5 'Overview of the Design Process for Mixed Method Evaluations'. Available at: http://www.nsf.gov/pubs/1997/nsf97153/chap_5.htm.

interesting kaleidoscope of the ways different people respond to this issue. The similarities and differences between them also have significant practical implications for the way disputes involving post-separation arrangements for children are handled. The extent to which there is common ground or marked differences in the views of the various professionals and the views of parents and children is likely to affect the way the various players construct the dispute and respond to the proposed solutions and approaches to involving children.

In general terms, there are good reasons for expecting that those involved in making decisions about the post-separation arrangements for children might come with different perspectives, and that those may in turn differ from those of children. Our interest is not in trying to reconcile the differences in views between the various players[6] but to understand the dimensions of the differences and the diversity of views, and the likely effect of that complexity on the way children's involvement in the decision-making process is provided for or denied.

Parents are likely to come to the process with distinctly different perspectives from those of family law practitioners (judges, lawyers and counsellors). Parents have an investment and emotional involvement in the process and in the outcome that is very different from the expected professional detachment of the practitioners. They also have much less knowledge about the formal decision-making processes associated with mediation and the courts. Their levels of comfort and familiarity with the process can therefore be expected to be considerably less, and their anxiety considerably higher than for the professionals. The way that parents and professionals frame the issues are also likely to be quite different, with parents more likely to put a moral framework around them, and the professionals, or certainly the lawyers and judges, more likely to use a legal framework. What is less clear is the extent to which parents and professionals see children's

---

[6] There is considerable debate in both the sociological and psychological literature about epistemology and methodology concerning the interpretation of data derived from various sources. In sociology this is referred to in broad terms as 'triangulation' and the debate concerns the various approaches and possibilities of interpretation and 'making sense of dissonant data' (Perlesz, A and J Lindsay, 'Methodological Triangulation in Researching Families: Making Sense of Dissonant Data' (2003) 6 *International Journal of Social Research Methodology* 25–40). The 'objective' position, looking for 'a better or more valid picture of reality' by comparing or combining perspectives, is generally contested with 'post-modern' acceptance that there are 'divergent realities' and some intermediate positions in between (Ribbens McCarthy, J, J Holland and V Gillies, 'Multiple Perspectives on the "Family" Lives of Young People: Methodological and Theoretical Issues in Case Study Research' (2003) 6 *International Journal of Social Research Methodology* 1–23). In psychology, the concern tends to focus on the validity of measures and accounts of family life that are based on only one 'informant', often the mother (Cook, W L and M J Goldstein, 'Multiple Perspectives on Family Relationships: A Latent Variables Model' (1993) 64 *Child Development* 1377–1388; Sobolewski, J M and V King, 'The Importance of the Coparental Relationship for Non-Resident Fathers' Ties to Children' (2005) 67 *Journal of Marriage and Family* 1196–1212); this is also a concern in sociology (Warin, J, Y Solomon and C Lewis, 'Swapping Stories: Comparing Plots: Triangulating Individual Narratives within Families' (2007) 10 *International Journal of Social Research Methodology* 121–134).

involvement in terms of children's rights and in terms of the possible emotional impact on children.

Parents and children are also likely to differ in their perceptions and expect-ations about the way decisions concerning post-separation arrangements for children are and should be made—as a function of their experiences, their gen-erational status, age, maturity, and access to information and power. There are a number of studies that indicate that parents and children within the same fam-ilies have overlapping but discrete perspectives on their family life and on other issues[7]—as do husbands and wives.[8] The different ways that family members frame issues can result in clouded communication and in conflict both in intact and separated families. Between parents and adolescents, for example, a common cause of conflict is parents' complaints about the state of adolescents' bedrooms. Whereas parents might see this as having a moral dimension, as a reflection of character and a lack of cooperation, for adolescents it is often a matter of per-sonal choice and an expression of independence.[9] In post-separation families, the different views held by mothers and fathers about their rights and obligations in relation to child support, and the perceived links between child support and contact, may be a source of considerable conflict between them. It may also be the source of perceived unfairness in child support policy for non-resident fathers who tend to see child support and contact as linked and conditional,[10] whereas child support policy around the world normally treats them as independent from each other.

Our interest is not just in the differences in perspectives *between* children, par-ents and the practitioners, however. It is also in the differences that lie 'within groups'. There is, for example, likely to be significant diversity *within* the vari-ous groups—among parents, particularly between resident and non-resident par-ents, and within the different groups of professionals. Judges, lawyers, mediators and counsellors may have a range of views about the appropriateness of involv-ing children. Understanding the differences in approaches within these groups

---

[7] Jessop, D J, 'Family Relationships as Viewed by Parents and Adolescents: A Specification' (1981) 43 *Journal of Marriage and the Family* 95–107; Cashmore, J and J Goodnow, 'Agreement between Generations: A Two-Process Approach' (1985) 56 *Child Development* 493–501; Tein, J-Y, M Roosa and M Michaels, 'Agreement between Parent and Child Reports on Parental Behaviors' (1994) 56 *Journal of Marriage and the Family* 341–355; Aquilino, W S, 'Two Views of One Relationship: Comparing Parents' and Young Adult Children's Reports of the Quality of Intergenerational Relations' (1999) 61 *Journal of Marriage and the Family* 858–870.

[8] Bernard, J, *The Future of Marriage* (Bantam Books, 1972); Jessop, n 10 above; Pahl, J, *Money and Marriage* (Macmillan, 1989).

[9] Steinberg, L, 'We Know Some Things: Parent-Adolescent Relationships in Retrospect and Prospect' (2001) 11 *Journal of Research on Adolescence* 1–19.

[10] Smyth, B and R Weston, *A Snapshot of Contemporary Attitudes to Child Support* (Research report no. 13, Australian Institute of Family Studies, 2005); Atkinson, A, S McKay and N Dominy, *Future Policy Options For Child Support: The Views of Parents* (Department for Work and Pensions Research Report no. 380, 2006); Lin, I-F and S S McLanahan, 'Parental Beliefs About Nonresident Fathers' Obligations and Rights' (2007) 69 *Journal of Marriage and Family* 382–98.

is also important in order to inform policy directions that can, as far as possible, reconcile divergent perspectives.

2.1.1 The importance of children's and parents' views

In an analysis of divorce in England over the last half of the 20th century, Smart pointed to significant changes in the management of divorce from the beginning to the end of that period, concluding that one of the most significant differences was 'the centrality of a new set of ideas about childhood and parent-child relationships', with changes in the notions of the welfare of the child.[11] More importantly, Smart argues, 'by the end of the 1990s the child emerges as a social actor whose wishes and feelings should be ascertained not simply as a minor whose welfare is safeguarded by his/her elders and betters'.[12]

The ethical and practical importance of hearing and taking children's views into account has also been highlighted by Smart, Neale and Wade who argue that children's viewpoints need to be included if family policy is to proceed from an ethical stance:[13]

… in order to treat children ethically we need to be able to hear what it is they value and to be able to see how they make sense of the social world … Children have standpoints which are not the same as adult standpoints; moreover they know a great deal about parenting and its consequences.

While children's views may differ from those of their parents, children may also hold quite different views from one another and it is important to explore and take account of these differences. There has quite justifiably been considerable criticism of references to 'the child' that carry with them concepts of the child as 'universal', homogeneous and as 'context-free'.[14] In reality, children can be expected to have a variety of views about what they would like to happen after their parents separate and whether and how they would like to be involved in the decision-making process. This is likely to depend, among other things, on the context and their expectations of what that might entail and what they think the consequences might be. These in turn may well depend upon children's

[11] Smart, C, 'Divorce in England 1950–2000: A Moral Tale. CAVA Workshop Paper 2' prepared for *Workshop One: Frameworks for Understanding Policy Change and Culture* (1999).
[12] Smart, n 11 above, p 15. See also Sawyer, C, 'Ascertaining the Child's Wishes and Feelings' (2000) 30 *Family Law* 170–174; Smart, C and B Neale, ' "It's My Life Too"—Children's Perspectives on Post-Divorce Parenting' (2000) 30 *Family Law* 163–169.
[13] Smart, C, B Neale and A Wade, *The Changing Experience of Childhood: Families and Divorce* (Polity Press, 2001) p 156.
[14] James, A and A Prout (eds), *Constructing and Reconstructing Childhood: Contemporary Issues in the Sociological Study of Childhood*, (The Falmer Press, 1997; 2nd ed); Greene, S, 'Child Development: Old Themes, New Directions' in M Woodhead, D Faulkner and K Littleton (eds), *Making Sense of Social Development* (Routledge and Open University Press, 1999) pp 250–268; Hogan, n 3 above; Lawrence, J, 'The Developing Child and the Law' in G Monahan and L Young (eds), *Children and the Law in Australia* (Lexis Nexis, 2008) pp 83–104.

experience of being involved, and on their age and maturity especially as these affect their understanding of the options.[15] Children construct their own understanding and views but these are context-dependent and developmentally driven. Exploring and understanding the diversity of children's views, and the factors that affect them, is therefore essential in developing policy and practice in relation to children's participation in such processes. Providing children with opportunities to participate requires understanding how, why and under what circumstances they wish to be involved.

It is equally important to understand how parents feel about children's involvement both within the family and in more formal decision-making processes. Within the family, parents can largely determine the level of involvement children have and what they are told. In processes beyond the family, parents are clearly in a position to resist and undermine children's involvement if they are uncomfortable with it. Their cooperation and involvement is necessary in terms of the information children receive as well as the programs, services and resources to which their children have access.

Practice in the area of children's participation may at times lag behind community attitudes or it may run ahead of them. If courts run ahead of community beliefs and attitudes concerning the involvement of children in the decision-making process, this may undermine confidence in the family law system generally, and may affect the perception of fairness of the outcomes of particular cases. When the issue at stake is how parenting disputes are decided, the views and perceptions of the parents and children involved in the case are of fundamental importance.

2.1.2 The importance of professionals' views: judges, lawyers and welfare professionals

The professionals involved in the family law system also need to have some confidence in the processes by which children's voices are heard, otherwise they may

---

[15] Many children in other research studies have indicated that they do wish to express a view, and have those views treated seriously and taken into account by those making decisions about their lives in various areas, such as child protection and adoption, not just in post-parental separation arrangements, but it is clear that others are reluctant to do so or do not see it as necessary (Morrow, V, *Understanding Families: Children's Perspectives* (National Children's Bureau, 1998); Murch, M, G Douglas, L Scanlan, A Perry, C Lisles, K Bader and M Borkowski, *Safeguarding Children's Welfare in Uncontentious Divorce: A Study of S41 of the Matrimonial Causes Act* (Lord Chancellor's Department, Research Series 7/99); Gollop, M, A B Smith and N J Taylor, 'Children's Involvement in Custody and Access Arrangements after Parental Separation' (2000) 12 *Child and Family Law Quarterly* 383–399; Smart and Neale, n 12 above; Bretherton, H, ' "Because it's me the Decisions are About"—Children's Experiences of Private Law Proceedings' [2002] 32 *Family Law* 450–457; Parkinson, P, J Cashmore and J Single, ' "Adolescents" Views on the Fairness of Parenting and Financial Arrangements after Separation' (2005) 43 *Family Court Review* 429–444; Cashmore, J and P Parkinson, 'Children's and Parents' Perceptions of Children's Participation in Decision-Making after Parental Separation and Divorce' (2008) 46 *Family Court Review* 91–104).

engage in passive or active resistance through professional channels of communication such as conferences and journals, as well as more informally through professional networks. They may also engage in practices that adopt the rhetoric but not the essence of participation for children. This is a recipe for disillusionment and cynicism. Change cannot wait for consensus of course, for that would always favour the option of maintaining existing practices as they are until there is an overwhelming pressure for change. However, in making changes, it is important to bring people along with those changes, explaining their rationale, dealing with concerns and responding to criticisms. Research on the views of professionals, as well as parents and children, may therefore be valuable in identifying both the extent of the likely welcome for change and the likely reasons for discomfort.

Another reason for policy and practice to take account of the views of those involved in the system is to ensure that counsellors, and mediators in particular, maintain motivation and commitment to the difficult work of resolving disputes about post-separation parenting. There is no reported shortage of family lawyers around the world, nor of people willing to take on judicial appointments. However, skilled and motivated social-science trained professionals working in the court system or in the organizations to which courts refer have many other options for their professional engagement. Working with high conflict parents involved in post-separation disputes is particularly challenging. Yet it is these professionals who are most valuable in helping to work with the parents who need therapeutic rather than legal interventions to move them on from their positions of entrenched conflict.

It is important therefore that counsellors and mediators in particular are comfortable with the roles they play in resolving family disputes. If they consider that either the system fails to listen to children's voices or places inappropriate pressures on children, then this may decrease their motivation and willingness to remain in this difficult work.

2.2 Research Method

Since our primary interest was in how parents, children and professionals perceive and construct children's involvement in post-separation parenting arrangements, our data collection was based on semi-structured interviews which included a combination of open-ended and more structured questions. Our analyses too included a combination of qualitative and quantitative methods. The focus of the qualitative analyses, using content analysis and NVivo, was on meanings, the interpretation of people's perceptions, and the underlying reasons for their attitudes, beliefs and feelings.[16] The focus of the quantitative analyses was more

---

[16] NVivo is a qualitative data analysis computer program that faciliatates the coding, exploration, comparison and pattern analysis of interviews, literature and even videoanalysis, like

on measurement and frequency, as a means of providing comparisons within and between groups.

2.2.1 The participants and the interviews

The study involved interviews with 47 children and young people and 90 parents as well as 42 lawyers, 41 mediators and counsellors and 20 judicial officers. While the professionals are, by nature of their work, specifically involved in cases that have become engaged in the family law system and dispute resolution process, the parents and children came from families who had engaged lawyers but were involved in a range of processes to sort out the arrangements for the children.

The children and their parents were recruited for the study through family lawyers, who were asked to write to up to 15 former clients who had resolved matters in the preceding 12 months. The lawyers were asked to include clients who had resolved matters with no more than counselling and mediation, as well as those who had experienced a more intense level of engagement with the family law system, and had at least had an independent expert report commissioned in preparation for a trial.

While much has been written about options for children's participation in more formal dispute resolution processes, a focus on the litigated cases is a very narrow one. In jurisdictions across the Western world, only about 5–10% of all the cases which are commenced concerning parenting after separation end in a trial. Research with parents and children in the general population of people who have had disputes about the post-separation parenting arrangements therefore provides a more comprehensive picture of the extent of children's participation in resolving those disputes than is possible by focusing on the cases that go to trial. Indeed, there has been some concern about the lack of opportunities for children to participate in informal dispute resolution processes before cases get to trial and in matters that do not get anywhere near the courts.[17] As Neale and Flowerdew point out:[18]

From a policy perspective, understanding how ordinary divorced families managed the changes in their lives has become just as important as understanding what happens in the 10% of families to seek professional help. The development of this *processual* [authors'

classifying, sorting and arranging information, allowing the exploration of trends, and building and testing theories.

[17] Lyon, C, E Surrey and J E Timms, 'Effective Support Services for Children and Young People when Parental Relationships Breakdown—A Child-Centred Approach' (Calouste Gulbenkian Foundation, 1999); Murch et al, n 15 above; Butler, I, L Scanlan, M Robinson, G Douglas and M Murch, 'Children's Involvement in their Parents' Divorce: Implications for Practice' (2002) 16 *Children and Society* 89–102; McIntosh, J and C Long, *Children Beyond Dispute: A Prospective Study Of Outcomes from Child Focused and Child Inclusive Post-Separation Family Dispute Resolution* (Final Report to the Attorney-General's Department, 2006).

[18] Neale and Flowerdew, 'New structures', n 2 above, at 26.

emphasis] approach acknowledges the negotiated character of family relationships, both within and across the generations, and seeks to understand fluidity and change as integral features of family life...

The children

The 47 children and young people from 28 families ranged in age from 6 to 18 and included ten sibling groups of two to four children. There were 29 girls and 18 boys. Their average age at the time of the first interview was 11.8 years (SD = 3.1). Their ages at the time their parents separated ranged from 5 months to 16 years, with a mean age of 7.1 years (SD = 4.6). There was no significant gender difference in age at separation or at interview.[19]

Just over half the children (25/47, 53%) had experienced contested proceedings, and 22 had not. A case was defined as a contested proceeding if it was resolved by means of a trial and final judgment. Many cases that are defined in this study as non-contested were contested at some stage; however they were resolved somewhere along the litigation pathway without requiring final adjudication. There may have been contested interim proceedings.

Either the parent or the children made substantive allegations of some form of family violence (allegations of violence between the parents) or abuse or neglect in 9 families affecting 19 children, and most of these cases (15/19) were contested.

Three-quarters of the children were living with their mother (n = 35, 74.5%) and just over 20% with their father (n = 10). Only two boys (in one family) were in shared alternate week arrangements.

Thirty-five children and young people were re-interviewed in 2005, 18–30 months after the first interview, to explore any changes in their arrangements since the first interview and their involvement in decision-making about any changes. In 12 cases, it was not possible to re-interview the children.

Parents

A total of 90 parents were interviewed; most of the mothers (39/43, 90.7%) were resident parents, and the majority of the fathers were non-resident parents (31/47, 66%). Seventy per cent of the parents were involved in contested matters. Both parents were included in three families where the children were also interviewed. One mother and six fathers were in shared parenting arrangements. Thirty-two parents (19 resident mothers, 6 resident and 7 non-resident fathers) from 25 families in which the children were interviewed, were re-interviewed at the same time as their children. A further 58 parents (with both parents in a further two families) were interviewed on one occasion but did not give permission for their children to be interviewed and were not re-interviewed.

---

[19] The average age at separation was 6.4 years for girls and 8.1 years for boys, and at the first interview, 11.7 years for girls and 11.9 years for boys.

The parents' interviews were concerned with background information about the separation and the way the arrangements for the children had been determined. We also explored what changes, if any, there had been since the separation. Parents were also asked a series of questions about what the children had been told, how they had reacted to the separation and the arrangements, and what their own views were about the appropriateness, and the possible risks and benefits, of involving children in the decision-making process, either within or beyond the family.

Lawyers

The 42 lawyers, 21 men and 21 women, were family law specialists. Twenty-two had some experience of acting as children's representatives as well as representing parents. The term 'child representative' refers to a legal representative appointed for the child who is independent of the parents. The child representative's role is to promote the child's best interests but also to put before the court the views of the child. The majority of parenting cases that go to trial in Australia involve a child representative. Child representatives are now known as independent children's lawyers.[20]

The lawyers' interviews explored a range of matters concerning children's involvement in decision-making about residence and contact disputes, whether and how the lawyers approach this with parents in more consensual and in contested matters, the perceived significance of children's views and the assessment of influences on those views. For lawyers who were child representatives, the questions concerned their views about their role, their communication with the child, and how they approached particular aspects such as ascertaining the children's views and their best interests.

Welfare professionals

Forty-one social-science trained professionals were interviewed about their role within the family law dispute resolution process and their views about children's participation. They were mostly women (30/41). Twenty-four were counsellors,[21] now known as 'family consultants',[22] working within four registries of the family courts. Their functions include mediation after a court application has been filed, and writing family reports for the court. They are known in this book as counsellors, to distinguish them from the community mediators. There were 17 such community mediators who worked for non-government organizations, largely funded by the federal government with the remit to run confidential

[20] Family Law Act 1975 (as amended by the Family Law Amendment (Shared Parental Responsibility) Act 2006), s 68LA.
[21] At the time of these interviews, their title within the Family Court was 'mediator', although their functions were by no means limited to mediation.
[22] Family Law Act 1975 (as amended by the Family Law Amendment (Shared Parental Responsibility) Act 2006), s 11B.

mediation and counselling services for separated partners and parents. They are collectively referred to in this book by the generic 'welfare professionals'.

The interviews with the welfare professionals concerned their views on children's involvement in decisions and dispute resolution processes about the residence and contact arrangements. They also explored their particular role within the court or in mediation within non-government agencies involved in dispute resolution. The most significant aspects of this concerned the way they went about obtaining the child's views, and for the court professionals, their thinking and practice concerning the way they assessed children's views and presented them to the court.

Judges

Interviews were conducted with 20 judicial officers, 10 men and 10 women, from the Family Court of Australia and the Federal Magistrates' Court, who were drawn from five registries across three different states in Australia.[23] Fourteen were judges of the Family Court of Australia and six were Federal Magistrates.[24] For ease of reference we will refer to them collectively as 'judges'.

The interviews explored a range of matters concerning children's participation in decision-making about residence and contact disputes, including the significance of children's views, the assessment of influences on those views, the direct involvement of children either through interviews in chambers or in court, and the role of child representatives.

2.3 Practical and Ethical Issues in Research with Children

There were a number of practical and ethical issues to consider in designing and carrying out the research. These included the format of the interviews for children, the timing of the interviews, informed consent and confidentiality. In addition, there is the overall question of the ethics of including children and young people in research of this kind, dealing with quite sensitive family-related issues. Our position on the last question is that it is not only ethical, but essential to include children, as long as it is conducted in an appropriate manner. Indeed, not to do so would perpetuate the notion that children can be the subject of policy and research, but not heard in their own right. The evidence from our research

---

[23] Newcastle, Parramatta and Sydney in New South Wales, Melbourne in Victoria and Adelaide in South Australia.

[24] Federal magistrates are judges with tenure under Chapter III of the Federal Constitution and have the same jurisdiction as members of the Family Court in resolving parenting disputes. By agreement between the two courts, cases scheduled to last longer than two days are normally heard in the Family Court. A small number of matters, such as applications to allow the sterilization of an intellectually disabled minor, are also heard only in the Family Court.

and other similar research[25] is that children generally appreciate the opportunity to have their say in the research process and, in ours and other research, have not been upset by the discussion of these matters. While ethics committees are quite rightly concerned about the possible distress or harm to children as a result of their involvement in research, there is increasing concern that the focus on protecting children from any risk of harm is overriding children's rights to participate in research—as it does in other areas of decision-making.

2.3.1 Consent for children's participation

The issue of consent for children's participation is a vexed one. The consent or cooperation of other parties including parents is generally required, but there is uncertainty in law and variability across jurisdictions as to the age at which children can consent on their own behalf without needing their parents' concurrence.[26] In this study, access to children was via family lawyers who sent the letters out to parents. The ethics conditions[27] for interviewing children provided that the researchers could interview the children with the consent either of both parents, or the permission of one parent without the refusal of the other, after that other parent was given the opportunity to object. The informed consent of children was also required. This approach was an agreed compromise on the initial expectation that the consent of both parents was required because, as other researchers have found, this would have resulted in a very restricted and probably unrepresentative sample of children.[28] Even so, children participated in the research in only about a third of the families in which one parent agreed to be interviewed. In 39 of the 83 families involved in the study, either the parent who was interviewed or their former partner who declined to participate refused permission for their children to participate. In four families, both parents refused consent for their children. The children ranged in age from 5 to 15 but most were

[25] Neale, B and C Smart, 'Agents or Dependants? Struggling to Listen to Children in Family Law and Family Research' (Working Paper 3, Centre for Research on Family, Kinship and Childhood, University of Leeds, 1998); Hogan, D M, D Halpenny and S Greene, 'Change and Continuity after Parental Separation: Children's Experiences of Family Transitions in Ireland' (2003) 10 *Childhood* 163–180; Taylor, N, 'What do We Know about Involving Children and Young People in Family Law Decision Making? A Research Update' (2006) 20 *Australian Journal of Family Law* 154–178.

[26] Fisher, C B, 'Integrating Science and Ethics in Research with High-risk Children and Youth' (1993) 7 *Social Policy Report* (no. 4); Halse, C and A Honey, 'Unraveling Ethics: Illuminating the Moral Dilemmas of Research Ethics' (2005) 30 *Signs: Journal of Women in Culture and Society* 2142–2162; Wiles, R, S Heath, G Crow and V Charles, *Informed Consent in Social Research: A Literature Review* (Methods Paper Series) (ESRC National Centre for Research Methods, undated). Available at: http://www.sociology.soton.ac.uk/Proj/Informed_Consent/litreview.rtf.

[27] The project was funded by the Australian Research Council and had ethics approval from the Human Ethics Committee of the University of Sydney; it was also endorsed by the Research Committee of the Family Court of Australia.

[28] Neale and Smart, n 25 above; personal communication, Anne Smith and Nicola Taylor, 2004.

under 10. In 13 families the children were under 6 and considered too young and in another three families, the children lived interstate and were not available for interview.

The main reasons that parents were not happy for their children to participate were that they thought they were too young or they did not want them to have to relive any of the upset or difficulties associated with the separation and subsequent arrangements. It is possible too, as Neale and Smart found, that some parents were apprehensive about what their children might say about problems within the family to an 'outsider'.[29] It is very likely that if the consent of both parents had been required, few children would have been able to participate.

Children's own consent or assent at least is of course also essential but it is not always clear how their consent—or assent—is obtained. In our research, for example, it is not clear how many parents asked their children before giving their consent or refusal on their behalf but the process was explained to children before the interview began and they were told they could stop at any time and not answer any questions as they wished.[30] The extent to which children feel comfortable doing this is, however, difficult to determine, especially if their parents have already given their approval. Some children did refuse to answer some questions or said they did not know. As Sandbaek, a Norwegian social researcher, points out, it is a 'challenge to make the contract with the child clear, either in terms of informed consent, or in terms of informed dissent from the children themselves'.[31]

Of course, our own criteria as researchers for including children in the study also need to be clear. Our letter of invitation to children and families indicated that we were interested in children who were aged between 7 and 15 years when their parents divorced, because we expected that children of this age would have been old enough to be involved in the post-separation arrangements and to remember what had occurred at that time. However, the youngest child we interviewed was 6 years old and nearly half the children were under 7 at the time their parents separated. We also included all children in the family if they were willing to participate rather than exclude some on the basis of age. In some families, some children agreed to participate and one or more siblings did not.[32]

---

[29] Neale and Smart, n 25 above, p. 21.

[30] Children were also read and asked to sign a form that included the following statement: 'It's OK for what we talk about to be tape-recorded. If I do not want to answer some or all of the questions, I don't have to and I can stop or turn the tape recorder off at any time.'

[31] Sandbaek admitted that in their study the researchers were concerned about asking children again at the beginning of the interview for their consent because of the risk of additional attrition of the sample (Sandbaek, M, 'Adult Images of Childhood and Research on Client Children' (1999) 2 *International Journal of Social Research Methodology* 191–202, at 196).

[32] The other important criterion for inclusion in the study was that there was no ongoing disputation involving legal action and none forthcoming, as far as could be anticipated. This was to prevent the children and the researchers becoming embroiled in further court action and to protect the confidentiality of the research materials which might otherwise be subject to subpoena.

2.3.2 Confidentiality and privacy of children's responses

As part of the process of obtaining informed consent, parents and children were informed that what they said would be confidential. Children were told, for example, that no one except the researchers would see or know what they said. This promise was backed up by court action to guarantee children's confidentiality. In one case early in the project, a parent sought access to his children's interview materials despite the fact that he had given an assurance that all court action was completed and none contemplated, and agreed to the confidentiality conditions of his children's involvement in the research. The University of Sydney backed us in defending the subpoena from the father, a self-represented litigant. The decision of the Family Court of Australia, *T v L* (2001) indicated that research conducted with children under express promises of confidentiality may be protected from subpoena in subsequent legal proceedings.[33] The Family Court struck down the subpoena on three grounds: public policy, estoppel and/ or waiver, and the lack of legitimate forensic purpose. The judge held that it was a 'fishing expedition' to subpoena material in case something comes out of it, and noted that the interviews were conducted for research purposes, not as an assessment for court purposes. However, the Court was satisfied on the first ground of public policy alone—the need for both researchers and participants to be able to rely on promises of confidentiality.[34] Collier J stated that:

> ...if projects of this kind, and I speak of this as a particular project, but I speak more widely of projects of this kind which, if I might say so with respect, are to be encouraged, then it is essential that people who wish to take part in these programs know that there is confidentiality. Equally, and possibly more significantly, it is of vital importance that the researchers know that when they conduct interviews in confidence as part of their research, that the confidentiality that they have set up as the basis of those interviews and the whole of the research cannot be impinged upon by the use of a subpoena in circumstances such as the present case. I would be satisfied, and find, that on the public policy aspect alone, the subpoena should be struck down.

In practical terms, children were interviewed without parents or siblings being present. Parents were aware that children had been promised confidentiality and were generally very respectful in withdrawing and leaving children to be interviewed in an open but private area of the family home while 'going about their business' elsewhere. Children who used the computer-assisted interview were also able to respond without verbalizing their responses if they wished to do so.

---

[33] The case was unreported, but the judgment is summarized in Parkinson, P, 'Research and Promises of Confidentiality to Children' (2002) 16 *Australian Journal of Family Law* 2–4. See also Alderson, P and V Morrow, *Ethics, Social Research and Consulting with Children and Young People* (Barnardos, 2004).

[34] Cashmore, J, 'Invited Commentary: Ethical Issues Concerning Consent in Obtaining Children's Reports on their Experience of Violence: Commentary on Carroll-Lind, Chapman, Gregory and Maxwell' (2006) 30 *Child Abuse and Neglect: The International Journal* 969–977.

Children and parents were also promised anonymity in relation to the reporting of their comments in the research report. They were told that 'if we use some of your answers in what we write, no one will know who said it'. In what is now commonplace practice, children have pseudonyms and in certain cases their particular details have been changed to protect their identity where the combination of information might be too identifying.

2.3.3 Format of interviews with children

The interviews concerned children's understanding of and participation in the decision-making about residence and contact issues following the separation of their parents, and included a mix of closed and open questions. Children were offered the opportunity either to talk directly with the interviewer or to respond to a specially designed computer-assisted interview. The computer-assisted interview was presented on a laptop computer using a child-friendly format which was largely self-directed and self-paced. The interviews were tape-recorded with the child's consent and transcribed (including the child's comments and conversation as they responded to the computer-assisted interview). Most children (29/47), especially those 12 years of age and younger (23/29), elected to use the computer-assisted interview. All were interviewed at their homes, without their parents or siblings being present.[35]

The introductory part of this interview aimed to engage children via both oral and visual presentation, and the use of a vignette concerning another child whereby both the age and gender of the child (Simon or Simone) were automatically adjusted to match their own. For example:

Simone is a girl about your age—she's 8 and her parents split up about 12 months ago. Simone knew they had been fighting a lot but she was surprised when they told her they were going to split up. She likes riding her bike and playing Nintendo with her friends and spending time with her parents.

Her parents are now trying to work out who Simone should live with. They can't agree and have gone to court to decide who she should live with and when she should see the other parent.

What would Simone say if she was asked which parent she wanted to live with?

Would that depend on who asked her?

How much say should she have deciding who she wants to live with?

Why do you think that?

Do you think it puts Simone in a difficult position to ask her what she wants?

What might she be worried about?

Should the court decide what is going to happen?

[35] Some quotations from the children are taken from their typed responses to the computerized questionnaire. Their spelling errors, if any were made, have been retained in the quotations.

What do you think the court needs to know when making the decision?

Should the court do what Simone wants?

Do adults really listen to what kids want?

Is Simone really old enough to know what is best for her?

What can Simone do if she wasn't happy with what was decided?

What could she do if she wasn't able to see her father/mother as much as she wanted?

These introductory questions were followed by questions about the children's own situation, with a visual backdrop that changed for each set of questions, using a theme that was specially designed to engage children. One of the reasons for using an introductory vignette was to invite children to reflect on the issues and to project their views into that context. We did not ask children what they wanted in their own situation. We did, however, ask them about their experiences, what arrangements had been made for them when their parents separated, what they were told about it, whether they had had any say in what those arrangements were, and how happy they were with them. If the post-separation arrangements were the subject of contestation, children were also asked about their contact with lawyers and court counsellors, and about their reaction to the court's decision.

The general indication from children was that they appreciated the opportunity to talk about these issues and to do so privately. While a few adolescents in very difficult circumstances indicated some distress about their parents' separation or the subsequent arrangements, they did not indicate any concern about the research process. Nearly all the parents and children who were able to be approached for a follow-up interview were very willing to participate again and some have kept in contact outside the interview process.

3

The Different Ways of Hearing the Voice of the Child

Separation is a catastrophic event, or a series of events, that happens *to* children. Like other catastrophes, it brings about major changes to their world, but happens entirely outside of their control. Sometimes there is warning, sometimes not. The orderly image of the 'good separation', in which the parents together sit the children down and calmly explain that they are going to live apart from now on, is discordant with the reality for many children, who find the process of separation, turbulent, confusing and traumatic.[1]

Some of these children and families will engage with the family justice system, using that term to include not only lawyers and courts but also mediators, and psychologists or psychiatrists who write reports for the courts. How will they then be treated in that system when parents are in dispute about the future of their children? Are they only objects of concern, or are they in some way involved in the process? How does the family justice system respond to their need for help through the turbulence, confusion and trauma of the litigation process?

In this chapter, we explore the different ways in which children's voices might be heard in the family justice system, and explain how they are heard within the Australian system as a background to the research presented in this book. There are a variety of approaches to the involvement of children around the Western world. Most of the focus has been upon hearing children in trials.

Fortin has identified a ladder of children's participation in family law proceedings.[2] On the bottom rung, children are not given any means of making their views known to the court. On the next rung, children's views are conveyed in a family report. On the next, children are given separate representation. On the highest rung, they litigate on their own behalf and may have initiated the proceedings themselves.

A situation where children are afforded no means of making their views known is clearly a violation of their Article 12 rights under the UN Convention on the Rights of the Child. Beyond this, there are many different views on how

---

[1] Mitchell, A, *Children in the Middle: Living Through Divorce* (Tavistock Publications, 1985) ch 5.

[2] Fortin, J, *Children's Rights and the Developing Law* (Lexis Nexis, 2003; 2nd ed) p 212.

children's voices should be heard in parenting disputes. Fortin's hierarchy is not necessarily a hierarchy of virtue. It is certainly a hierarchy of involvement. Yet often the issues are presented as if greater participation and representation for children is an unqualified virtue. Alternatively, the issues are presented in terms of binary choices between irreconcilable alternatives: welfare versus rights, protection versus participation, objects of concern versus social actors, a best interests model versus direct instructions. One position is often painted as the outmoded traditional one and the other as the progressive option.[3]

Such a binary analysis of the complex issues surrounding children's participation in legal proceedings is usually unhelpful once it is taken as a given that in every case, by one means or another, evidence should be given of any views that the child may have concerning the family situation or the preferred outcome. A binary approach to the means of ensuring that such evidence is given suggests that one view needs to prevail over the other; it involves an assumption that one perspective must be 'right' and the other 'wrong', which fails to acknowledge the legitimacy of the concerns that underlie different perspectives, and it suggests that across the range of children involved in family law proceedings, and the spectrum of childhood, a 'one size fits all' approach is appropriate.

The reality, perhaps, is that the smorgasbord of ways of hearing the voices of children in legal proceedings should be seen as offering means that ought to be available within legal systems and that should be utilized in a flexible way depending on the circumstances of the case and the needs of the child. The extent to which such means are available in a given jurisdiction will depend not only on the views of professionals and governments concerning the appropriateness of different means of children's participation but also the resources that are and ought to be made available for the purpose.

Behind all the abstract debates about best models for children's participation lie three fundamental and practical questions. Who should pay, how should scarce resources best be targeted and why should one model which may bring benefit to some children be preferred over another use of the funds that may also provide a benefit to the same target population of children? If one method of hearing the voice of the child is more cost-effective than another, should cost be a material factor in making the decision about the preferred option? The cost-effectiveness of different forms of intervention to support children is rarely, it seems, considered in the legal literature; but it is always an issue to be addressed when claims are being made for resources from taxpayer funds or further calls are being made on scarce court resources or judicial time. Advocates are free from the need to worry about costs and alternate uses of scarce resources; governments are not.

---

[3] See, for example, the review of the (mostly Canadian and American) literature in Bessner, R, *The Voice of the Child in Divorce, Custody and Access Proceedings* (Family, Children and Youth Section, Department of Justice, 2002).

3.1 Legislative Principles for Participation

Litigation is a process which is often lengthy, and in which numerous professionals may interact with the parents and children over the course of time. Children can suffer considerably through that period. In a recent study in Australia, McIntosh found that over 40% of children going through the adversarial trial process had scores in the borderline or abnormal range for symptoms of emotional distress.[4]

Despite the difficulties for children when parents are going through the litigation process, little attention has been paid by legislatures to the needs of children for information and support through that process, or concerning their right to participate. This may be contrasted with legislation in the child protection system. For example, in British Columbia, one of the service delivery principles of the Child, Family and Community Service Act 1996 is that 'families and children should be informed of the services available to them and encouraged to participate in decisions that affect them'.[5] In New South Wales, the Children and Young Persons (Care and Protection) Act 1998 contains a 'principle of participation'[6] which applies to all children who are affected by child protection interventions.[7] It imposes upon the head of the responsible child welfare department the duty to provide a child or young person with:

(a) adequate information, in a manner and language that he or she can understand, concerning the decisions to be made, the reasons for the Department's intervention, the ways in which the child or young person can participate in decision-making and any relevant complaint mechanisms;

(b) the opportunity to express his or her views freely, according to his or her abilities;

(c) any assistance that is necessary for the child or young person to express those views;

(d) information as to how his or her views will be recorded and taken into account;

(e) information about the outcome of any decision concerning the child or young person and a full explanation of the reasons for the decision;

(f) an opportunity to respond to a decision made under this Act concerning the child or young person.

By way of contrast, family justice systems do not have the same kind of organizational coherence as child protection services, and there may not be a perception

---

[4] McIntosh, J, *The Children's Cases Pilot Project: An Exploratory Study of Impacts on Parenting Capacity and Child Well-Being* (Family Transitions, 2006) p 29.

[5] Child, Family and Community Service Act, RSBC 1996, Ch 46, s 3.

[6] Children and Young Persons (Care and Protection) Act 1998, s 10.

[7] Parkinson, P, 'The Child Participation Principle in Child Protection Law in New South Wales' (2001) 9 *International Journal of Children's Rights* 259–272.

that it is a system that has children as direct, or at least indirect clients. While there is a small but growing awareness of children's informational and support needs within family justice systems,[8] the focus of legislation concerning disputes between parents is typically on how judges should decide cases, and what processes need to be followed for them to do so, rather than on how the service system associated with that dispute resolution role deals with the parents and children who are involved in the disputes. Typically, statutory checklists require courts, in determining the best interests of the child, to ascertain the 'wishes' or 'views' of the child in regard to the respective proposals of the parents. That is a limited perspective on children's participation, and it has its main application in cases which go to trial or which proceed far enough along the litigation pathway for evidence to be ascertained about the children's perspectives.

Douglas and colleagues have called for a more holistic approach to the well-being of children who are involved in family law disputes, seeing the issues from a child welfare and mental health perspective.[9] They argue that courts should have a role in supervising post-separation parenting arrangements reached by agreement between parents, to ensure that they have been arrived at jointly and after consideration of the child's expressed wishes and feelings (and where that is not the case, the reasons why the child has not been consulted).[10]

Legislative principles for children's participation are not the only way in which a culture can be created that meets children's informational and support needs while their family is involved in parenting proceedings, but it is often a useful catalyst for attention to be paid to these issues. Statutory obligations also provide a basis to claim appropriate levels of funding for services both within and outside the court system to meet children's needs. When governments seek to cut costs, and impose 'efficiency dividends' on courts, discretionary expenditure which is not part of the core business of the family justice system goes first. A focus on safeguarding the welfare of children when there are parenting disputes ought to be defined within the core business of the courts which are called upon to resolve those disputes.

The European Convention on the Exercise of Children's Rights, discussed in Chapter 1, may be a catalyst for a broader approach to children's participation amongst signatory countries.[11] The object of the Convention is to grant children

[8] Taylor, N, 'What do We Know about Involving Children and Young People in Family Law Decision Making? A Research Update' (2006) 20 *Australian Journal of Family Law* 154–178, at 173–175.

[9] Douglas, G, M Murch and A Perry, 'Supporting Children When Parents Separate—A Neglected Family Justice or Mental Health Issue?' (1996) 8 *Child and Family Law Quarterly* 121–135. See also Lowe, N and M Murch, 'Children's Participation in the Family Justice System—Translating Principles into Practice' (2001) 13 *Child and Family Law Quarterly* 137–158; Fortin, n 2 above, pp 204–210.

[10] Douglas, G, M Murch, L Scanlan and A Perry, 'Safeguarding Children's Welfare in Non-Contentious Divorce: Towards a New Conception of the Legal Process' (2000) 63 *Modern Law Review* 177–196, at 194–195.

[11] ETS 160. The Convention was made at Strasbourg on 25 January 1996.

procedural rights and to facilitate the exercise of these rights by ensuring that children are informed and allowed to participate in family proceedings affecting them. Article 3 provides:

A child considered by internal law as having sufficient understanding, in the case of proceedings before a judicial authority affecting him or her, shall be granted, and shall be entitled to request, the following rights:
(a) to receive all relevant information;
(b) to be consulted and express his or her views;
(c) to be informed of the possible consequences of compliance with these views and the possible consequences of any decision.

Article 3 lays emphasis on information, for this is an important first step in participation, and the need for this has been borne out by much research.[12] The Article 3 rights do not only concern hearing the voice of the child in the trial. The child is given information rights as well as the right to be consulted and heard. This applies to the process prior to the trial. Article 6 reinforces this obligation, requiring the judge to ensure that the child has received all relevant information when the matter comes to trial. Children's rights to information and participation have also been reinforced by Article 6 of the European Convention on Contact Concerning Children.[13]

3.2 Child-inclusive Mediation

Alternative dispute resolution has long played an important part in the resolution of parenting disputes. Jurisdictions across the Western world encourage parents to mediate or have other systems and structures in which attempts can be made to conciliate the dispute between them. Traditionally the role of the mediator has been to act as a neutral facilitator of negotiations between the parents.

Practice has varied widely both within and across jurisdictions on the involvement of children in the mediation process. There are a variety of ways in which children can be included.[14] They might have separate meetings with the

---

[12] O'Quigley, A, *Listening to Children's Views: The Findings and Recommendations of Recent Research* (Joseph Rowntree Foundation, 2000); Butler, I, L Scanlan, M Robinson, G Douglas and M Murch, *Divorcing Children: Children's Experience of their Parents' Divorce* (Jessica Kingsley, 2003) pp 186ff; Douglas, G, M Murch, C Miles and L Scanlan, *Research into the Operation of Rule 9.5 of the Family Proceedings Rules 1991* (Report to the Department of Constitutional Affairs, 2006) pp 187ff.

[13] The Council of Europe Convention on Contact Concerning Children is concerned with transfrontier and other issues relating to contact between children and their parents when the parents live in different member states of the Council of Europe. The Convention is available at: http://conventions.coe.int/Treaty/en/Treaties/Html/192.htm.

[14] Paquin, G, 'Protecting the Interests of Children in Divorce Mediation' (1987–88) 26 *Journal of Family Law* 279–315, at 305–313.

mediators, meetings together with the parents, or both.[15] Another option is for a child advocate to participate in mediation sessions, having spoken with the child beforehand.[16] In jurisdictions that require the mediator to make recommendations to the court if the mediation itself does not result in a settlement, the mediator is likely to need to talk with the child for the purpose of determining his or her views and to formulate proposals that the mediator considers are in the best interests of the child.[17]

The debate on the involvement of children has in the past been polarized between two positions. Meggs summarizes the arguments as follows:[18]

The main argument against involving children in divorce mediation is that it is wrong to ask a child to choose which parent's position the child favours when he or she has a deeply divided sense of loyalties.[19]

Another argument is that it is for the parents and not the children to decide what arrangements should be made for the parenting of the children.

The main argument in favour of involving children in divorce mediation relies on the belief in children's rights. The children's rights argument implies that children are rational beings who can and should be invited to make a choice not only between two parents but also about the access arrangements.

These positions reflect the two poles of opinion on the issue of children's participation in making parenting arrangements after separation more widely.[20] On the first view, the purpose of involving children is to ascertain their wishes concerning the outcome of the dispute. This may indeed put them in a position of divided loyalties. The other position involves an assertion of rights and of children's competence to make rational decisions.

Recently in Australia there has been a concerted effort to include the voices of children in the mediation process without using this as a means of ascertaining their views or assuming that children of a particular age or stage of development are competent to make rational choices.

In child-inclusive mediation as practised in Australia, a specialist practitioner who has been trained in this work talks to the children privately.[21] He or she

---

[15] On an evaluation of the involvement of children in a conciliation service in Scotland, see Garwood, F, 'Children in Conciliation—The Experience of Involving Children in Conciliation' (1990) 28 *Family and Conciliation Courts Review* 43–51. See also Bienenfeld, F, 'The Power of Child Custody Mediation' (1985) 9 *Mediation Quarterly* 35–47.

[16] Paquin, n 14 above, at 311–313.

[17] See, for example, Paquin, G, 'The Child's Input in the Mediation Process: Promoting the Best Interests of the Child' (1988) 22 *Mediation Quarterly* 69–81.

[18] Meggs, G, 'Issues in Divorce Mediation Methodology and Ethics' (1993) 4 *Australian Dispute Resolution Journal* 198–209, at 206.

[19] Citing Kaslow, F and L Schwarz, *The Dynamics of Divorce: A Life Cycle Perspective* (Brunner/Mazel, 1987) p 117.

[20] See Chapter 1.

[21] The process is described in detail in McIntosh, J, *Child Inclusion as a Principle and as Evidence-Based Practice: Applications to Family Law Services and Related Sectors* (AFRC Issues no 1, Australian Family Relationships Clearinghouse, 2007). See also Hewlett, W, 'Accessing the

is known as a child consultant. This involvement requires the consent of both parents and at least one child should normally be of school age. The subject matter of the discussions will vary from child to child and family to family, but the objective of child-inclusive mediation is not to ascertain the 'wishes' of the children. Rather it is to explore more widely their perspectives and experiences of the current living and visiting arrangements and the conflict between the parents, as well as their hopes for the future.[22]

The consultant discusses with the children what can be fed back to the parents from their conversation or activities. The child consultant then meets with the parents to give feedback from the children's session, acting as a kind of ally to the children while helping the parents to reflect upon their children's needs.[23] Children's 'voices' may be heard through drawings, or through statements about how they are feeling about the conflict between their parents. They might express particular needs. What may, for example, be fed back to the parents is that their children are deeply distressed by the ongoing conflict. This may lead to the parents' softening their individual positions and to a greater willingness to compromise in order to reach a resolution. The children might express their views on how their parents' arguments at changeover time are affecting them, and this might lead to different changeover arrangements being made or different behaviour by the parents on such occasions.

Child-inclusive mediation therefore does not need to involve the children in expressing a view on the choices as the adults see them. Rather it provides children with an opportunity to give their perspectives on how they are feeling about the situation, which may in turn persuade the adults to change their positions and their behaviour. Richards has criticized the idea that mediators should talk with children and then bring their perspectives back to the parents, because, in his view, this is inconsistent with the mediator's neutrality.[24] In the Australian model, it is not the mediator who talks with the children and so the mediator's own neutrality is preserved.

McIntosh identifies the key elements of child-inclusive mediation as follows:[25]

- consulting with children in a supportive, developmentally appropriate manner about their experiences of the family separation and dispute;
- ensuring that the style of consultation avoids and removes any burden of decision-making from the child;
- understanding and formulating their child's core experience within a developmental framework;

Parental Mind through the Heart: A Case Study in Child-Inclusive Mediation' (2007) 13 *Journal of Family Studies* 94–103.
    [22] McIntosh, n 21 above, p 8.
    [23] McIntosh, n 21 above, p 8.
    [24] Richards, M, 'But What about the Children? Some Reflections on the Divorce White Paper' (1995) 7 *Child and Family Law Quarterly* 223–227, at 224–225.
    [25] McIntosh, n 21 above, p 5.

- validating children's experiences and providing basic information that may assist their present and future coping;
- forming a strategic therapeutic loop back to the child's parents by considering with them the essence of their child's experience in a manner that supports them to hear and reflect upon their child's needs; and
- ensuring that the ongoing mediation/litigation process and the agreements or decisions reached reflect at core the psycho-developmental needs of each child.

In an evaluation study, McIntosh and Long reviewed the outcomes of cases where there was child-inclusive practice compared with child-focused practice.[26] McIntosh and Long's evaluation shows that child-inclusive mediation has much more beneficial results for parents and children than mediation in which the children's voices were not heard.[27] Both mothers and fathers in the child-inclusive mediation group reported significantly greater satisfaction with their children's living arrangements one year after the mediation and also with the contact arrangements. The children in this group were also significantly more content and less inclined to want a different arrangement than those in the other mediation group. There was also greater stability in the lives of the children in the child-inclusive mediation group. The pattern of overnight contact remained stable over the year whereas it varied significantly for the group who went through the child-focused mediation.

It is significant that the amounts of overnight contact that fathers had in the child-inclusive mediation group were actually lower than that in the other group; yet their satisfaction with the arrangements was higher. The research has also found that the arrangements reached after child-inclusive mediation were more durable than those in the other group. The child-focused mediation group were more likely to have changed the arrangements or litigated to bring about new arrangements than the group that went through child-inclusive mediation. Children in the child-inclusive mediation also reported a more available relationship and greater closeness to their fathers one year later than did the children in the other mediation group.[28]

An evaluation of a pilot family mediation program in Hong Kong asked parents about the involvement of children. While many were opposed to interviews with their children, some did express support for this. Some parents even wanted

---

[26] In child-focused mediation, the mediator does not adopt a neutral stance. He or she tries to help the parents reach an agreement which is in the best interests of the children concerned and therefore takes a proactive approach to helping the parents reach the kind of agreements which are likely to be more beneficial for the children.

[27] McIntosh, J and C Long, *Children Beyond Dispute: A Prospective Study Of Outcomes from Child Focused and Child Inclusive Post-Separation Family Dispute Resolution* (Final Report to the Attorney-General's Department, 2006). See also McIntosh, J, Y Wells, B Smyth and C Long, 'Child-Focused and Child-Inclusive Divorce Mediation: Comparative Outcomes from a Prospective Study of Postseparation Adjustment' (2008) 46 *Family Court Review* 105–124.

[28] McIntosh and Long, n 27 above.

children to attend mediation sessions. Children expressed a clear wish to be involved in the mediation process.[29]

Child-inclusive mediation is in its infancy still in Australia and elsewhere but the success of the practice so far suggests that the participation of children in the mediation process in a sensitive way offers real benefits to children and parents. Parents may be able to reach a better level of agreement and alliance when it comes to their children's needs if they can hear the voices of their own children spoken to a neutral third party who is sensitive to their circumstances and views. Child-inclusive mediation does appear to have powerful effects in reducing the level of angst between the parents and in allowing more durable and workable agreements to emerge.

Child-inclusive mediation is now offered in a range of different mediation services across Australia. These include the Family Relationship Centres (FRCs). These centres, which have been established all over the country since July 2006, are highly visible and accessible places where people can go to get help in the process of separation or indeed if they have other difficulties in their family life. They have been devised as a first resource for people going through separation, providing them with information, advice and three hours of free mediation to develop parenting arrangements after separation.[30] Given the establishment of these free mediation services around the country, parents are now required to engage in some process of mediation, either through the FRCs or another approved counselling and mediation organization, before filing court applications. This pre-filing requirement does not apply where there are concerns about violence or abuse, or in relation to urgent matters. There are also certain other grounds of exemption.[31]

3.3 Family Reports

The most common way in which children's voices are heard in legal proceedings is through a social-science trained professional who prepares a report for the court on the family situation, making recommendations about what he or she considers is in the best interests of the child. In North America, such professionals are often known as custody evaluators. In England, such reports are prepared by a Children and Family Reporter whose qualifications include training in child development.[32] In other jurisdictions, they have other descriptions. In this book, these reports will be known generically as family reports.

---

[29] Chan, Y, R Chun, G Lam and S Lam, 'The Development of Family Mediation Services in Hong Kong: Review of an Evaluation Study' (2007) 29 *Journal of Social Welfare & Family Law* 3–16, at 9–10.

[30] Parkinson, P, 'Keeping in Contact: The Role of Family Relationship Centres in Australia' (2006) 18 *Child and Family Law Quarterly* 157–174.

[31] Family Law Act 1975, s 60I.

[32] Lowe and Murch, n 9 above; Bretherton, H, ' "Because it's me the Decisions are About"— Children's Experiences of Private Law Proceedings' (2002) 32 *Family Law* 450–457.

The family report usually examines all aspects of the family situation relevant to the decision to be made about the parenting arrangements. The children's views and perspectives may be a part of this, but are not heard in isolation from an assessment of the parent-child relationships taken as a whole. The use of family reports to ascertain the wishes and feelings of children reflects a view that it is better to rely on the work of trained experts to interview children and to interpret their wishes and feelings to the court. Not only are such professionals regarded as better able to interview children, but they are also seen as better qualified to interpret their views in the light of all the circumstances.[33]

In Australia, the Family Court has employed counsellors ever since its inception in 1976.[34] These counsellors, who are trained in psychology, social work or related disciplines, are now known as family consultants. They have two main roles. The first is a conciliation role to help resolve parenting disputes by agreement. The second is to write family reports and to give evidence in court. This latter role can also be fulfilled by counsellors employed on a contract basis.

Until 2006, the normal practice in Australia was that the mediators who sought to conciliate the dispute and those who wrote family reports were not the same people because the conciliation was confidential and privileged. Indeed the practice was to have a Chinese Wall between the counsellors fulfilling each role, with no communication allowed between them. However, this has changed with the establishment of the FRCs, beginning in July 2006, and the requirement since July 2007 to attend mediation in a parenting dispute before being permitted to file in court, unless one of the grounds of exemption could be shown.

With the emergence of mandatory pre-filing mediation, the family courts took the view that they no longer needed to engage in confidential mediation after a parent has filed an application in the court. Indeed, legislation in 2006 provided that the work that family consultants in the court system do with parents would not be confidential. The result has been the development of a new model of engagement with children and families when parents are involved in litigation about parenting disputes. The same family report writer will seek to conciliate the dispute, but if that is unsuccessful will then prepare the report for the court. In that process, he or she will normally see the children in a process that is similar to child-inclusive mediation.[35] This means that the family deals throughout the court process with the same person and that the family consultant builds up a picture of the family and the children through the process rather than coming cold to the family in writing a family report for the court.

[33] Bala, N, 'Assessments for Postseparation Parenting Disputes in Canada' (2004) 42 *Family Court Review* 485–506.

[34] For a history of the Family Court of Australia, see Starr, L, *Counsel of Perfection* (Oxford University Press, 1996).

[35] The 'Child Responsive Model', as it is known, which was piloted in Melbourne, is described in McIntosh, n 21 above, p 11. See also McIntosh, J, D Bryant and K Murray, 'Evidence of a Different Nature: The Child-Responsive and Less Adversarial Initiatives of the Family Court of Australia' (2008) 46 *Family Court Review* 125–136.

It is possible also for parties to agree on their own expert to prepare a family report. In some cases, where complex issues such as alleged child abuse or parental alienation are involved, the court will appoint an independent expert such as a child psychiatrist with special expertise on the issues arising in that family.

Family reports, or reports of independent experts, are not prepared in every case that goes to trial in Australia. The courts have to deal with the need to ration scarce resources and where the issues in a case are relatively confined, such as cases in which the issue is how much parenting time the non-resident parent should have, the court may decide not to order a report.[36] Nevertheless, the majority of cases that go to trial will have a family report or expert report, and the normal practice is that the report writer will convey the views of children old enough to give expression to them.

3.4 Child Representatives

In some jurisdictions, counsel for the child may be appointed to represent the child or children separately from the parents. The lawyer appointed to represent the child may be known by different names in each jurisdiction. Common terms include counsel for the child, separate representative, child representative and independent counsel. In Australia, the terminology was changed in 2006 and the term used in the legislation is now 'independent children's lawyer'. In this book, the generic term 'child representative' will be used.

Practice concerning the appointment of a lawyer for children varies widely. In New Zealand, for example, child representatives are appointed in almost all cases that go to trial in children's family law matters. Section 7 of the Care of Children Act 2004 creates a strong presumption in favour of appointing a lawyer to act for a child in any proceeding involving the day-to-day care, or contact with the child, if that proceeding is likely to result in a hearing. Such an appointment should be made unless it would serve 'no useful purpose' (s 7(2)). The lawyer must meet with the child for the purpose of obtaining their views (s 7(3)).

In England and Wales, by contrast, the appointment of a child representative remains uncommon in private law disputes between parents. A tandem model usually operates under rule 9.5 of the Family Proceedings Rules 1991. A guardian *ad litem* is appointed who is usually an officer of the Children and Family Court Advisory and Support Service (CAFCASS) or the National Youth Advisory Service (NYAS).[37] The guardian *ad litem* then instructs a solicitor. The

---

[36] A Practice Direction of the Family Court stipulates that a family report should not be ordered unless there is no other relevant independent expert evidence: Practice Direction No 3 of 2006, para 6.3.

[37] The detailed provisions for children's representation are under review by the government following a consultation process in 2006. See *Separate Representation of Children: Summary of Responses to a Consultation Paper* (Ministry of Justice, London, 2007).

child becomes a party to the proceedings through the guardian but does not give instructions or evidence.[38] In some cases a lawyer may be appointed directly without having a guardian *ad litem* to instruct.[39] Wall LJ has summarized the benefits of the tandem model:[40]

The child has the input of expertise from the different disciplines of lawyer and guardian, who are able, with the court's permission, to call on additional expertise and advice where necessary…Children are not required to give evidence and be cross-examined: they do not have access to the sensitive documentation generated by the case. This system is, of course, paternalistic in approach, but it usually works well, in my experience, even in cases where the child has sufficient understanding to participate in the proceedings concerned without a guardian.

Thorpe LJ did note in the same case, however, that this is a 'Rolls-Royce' model.[41] The nature of such models is that there often has to be a trade-off with breadth of coverage. Cost has been a major concern in trying to limit the appointment of guardians *ad litem* in the UK to only the most difficult cases.[42] The rate of appointment of a guardian *ad litem* in private family law cases varies around the country from about 2% of cases to 10%.[43] Although there are numerous grounds on which a guardian *ad litem* can be appointed,[44] Douglas et al found that the main reasons why a guardian was appointed were that there were protracted disputes between the parties often involving a number of separate applications.[45] Giving children a voice was certainly one of the reasons for appointment, but in general, a welfare motivation was most prevalent.

In Australia, there is no right to independent representation for children, but it is very common for a child representative to be appointed in complex cases,[46] and most cases that go to trial have some level of complexity to them. The 20 judges who participated in this study from around the country typically reported that most trials they conducted had a child representative. The child representative is appointed on the order of the court by the relevant Legal Aid Commission in that state or territory. Each Commission has a panel of private lawyers who have been trained in child representation. In addition, many of Legal Aid's in-house lawyers have been trained in child representation.

---

[38] *L v L (Minors) (Separate Representation)* [1994] 1 FLR 156.

[39] Fortin, n 2 above, p 213.

[40] *Mabon v Mabon* [2005] Fam 366 at 375.

[41] [2005] Fam 366 at 372.

[42] Douglas et al, n 12 above, p 29.

[43] Douglas et al, n 12 above, p 44. See also Bellamy, C and G Lord, 'Reflections on Family Proceedings Rule 9.5' (2003) 33 *Family Law* 265–269.

[44] See President's Direction: *Representation of Children in Family Proceedings pursuant to Family Proceedings Rules 1991, r 9.5* [2004] 1 FLR 1188.

[45] Douglas et al, n 12 above.

[46] The guidelines for when a child representative should be appointed were given by the Full Court of the Family Court in *Re K* (1994) 117 Fed LR 63. Sometimes they are appointed also in cases falling outside these guidelines. The statutory power is contained in the Family Law Act 1975, s 68L.

The cost of the lawyer is borne either by the parties, if they are funding the litigation themselves, or by Legal Aid. Parties are required to share the cost of the child representative equally on a stage of matter basis, that is, there is a fee for the work leading up to a trial and a further sum payable if the matter goes to trial. If Legal Aid is supporting one of the parents, then it will bear the half share of the costs attributable to its client.

In Australia, the role of the child representative is as a best interests representative.[47] That role has now been codified by statute. The Family Law Act 1975 provides that the independent children's lawyer must:[48]

(a) form an independent view, based on the evidence available to the independent children's lawyer, of what is in the best interests of the child; and
(b) act in relation to the proceedings in what the independent children's lawyer believes to be the best interests of the child...

The specific duties of the independent children's lawyer are as follows:[49]

The independent children's lawyer must:
(a) act impartially in dealings with the parties to the proceedings; and
(b) ensure that any views expressed by the child in relation to the matters to which the proceedings relate are fully put before the court; and
(c) if a report or other document that relates to the child is to be used in the proceedings:
    (i) analyse the report or other document to identify those matters in the report or other document that the independent children's lawyer considers to be the most significant ones for determining what is in the best interests of the child; and
    (ii) ensure that those matters are properly drawn to the court's attention; and
(d) endeavour to minimise the trauma to the child associated with the proceedings; and
(e) facilitate an agreed resolution of matters at issue in the proceedings to the extent to which doing so is in the best interests of the child.

It is not the child representative's role to give evidence of the views of the child. Counsel cannot be both an advocate and a witness.[50] The advocate must seek to ensure that the views of the child are presented to the court in admissible form.

There has been a long-standing debate around the world about the role of child representatives. Three discrete purposes for separate representation may be identified in practice, although a child representative may fulfil more than one of those purposes (and perhaps all of them) in a given case. These are a welfare role, a counsel assisting role and a role in giving the child a voice in the proceedings.

---

[47] See Keough, W, *Child Representation in Family Law* (Law Book Company, 2000); Blackman, L, *Representing Children and Young People: A Lawyers' Practice Guide* (Victoria Law Foundation, 2002) ch 11.
[48] Family Law Act 1975, s 68LA(2).
[49] Family Law Act 1975, s 68LA(5).
[50] See, for example, *Strobridge and Strobridge* (1994) 18 OR (3rd) 753.

There is a welfare orientation evident, for example, in many of the reasons for appointing a separate representative in both England and Wales in Australia. These reasons focus on cases of particular difficulty, for example, where there are allegations of child abuse or there is an intractable contact dispute, and where there is a significant risk of harm to the child. Here, the child representative has a protective role, by directing the court to the decision which will most protect the child from harm.

The second role is one of an amicus curiae, to ensure that all relevant evidence is presented to the court. This role can be of particular assistance to the court when neither parent is legally represented. The child representative may also be able to act as an honest broker to help resolve cases where the parents are locked in intractable conflict, and may assist the parents and the court by having a neutral role in the proceedings. An example, in the English Practice Direction, is where there are international complications (other than in international child abduction cases), and where it may be necessary for there to be discussions with overseas authorities or a foreign court. In such circumstances, an independent lawyer for the child may better be able to conduct such negotiations than a lawyer for one of the warring parents.

These two roles are encapsulated in the best interests model for counsel's role which prevails in Britain and Australia. The lawyer calls evidence, conducts cross-examination, and makes submissions to the court on what he or she considers is in the best interests of the child.

The third possible role of the child representative is to be an advocate for the child's views and desired outcome of the case. In New Zealand, section 6 of the Care of Children Act 2004 gives particular statutory emphasis to the importance of children's voices. It provides that a child must be given reasonable opportunities to express views on matters affecting the child; and that any views the child expresses (either directly or through a representative) must be taken into account. The importance of children's voices is also reflected in the English Practice Direction concerning the circumstances in which consideration should be given to the appointment of a guardian *ad litem*. These include:

- where the child has a standpoint or interests which are inconsistent with or incapable of being represented by any of the adult parties;
- where the views and wishes of the child cannot be adequately met by a report to the court; and
- where an older child is opposing a proposed course of action.

The debate on what the role of the child representative ought to be has become quite polarized in the same way as characterizes so much of the literature on children's participation. The two alternative options are a best interests role and a direct representation role. However, there is not necessarily such a difference between the two positions. The advocate who is seeking to promote the best interests of the child needs to know how the child feels about the situation. The older the children, the greater weight needs to be placed upon their preferences out of respect for their choices, having due regard to their age, their stage of cognitive development and the nature of the choices to be made. Those preferences also need to be considered because a child who is profoundly unhappy with the arrangements may act to resist their continuation. The child representative is therefore likely to see it as his or her role to advocate for the child's preferences if he or she has them, whether or not a 'best interests' or 'instructions' model is used.

The essential difference between the 'best interests' approach and the direct representation model is that the direct representation model more obviously facilitates the participation of some older children who have a clear position on the outcome that they prefer. They have an advocate in the proceedings who is putting forward their views. This, however, may not necessarily be a good thing in parenting cases. The child is likely to have an ongoing relationship with both parents, and will be dependent upon them both, long after the lawyer has ceased his or her work. Many children will want to have their say, but having an advocate in a court case for their views may be to engage in a more confrontational stance than they really want in the circumstances. Having a speaking part in the play is a little different from being centre stage, and children will react in different ways to having such a major role in the litigation.

There are, nonetheless, some weaknesses in the best interests model. Where a child representative is appointed for reasons concerning the child's welfare, or in order to provide an amicus curiae role for the court in complex cases, he or she can in theory fulfil the role without involving the child. It should not be thought therefore, that just because a child representative has been appointed, the child has a greater voice in the proceedings than if counsel had not been appointed. The child representative is not there to give evidence of the child's views, and does not need to make submissions in accordance with the child's views. It follows that appointing a child representative is not necessarily a means of fulfilling his or her rights under Article 12 of the UN Convention on the Rights of the Child.

3.5 Children as Parties to Proceedings

Do children have the right to become parties to family law proceedings with the same right of access to all the documents and evidence as the other parties, the right to give evidence and be subject to cross-examination, and the right to direct his or her representation? This is the logical endpoint of the direct representation model for the role of child representative. However, in jurisdictions where a best interests model is adopted for that role, direct representation of the child as a party to the proceedings is more commonly presented as an alternative to a court-appointed child representative.

In rare cases, the court may appoint a direct representation lawyer in addition to the best interests representative. This has happened, for example, in two Australian cases. In the first, a 14-year-old girl was allowed to become a party and to have her own solicitor when she had differences with the lawyer appointed to represent her.[51] The child's court-appointed representative was allowed to remain in the case as a best interests advocate. In another case which concerned the donation of bone marrow by a 10-year-old child, the judge ordered that the child be made a party and given a lawyer who would act on his instructions, as well as having a next friend, the Public Trustee, who was represented in the proceedings.[52] This is another Rolls-Royce model which could only be rarely justified given the costs involved.

Can children initiate an appplication? In England and Wales,[53] section 10(8) of the Children Act 1989 provides that a child is able to apply for a parenting order as long as he or she seeks leave from a court. The court should give such leave if it is satisfied that the child has sufficient understanding to make the proposed application.[54] Such leave needs to be granted by the High Court. Children may also initiate proceedings in Australia.

The issue of allowing children to become parties on a direct representation basis was considered by the English Court of Appeal in *Mabon and Mabon*.[55] Thorpe LJ described the tandem model as 'essentially paternalistic'.[56] He noted that in certain cases the guardian's view of the child's best interests may conflict with the child's wishes. He wrote:[57]

Although the tandem model has many strengths and virtues, at its heart lies the conflict between advancing the welfare of the child and upholding the child's freedom of expression and participation. Unless we in this jurisdiction are to fall out of step with similar societies as they safeguard Article 12 rights, we must, in the case of articulate teenagers, accept that the right to freedom of expression and participation outweighs the paternalistic judgment of welfare.

Wall J commented:[58]

I do not agree with the judge that the only advantage from independent representation was 'perhaps the more articulate and elegant expression of what I already know'. That analysis overlooks, in my judgment, the need for the boys on the facts of this particular case to emerge from the proceedings (whatever the result) with the knowledge that their

[51] *Pagliarella and Pagliarella* (1993) FLC 92-400.

[52] *Re GWW and CMW* (1997) FLC 92-748.

[53] For a comparison with Sweden, see Ryrstedt, E and T Mattsson, 'Children's Rights to Representation: A Comparison between Sweden and England' (2008) 22 *International Journal of Law, Policy and the Family* 135–147.

[54] See also Family Proceedings Rules 1991, r 9.2A. For commentary on children initiating proceedings, see Sawyer, C, 'Applications by Children: Still Seen But Not Heard?' (2001) 117 *Law Quarterly Review* 203–207.

[55] [2005] Fam 366.   [56] [2005] Fam 366 at 372.

[57] [2005] Fam 366 at 373.   [58] [2005] Fam 366 at 376.

position had been independently represented and their perspective fully advanced to the judge.

Wall J's focus on the importance of children's participation in terms of their acceptance of the result offers a vital perspective on children's participation. Having an advocate for a child may or may not help the judge to make a better decision than he or she would have made knowing the child's views and perspectives only from a family report. However, it may in certain cases lead to a better outcome, by giving young people the knowledge that their perspective has been heard in circumstances where the benefits of so doing outweigh the damage that might be done to the parent-child relationship.

3.6 Judicial Interviewing

One of the areas in which practices vary the most between jurisdictions is in the use of judicial interviews with the children who are the subject of parenting disputes. For many years, it was an acceptable practice in common law countries that judges could interview children in chambers when seeking to reach decisions about children's welfare.[59] While in some jurisdictions, that continues to be a common practice,[60] the accepted view in most modern common law jurisdictions is that it is better to rely on the work of trained experts to interview children and to interpret their wishes and feelings to the court. Writing in 1983, three Canadian judges explained why the practice of judicial interviewing should be regarded as undesirable:[61]

The interview is conducted in an intimidating environment by a person unskilled in asking questions and interpreting the answers of children. In the relatively short time these interviews take, it is difficult to investigate with sufficient depth and subtlety those perceptions of a child which explain, justify or represent the child's wishes. Moreover, the interview may be perceived as a violation of the judge's role as an impartial trier of fact

[59] Jones, J C, 'Judicial Questioning of Children in Custody and Visitation Proceedings' (1984) 18 *Family Law Quarterly* 43–91; Lombard, F, 'Judicial Interviewing of Children in Custody Cases: An Empirical and Analytical Study' (1984) 17 *UC Davis Law Review* 807–851; Scott, E S, N D Reppucci and M Aber, 'Children's Preferences in Adjudicated Custody Decisions' (1988) 22 *Georgia Law Review* 1035–1078; Hale, B, 'Children's Participation in Family Law Decision-Making: Lessons from Abroad' (2006) 20 *Australian Journal of Family Law* 119–126.

[60] Atwood, B, 'The Child's Voice in Custody Litigation: An Empirical Survey and Suggestions for Reform' (2003) 45 *Arizona Law Review* 629–690; Davies, C, 'Access to Justice for Children: The Voice of the Child in Custody and Access' (2004) 22 *Canadian Family Law Quarterly* 153–175. The authorization to interview children in chambers exists in most US jurisdictions. See American Law Institute, *Principles of the Law of Family Dissolution: Analysis and Recommendations* § 2.14 cmt a (2002).

[61] Abella, R S, C L' Heureux-Dubé and M L Rothman, 'A Code of Recommended Procedures in the Resolution of Family Law Disputes' in R S Abella and C L' Heureux-Dubé (eds), *Family Law: Dimensions of Justice* (Butterworths, 1983) p 329.

who does not enter the adversarial arena. The impartiality may also be compromised by the judge assuming the role of inquisitor in questioning children.

In addition to these issues, there is the question of whether judges are competent to interview children and to assess their views. As Kelly writes:[62]

Judges are not trained in child interviewing skills, and generally lack knowledge about developmental differences in cognitive, language and emotional capacities. Thus, it is hard for even the most experienced judge to place children's responses in an appropriate context and evaluate the weight that should be given to their wishes.

For these reasons, judicial interviews with children have been regarded by many people as anachronistic.[63]

However, a different view has been taken in Continental Europe. Article 6 of the European Convention on the Exercise of Children's Rights provides that in a case where the child is considered by internal law as having sufficient understanding the judge must 'consult the child in person in appropriate cases, if necessary privately, itself or through other persons or bodies, in a manner appropriate to his or her understanding, unless this would be manifestly contrary to the best interests of the child'. The judge must also allow the child to express his or her views and give due weight to the views expressed by the child.

In common law countries thinking on this issue has also begun to change again. There is now increasing discussion of the potential benefits of judicial conversations with children as part of the process of judicial decision-making in parenting proceedings,[64] and a growing view that this practice may, with certain safeguards, be appropriate as a way of recognizing children's right to be heard.

In England and Wales, the President of the Family Division has indicated his belief that in certain circumstances, judges ought to see children in private,[65] and a member of the House of Lords with extensive experience as a judge in family law matters has also indicated her support for the practice, saying that she has never refused to do so when asked by counsel to talk with a child.[66] In England and

---

[62] Kelly, J B, 'Psychological and Legal Interventions for Parents and Children in Custody and Access Disputes: Current Research and Practice' (2002) 10 *Virginia Journal of Social Policy & Law* 129–163, at 154.

[63] Starnes, C, 'Swords in the Hands of Babes: Rethinking Custody Interviews after Troxel' (2003) *Wisconsin Law Review* 115–169.

[64] Lyon, C, 'Children's Participation in Private Law Proceedings with Particular Emphasis on the Questions of Meetings Between the Judge and the Child in Family Proceedings' in The Rt Hon Lord Justice Thorpe and E Clarke (eds), *No Fault or Flaw. The Future of the Family Law Act 1996* (Jordans, 2000) pp 67–79; Bessner, n 3 above; Tapp, P, 'Judges are Human Too: Conversation between the Judge and a Child as a Means of Giving Effect to Section 6 of the Care of Children Act 2004' (2006) *New Zealand Law Review* 35–74; Crichton, N, 'Listening to Children' (2006) 36 *Family Law* 849–854; Raitt, F, 'Hearing Children in Family Law Proceedings: Can Judges Make a Difference?' (2007) 19 *Child and Family Law Quarterly* 204–224.

[65] Potter, M, 'The Family in the 21st Century' paper at *17th World Congress of the International Association of Youth and Family Judges and Magistrates* (Belfast, 28 August 2006). Available at: http://www.judiciary.gov.uk/publications_media/speeches/2006/sp280806.htm.

[66] Hale, n 59 above, at 125.

Wales, the option has been canvassed as an alternative to the use of interviews by CAFCASS professionals—expert report writers with social-science training.[67] However, a majority of respondents to a government consultation paper did not support the option of children speaking to a judge in private because it cannot be tested in evidence.[68] In Scotland, the majority of judges interviewed in a recent study said they were happy to speak with children if that is what the children wanted.[69]

In New Zealand, there is an increasing use of judicial interviews.[70] Tapp's analysis of 829 family law judgments in New Zealand during the 1990s indicates that judicial interviews were used to ascertain the views of the child in about 22% of the 130 judgments where it was possible to determine how the child's views were ascertained.[71]

This option has also begun to be used a little more frequently now in Australia than in previous years, although such interviews are still very unusual. The power to interview children in chambers has long been part of the law.[72] While it was not an uncommon practice among State Supreme Court judges exercising jurisdiction under the Matrimonial Causes Act 1959, the practice gradually disappeared with the advent of the Family Law Act 1975,[73] and the involvement of social-science trained professionals in the work of counselling and dispute resolution. In particular, the establishment of a Counselling Service as part of the Family Court when it opened its doors in 1976 gave to the Court a body of professional staff who could assess family relationships, talk with the children and prepare a Family Report for the Court.

Thinking about this issue has begun to change in recent years and a vigorous debate has emerged among Australian judges about whether it is ever appropriate for judges to interview children and, if so, in what situations and under what conditions. The reasons for this new debate in Australia about the appropriateness of interviewing children can be traced to two related developments that occurred at about the same time in 2004. The first was a change to the relevant provision of the Family Law Rules. The Family Law Rules 2004 continued the provision

---

[67] Hunter, R, 'Close Encounters of a Judicial Kind: "Hearing" Children's "Voices" in Family Law Proceedings' (2007) 19 *Child and Family Law Quarterly* 283–303.

[68] Ministry of Justice, n 37 above. This was also the view of most of the 35 District Court judges interviewed by Murch and colleagues in the late 1990s (Murch, M, G Douglas, L Scanlan, A Perry, C Lisles, K Bader and M Borkowski, *Safeguarding Children's Welfare in Uncontentious Divorce: A Study of S41 of the Matrimonial Causes Act* (Lord Chancellor's Department, Research Series 7/99) p 181).

[69] Raitt, n 64 above, at 209.

[70] Boshier, P, 'Involving Children in Decision-Making: Lessons from New Zealand' (2006) 20 *Australian Journal of Family Law* 145–153; Tapp, n 63 above.

[71] Tapp, n 64 above.

[72] The power to interview children in chambers is currently contained in Family Court Rules 2004, r 15.02.

[73] For discussion and citation of early examples of judicial interviews under the Family Law Act 1975 see *Ryan and Ryan* (1976) FLC 90–144 at 75,705–708.

in the previous Family Law Rules that judges could interview children in chambers. However, under the previous Rules, such interviews were not admissible in evidence. The 2004 Rules removed this exclusion, and gave conditions under which such interviews were to be conducted. By implication, rather than express provision, this meant that a judge could rely on the contents of such an interview in giving reasons for judgment.

The second influence was the Children's Cases Program which began operating as a pilot program in the Sydney and Parramatta registries of the Family Court of Australia in 2004.[74] This innovative program, aimed at reducing the adversarial nature of children's cases, contained many features that differentiate the process from a traditional trial. The process involves the judge swearing in the parties at the start of the case so that anything said thereafter is evidence in the case. The parties are each given an opportunity to explain at the beginning of the hearing what the dispute is about. The judge then seeks to resolve the dispute by agreement. If the matter needs to progress to an adjudication, the judge determines what evidence will need to be adduced. The Program also utilizes introductory questionnaires to gain a lot of the basic information about the case. Most of the rules on admissibility of evidence that apply in civil proceedings were excluded in the pilot program by consent of the parties, and instead the judge admitted the evidence giving it such weight as is appropriate in the circumstances.

This Program has now been mainstreamed with legislative support[75] so that it no longer relies upon the consent of the parties.[76] It is not a necessary feature of this program that judges should interview children in determining the matter. However, it was specifically included as one of the options that judges could consider in the pilot. In developing the model for the Children's Cases Program, a delegation from the Family Court visited Germany, where interviewing children in family law disputes is common.

The debate in Australia is occurring in a different context from the discussions in the past. Now the issue is whether there is a role for judicial conversations with children *in addition* to hearing children's voices through a court report by a counsellor, psychologist or psychiatrist.[77] These debates are considered further in Chapter 7.

---

[74] Sandor, D, 'A More Future-Focused Approach to Children's Hearings in the Family Court' (2004) 18 *Australian Journal of Family Law* 5–12; Bryant, D, 'The Role of the Family Court in Promoting Child-Centred Practice' (2006) 20 *Australian Journal of Family Law* 127–144.

[75] Family Law Amendment (Shared Parental Responsibility) Act 2006, inserting a new Division 12A into Part VII of the Family Law Act 1975.

[76] Hunter, R, 'Child-Related Proceedings under Pt VII Div 12A of the Family Law Act: What the Children's Cases Pilot Program Can and Can't Tell Us' (2006) 20 *Australian Journal of Family Law* 227–248.

[77] Crosby-Currie found that mental health practitioners in her study of US judges, attorneys and mental health practitioners were more attentive to due process protections in relation to interviews with children than judges were, and argued that both types of 'interview' were useful and that 'the choice of one type of interview to the exclusion of the other might be inappropriate' (Crosby-Currie,

3.7 Evidence from Children

Giving evidence in court is a further way in which children may participate in family law proceedings. It is possible in Australia for children to give evidence, but it is extremely unusual, and it requires the leave of the court.[78]

Historically, judges have taken a strongly protective stance. In a leading English case, *Re M (family proceedings: affidavits)*[79] a 12-year-old girl was refused leave to file an affidavit setting out her views which differed from the court welfare officer's assessment of her best interests. On an appeal in the case, Butler Sloss LJ wrote:[80]

... it is not fair on children that they should be dragged into this arena, that they should be asked specifically to choose between two parents, both of whom they love, and they ought not to be involved in the disputes of their parents.

This assumes, of course, that the child has an ongoing relationship with both parents that needs protection. In cases where there is an irretrievable breakdown in the relationship with one parent, due to violence, abuse or otherwise, the case for protection from giving evidence may not be nearly as great.

The question whether a child under 18 should be allowed to file an affidavit and to give evidence as a witness was also considered in the 1978 case of *Foley and Foley* in Australia. Lambert J said that in deciding whether to admit or refuse evidence by affidavit or orally from a child under 18, the following factors should be considered:[81]

(1) The nature and degree of cogency of the evidence it is sought to adduce through the child.
(2) Whether such evidence is reasonably available from an alternative source.
(3) The maturity of the child.

C A, 'Children's Involvement in Contested Custody Cases: Practices and Experiences of Legal and Mental Health Professionals' (1996) 20 *Law and Human Behavior* 289–311, at 308).

[78] Family Law Act 1975, s 100B provides:
(1) A child, other than a child who is or is seeking to become a party to proceedings, must not swear an affidavit for the purposes of proceedings, unless the court makes an order allowing the child to do so.
(2) A child must not be called as a witness in, or be present during, proceedings in the Family Court, or in another court when exercising jurisdiction under this Act, unless the court makes an order allowing the child to be called as a witness or to be present (as the case may be).
[79] [1995] 2 FLR 100.
[80] [1995] 2 FLR 100 at 103. See also *In the Marriage of Borzak* (1979) 5 Fam LR 571 at 575 in which Wood SJ of the Family Court of Australia said that the prohibition against calling a child as a witness 'is designed to prevent a child under 18 from giving evidence for or against either of his parents'; Watson J, referring to the relevant provision in the regulations, said that it was 'obviously designed for the protection of children and for their removal as far as possible from forensic partisanship in spousal conflict': *In the Marriage of Cooper* (1980) 6 Fam LR 288 at 289.
[81] *Foley v Foley* (1978) 4 Fam LR 430 at 432; (1978) FLC 90-511 at 77,680.

(4) The nature of the proceedings, and the relationship of the child to persons affected by those proceedings.

He noted also that:

...the court should weigh the value of the evidence to the determination of the issues between the parties against the possible detriment to the child in being thus involved in the adversary procedures between the parties. This necessarily involves some consideration of the prospects of a continuing relationship between the child and the parties following the necessary determination of the issues between the parties.

Very few of the Australian judges who were interviewed for the purposes of this study reported that they had allowed children under 18 to give evidence. A few judges indicated that they have done so on occasions, for example, where a change of name is involved for an adolescent child and where hearing directly from the child or young person who is 15 or 16 years old would settle the matter in the minds of parents that the child has a firmly expressed view about their identity which should not be contradicted by the decision of the court.[82] In one reported case, an 11-year-old girl intervened through a next friend in a child abduction case involving another child of her mother. She gave evidence and was cross-examined.[83]

Because, under Australian law, evidence from adults of what children say may be admitted as an exception to the normal rules of evidence concerning hearsay,[84] it is usually possible for evidence of what children have seen and heard to get into court in some other way.

3.8 The Filtering of Children's Voices

At the heart of the debates about children's participation is a tension between the filtered and direct involvement of children in family law proceedings. The prevailing view to date[85] has been a protectionist view. Whereas that once excluded children's voices, except in the case of judicial interviews with articulate older

---

[82] Nicholson, a former Chief Justice of the Family Court of Australia, states: 'There may be children, who wish to give evidence and if they do, it is difficult to see the rationale for preventing them doing so. To refuse them this right may well be a breach of their entitlements under UNCROC and may effectively prevent the court ascertaining their wishes.' (Nicholson, A (Chief Justice, Family Court of Australia), *Children and Young People—the Law and Human Rights* (Sir Richard Blackburn Lecture, Canberra, 14 May 2002) Available at: http://law.anu.edu.au/cipl/Publications/OccasionalPapers/nicholsonMay02Blackburn.pdf.

[83] *A and GS* (2004) FLC 93-199 at 79,280.

[84] See Family Law Act 1975, s 68ZV(2): 'Evidence of a representation made by a child about a matter that is relevant to the welfare of the child or another child, which would not otherwise be admissible as evidence because of the law against hearsay, is not inadmissible in the proceedings solely because of the law against hearsay.' On the earlier law, see *Barnett and Hocking* (1983) FLC 91-331.

[85] See Chapter 1.

children, now the protectionist stance is that children's voices should be heard in a way that still shields them from the heat of battle. The family report is the main vehicle for this, and appointing a child representative is another way in which children's voices may be heard through the submissions of counsel, whether or not counsel is an advocate for the child's preferred outcome.

The filtering of children's voices has the benefit not only of shielding them from the centre of the conflict but also allowing their voices to be articulated by a social-science trained professional who can be sensitive to the parent-child dynamics in terms of how those views are presented. The family report writer can also place the child's perspective in the context of all the family relationships and comment where a child's views may be the consequence of pressure from a parent or be inconsistent as a reaction to loyalty conflicts.

Perhaps that is also the disadvantage; for the filtering means that children's voices may only be heard with qualifications and caveats. The direct representation approach allows the child's viewpoint to be heard in an unfiltered way, but also without shielding them from the conflict. The tension between protection and participation is not one that can be resolved by argument and nor should it be determined on a win-lose basis. Both perspectives are important to determining the issue of children's participation, and neither is free from detriments or difficulties. The challenge is to work through how best to manage the tension, rather than resolving it through disregarding one or other orientation.

4

Children's and Parents' Views of Children's Participation

Children's involvement in relation to the post-separation arrangements concerning them can take a number of forms, depending on the circumstances, as outlined in Chapter 3. Children may be consulted in the course of negotiations between their parents on contact arrangements where the issue of primary residence is not in dispute; they might be interviewed by a counsellor and their views fed back to their parents in the course of mediation; they might have their views included in a family report; and they might be involved in the trial process as well, at least through having an independent lawyer to represent them, and perhaps also by having the opportunity to talk with the judge (see Chapter 7).[1]

The extent to which children are involved in any real sense, however, depends on a number of factors, not least the extent to which the adults involved, and particularly the parents, allow this to happen. Apart from the situation in which older children and adolescents 'vote with their feet' or refuse to cooperate with their parents' arrangements, children generally have to rely on the adults involved to hear their voices and accommodate their choices. Where parents and the other adults who are involved doubt children's competence or suspect their motivation for involvement, they can often play a key gate-keeping role by preventing those views from being heard or being taken seriously. A receptive audience is therefore the main prerequisite for children's involvement, and so some understanding of parents' views and also those of the legal and social work/social science professionals who are involved in making decisions about children's post-separation arrangements is important. Parents' views are considered in this chapter, and judicial and professionals' views in Chapters 5 and 6. While the burgeoning literature on children's participation has cited the underlying attitudes of adults in general, and the social construction or models of children in law and psychology in particular, as one of the significant barriers to participation, there have been

---

[1] See also Cashmore, J and P Parkinson, 'Hearing the Voices of Children: The Responsibility of Courts in Relation to Criminal and Family Law' (2007) 15 *International Journal of Children's Rights* 43–60; Parkinson, P and J Cashmore, 'Judicial Conversations with Children in Parenting Disputes: The Views of Australian Judges' (2007) 21 *International Journal of Law, Policy and the Family* 160–189.

few studies which have included parents' views, and compared them with children's views.[2]

4.1 Preconditions for Children's Participation

In addition to parents and other adults who are willing to facilitate children's participation, there are a number of other preconditions for effective participation by children in the decision-making process.[3] This does not presuppose that they will be the decision-maker but rather, a contributor to the process.

Early in the process, children need information that is appropriate to their level of understanding and circumstances about what is happening and likely to happen, about the various options, how the decisions might be made, and what their involvement might be, and perhaps some indication of their parents' views on these issues. At the simplest level, there is some indication from research that parents often believe they have told their children what is happening and explained what is likely to happen, but children often provide accounts that differ from their parents' accounts of what they were told or even whether they were told.[4]

Secondly, if children are to be involved, they need to have the opportunity to do so and some choice about how they might be involved, including the option of not being involved at all. The opportunity and choice also requires some honesty about the options and the extent to which their involvement will be possible. As research with children in out-of-home care has shown, children and young people are likely to become disillusioned about participating if they believe that their involvement is pointless or merely tokenistic because there is no real choice

---

[2] James, A and A Prout (eds), *Constructing and Reconstructing Childhood: Contemporary Issues in the Sociological Study of Childhood* (Falmer Press, 1990); Mayall, B (ed), *Children's Childhoods: Observed and Experienced* (Falmer Press, 1994); King, M and C Piper, *How the Law Thinks about Children* (Ashgate, 1995); Treseder, P, 'Involving and Empowering Children and Young People: Overcoming the Barriers' in C Cloke and M Davies (eds), *Participation and Empowerment in Child Protection* (Wiley, 1995) pp 207–231; Marshall, K, *Children's Rights in the Balance: The Participation-Protection Debate* (The Stationery Office, 1997); Trinder, L, 'Competing Constructions Of Childhood: Children's Rights And Children's Wishes In Divorce' (1997) 19 *Journal of Social Welfare and Family Law* 291–305. For a study of parental attitudes, see Smart, C and B Neale, *Family Fragments?* (Polity Press, 1999), and for children's experience and a chapter comparing parents' and children's attitudes and experiences, see Smart, C, B Neale and A Wade, *The Changing Experience of Childhood: Families and Divorce* (Polity Press, 2001).

[3] Lansdown, G, *Taking Part: Children's Participation in Decision-Making* (Institute of Public Policy Research, London, 1995); Treseder, n 2 above.

[4] Children in a number of studies have said they were told very little about their parents' separation, and what was happening (see Gollop, M, A B Smith and N J Taylor, 'Children's Involvement in Custody and Access Arrangements after Parental Separation' (2000) 12 *Child and Family Law Quarterly* 383–399; Dunn, J and K Deater-Deckard, *Children's Views of Their Changing Families* (Joseph Rowntree Foundation, 2001); Butler, I, L Scanlan, M Robinson, G Douglas and M Murch, *Divorcing Children—Children's Experience of their Parents' Divorce* (Jessica Kingsley, 2003)).

or no other option available.[5] When they were involved in decision-making processes, some young people in care were also unhappy that they were not given enough notice or time to think things through.

Thirdly, children often need support or 'scaffolding' to facilitate the process and to allow them to express their views appropriately. In formal processes, this means that the adults involved need to have the resources and skill to structure the process so that children feel they can participate safely.

Finally, children need to be able to understand and trust the way any information they provide may be used. If confidentiality is not guaranteed, children need to know that and take it into account in assessing whether they will participate and what they will say. As Kroll pointed out, sometimes, when difficult decisions have to be made, children may prefer a responsible adult and someone they trust to make a decision without implicating them in the process, especially if this preserves the relationships with their parents.[6] This does not mean, however, that they may not change their minds or wish to be involved later in a different way. Their views may also differ from those of their parents.[7]

This chapter will therefore outline children's views and those of their parents in relation to children's involvement in the decision-making process, taking into account the various pre-conditions for their involvement. It also distinguishes between several aspects of children's agency: the extent to which children wish to have any influence or involvement, the extent to which children and their parents think children should be involved, and the extent to which they actually were involved and had any influence over the arrangements.

4.2 Children's Views

Most children (91%, 40/44 who gave clear answers)[8] said that they should be involved, though not necessarily in *making* the decisions, with only a few, mostly

---

[5] Aldgate, J and J Statham, *The Children Act Now: Messages from Research* (The Stationery Office, 2001).

[6] Kroll, B, 'Working with Children' in F Kaganas, M King and C Piper (eds), *Legislating for Harmony: Partnership under the Children Act 1989* (Jessica Kingsley, 1995) pp 89–101.

[7] Smart et al, n 2 above.

[8] Both children and parents were asked several questions about the appropriateness, benefits and disadvantages of children having a say in the post-separation arrangements for residence and contact. For older children and parents, these took a general format (Do you think it is appropriate for you/children to 'have a say' in what is decided? Why/why not? Some people say it isn't fair to ask children what they want, that it puts you/children in a difficult position? What do you think?). For younger children, the questions were related to a vignette about a child of their own age and gender (Do you think Simon/e should say what s/he wants?/Do you think it puts Simon/e in a difficult position? What might s/he be worried about?).

younger children not wanting to be involved at all.[9] The strength of their views varied, however, with their experience—whether they were involved in contested proceedings and whether they had been exposed to violence, abuse or high levels of conflict between their parents. Children's views also varied within families, with some younger children being content with the contact or residence arrangements but older siblings seeking to change them, reflecting the inflexibility of orders and some parents' expectations.

Most children said that children over the age of seven should and could be asked, with only two (4%) specifying a younger age. Almost a third (14, 30%) said that there was no specific age for children knowing what they want but that children need to be old enough to understand 'what is going on'. Of those who specified a particular age or age range, the most common was from 7 to 10 years (13, 28%). There was no correlation between the age of the child and the age they nominated as appropriate for being involved ($r = .08$). Some children nominated their own age or a younger age as appropriate but more commonly children nominated ages that were substantially younger than their own or refused to specify a minimum age.[10] For example:

Well, it all depends on how old the kid is. I suppose I would have liked [to be asked] when I was 12 or something, and I knew what I wanted. *At what age do you think?* About 9 or 10. (Jade, 13, contested)

I don't think there is a 'too young'. I mean, even when I was three, I had pretty clear ideas of what I wanted and what I didn't, and even if they were based on completely stupid things, they should at least be considered. (Rani, 14, contested)

I think that it's fair to ask them because it doesn't matter how old they are just as long as they know what they want. (Kelly, 12, contested)

There were no significant differences between boys or girls, or between contested and non-contested matters though there was a non-significant trend ($p = .08$) for children in contested cases to nominate a younger age than those in non-contested ages. Only four children said they were too young to know what was best and to be involved; all four were under 10 in non-contested cases.

Just over half the children (23, 52%) gave quite strong and unequivocal responses indicating that children should be involved because 'it is their lives' that are affected; in the words of a 12-year-old in a contested matter: 'they are

---

[9] See Smart et al, n 2 above, for a very similar finding: 'only the very youngest in our sample felt that the decision should only be taken by the mother and father because it would be too hard for the child. The others thought that the child should either be able to choose themselves (some were adamant about this) or they wanted a group decision in which the child's views could be aired and taken into account.' (p 103).

[10] Similarly, many children in a Canadian study 'felt that, even at a young age, they knew enough about what was going on that they should be able to speak with decision-makers. Young people spoke about knowing "what is really going on" and that this information should be valuable to decision-makers' (Williams, S, *Through the Eyes of Young People: Meaningful Child Participation in Family Court Processes* (International Institute for Child Rights and Development, 2006) p 26).

the ones who are stuck in the middle of it'.[11] The majority of these children[12] were involved in contested matters, especially where there was violence, abuse or high levels of conflict. These children were less likely to be concerned that saying what they wanted would put them in a difficult position. As those on the inside, they knew what was going on, and like some of the children cited in English[13] and New Zealand[14] studies, the children who had experienced violence, abuse or conflict had less reason to respect their parents' feelings or trust their parents' capacity to consider their needs and care for them. Although a few were clearly concerned about the consequences of making their parents angry, these children were much more likely to 'insist that they should be able to make an autonomous choice about residence and contact'.[15]

The next largest group (17 children) gave more qualified responses, with some saying that they wanted to be involved but did not want to make the decision themselves (14 children, 32%); others said that it depended on the circumstances and exactly what decision needed to be made (3 children). These children were more likely to be involved in non-contested matters without high levels of conflict or violence (12/17). The difference in children's views between those in contested and non-contested cases was significant.[16] Whereas those in contested matters were more likely to say they wanted to have a say, and to be involved in the decision-making, children in non-contested matters were more likely to see it as a shared process, or, like Cassandra, as one that was more their parents' responsibility:[17]

Simone should have some say but it's more the parent's decision. They should listen to her just to mix with their idea what the child thinks. (Cassandra, 9, non-contested)

The ambivalence of some children was captured well by one teenager caught in the aftermath of a high conflict separation:

I'm not happy that I have to make the decisions but I'm happy that I could make the decisions. (Hilary, 14, contested)

---

[11] For similar comments concerning the strength of children's views, see Smart et al, n 2 above, pp 98, 104.

[12] That is 18 of the 25 children involved in contested matters (72%).

[13] Neale, B and C Smart, *Good to Talk: Conversations with Children after Divorce* (Report for the Nuffield Foundation, 2001).

[14] Gollop et al, n 4 above.

[15] Like those referred to by Taylor (Taylor, N, 'What do We Know about Involving Children and Young People in Family Law Decision Making? A Research Update' (2006) 20 *Australian Journal of Family Law* 154–178, at 163).

[16] $\chi^2 = 10.8$, 2 df, $p = .004$, odds ratio = 8.6.

[17] This is similar to the children and adolescents in other studies: Gollop et al, n 4 above; Smart, C and B Neale, ' "It's My Life Too"—Children's Perspectives on Post-Divorce Parenting' (2000) 30 *Family Law* 163–169; Parkinson, P, J Cashmore and J Single, 'Adolescents' Views on the Fairness of Parenting and Financial Arrangements after Separation' (2005) 43 *Family Court Review* 429–444. It is also consistent with the analysis by Smart et al of children's preference for some voice in collaborative decision-making and negotiations in a 'moral conversation' over the need to make a choice (Smart et al, n 2 above, pp 100–104).

4.2.1 Children's reasons for wanting to have a say

There were several consistent themes in children's comments about the benefits of being involved: the need to be acknowledged, the belief that this would ensure more informed decisions and better outcomes, and the view that they had the right to determine the arrangements that would affect them most.

Being acknowledged

The need for some acknowledgement and recognition that 'it is their lives' that are affected by the decisions that are made about them was the most commonly expressed reason for children wanting to have some say in what happened.[18] For Sandi, for example, being involved and asked for her opinion by her parents was a clear mark of her parents' respect and care for her, consistent with the 'ethic of care' and 'ethic of respect' outlined by Smart and her colleagues:[19]

I think it's important that they've asked us our opinion on it before they've made a decision. And they've made us feel like they actually do care about us, whereas before...when it first happened you felt like you were nothing...and then once they start involving you in it you realise that they do care, they want to know our opinion, they want to make sure that we're okay with it before they do it. (Sandi, 18, at the second interview)

Hilary, 14, referred to the importance of her feelings being acknowledged as well as the informational value of her views. She was disillusioned with her father when she became aware of clear evidence of his dishonesty in his adult relationships.

Well every living thing has feelings whether u r young or old. We know whose [sic] been nice or mean to us—shore [sure] we might be a bit bias[sic] to the parent whose [sic] not the bad guy but the parents can tell the judge their side. (Hilary, 14, contested)

Other children referred to feeling better if they knew what was going on and had some control over the situation, rather than being entirely at the 'mercy' of their parents' actions and decisions, especially in contested matters and when this involved a substantial move away from their family home. Rani's comment about her resentment of the process was a clear expression of her concerns about procedural justice. In a lengthy dispute about contact, 14-year-old Rani was unhappy that she had been excluded from the court process. Although there was a child representative and a family report presenting 'her best interests', she did not feel that her voice was 'properly heard'.

I know if I got a judgment that I wasn't completely happy with, but I had an active role in the process, I might not have resented it so much, because I would have felt, OK at least my voice was properly heard.

---

[18] This view was expressed by children in studies in England and Wales, Australia, Canada and New Zealand. See Gollop et al, n 4 above; Smart et al, n 2 above; Butler et al, n 4 above; Parkinson et al, n 17 above; Taylor, n 15 above; Williams, n 10 above.

[19] Smart et al, n 2 above, pp 93–100.

Better decisions, better outcomes

Related to the view that it is their lives that are affected, children ranging in age from 8 to 16 in both contested and non-contested cases saw their views as contributing to better decisions and more workable arrangements that they could be happy living with. Some children like 9-year-old Bianca were concerned that parents know what they want so they can make the 'right decision'.

[Simone should have] quite a bit of say because if her parents said what thay thort [sic] if they made a mistake, Simone mite [sic] be sad. (Bianca, 9, contested, in response to the vignette-related questions about Simone)

In the strongest expression of this view, five children, like Emma, proposed that their views should prevail, especially in relation to the practicality and ease of the arrangements and them refusing contact.

I think that it's important for them to have a say because it's their lives and they're going to have to deal with it and it's a choice that I think personally is up to them. It's not whether the parents want them to be with them because I'm hoping both of the parents want to be with their kids. It should be what the child thinks is best for themselves and how it's going to be easier. Like I wanted to stay in the same school and the same area and my Dad is now living [much further away] so that's what makes it hard to go and see him often, 'cause we have to get back to school and that means getting up early and being in traffic and stuff and so that's a choice that we made. (Emma, 13, non-contested matter)

A number of children also indicated, however, that they were concerned about the fairness of the arrangements for their parents and their siblings, not just themselves, and generally said that it was important for siblings to stay together.[20]

4.2.2 Children's reasons for not wanting to have a say

While only four children (9%) said they thought it was *not* fair to ask children what they want to happen in relation to the residence and contact arrangements, the majority (70%) indicated that 'being asked' does put them in 'a difficult position'. There were several reasons for their discomfort, especially if their views were to become known to their parents. For this reason, a number of children were keen that their parents would not know what they said, and this was one of the reasons children thought it would be useful for children to speak directly with the judge.[21]

Unwilling or unable to choose

Several children spoke quite explicitly about their unwillingness or inability to choose between their parents. Daniel, 16, who was in a shared care/equal time

---

[20] This is consistent with other findings concerning children's views on fairness within the family, and in particular with an 'ethic of care' and an 'ethic of fairness' in children's reasoning on similar issues (see Smart et al, n 2 above, pp 93–97). See also Parkinson et al, n 17 above.

[21] See Chapter 7.

arrangement, was very clear about the difficulty and unfairness of 'asking the child to choose between their parents, something which is not possible to do'. Jade, 13, was equally unwilling to say who she wanted to live with although she was keen to be heard in relation to the contact arrangements and was happy for these to be resolved through the court process.

Well, it is [unfair] if like, say if they've just split up, and they ask you then who you want to live with. But like when Mum and Dad went to court, Mum asked me 'cos that was the whole reason it went to court because I said that's what I wanted, so that was OK. It's kind of hard to say but it's not like that really big decision 'cos if I chose Mum, that would be slack to Dad, and if I chose Dad, that would be slack to Mum. (Jade, 13, contested matter)

Like the children in other studies, some were explicit in saying that they did not want to have to deal with any emotional pressure from one or both parents to say what they want.[22]

The consequences of 'choosing'

In explaining their reluctance or inability to choose, a number of the children who indicated that being asked what they wanted put them in a difficult position referred to the consequences for their parents ('being hurt or upset' or 'causing bigger fights', 35%).[23] Ten-year-old Heidi was concerned, for example, about 'making her parents sad' and that 'they might miss her' but she was still adamant after protracted contested disputes that children should have 'a lot of say' because 'it is their life'. One 11-year-old whose father had attempted suicide was clearly reluctant to 'get too involved' because of her concern about 'what might happen in the future'; she still said, however, that children should have a say. Others mentioned the risk of making the wrong decision (27%). Terri, 16, for example, was concerned that, in addition to being too difficult and upsetting to ask children about the arrangements, there might be some recovery possible from the 'wrong decision':

... if you don't like it, you can still go back and change the decision or whatever. So it's not like full-set in the ground.

Terri's comment is similar to those of other children in this study and children interviewed by Smart and her colleagues who believed that it should be possible for children to 'try things out' before settling on an arrangement. 'Trying things out' or 'experimenting' also means that children have a chance to reality test the options; 'wrong decisions' should be less likely and less of a concern.[24]

---

[22] Neale, B and C Smart, 'Agents or Dependants? Struggling to Listen to Children in Family Law and Family Research' (Working Paper 3, Centre for Research on Family, Kinship and Childhood, University of Leeds, 1998); Gollop et al, n 4 above; Butler et al, n 4 above.

[23] The children interviewed by Smart et al in several studies were also 'fully aware of the consequences of "choosing" one parent over the other' (Smart et al, n 2 above, pp 101–102).

[24] Smart et al, n 2 above, pp 101–102.

Four children involved in highly contested matters, including three who had been exposed to serious violence or abuse, were concerned about more direct and immediate consequences—that a parent might 'hit', 'hurt' or 'not let them in the house'. Despite their fears about being hurt, these children still wanted to have a say and thought that it was appropriate that they should do so.

Mike, 11, for example, whose father successfully contested residence after several years of substantiated abuse, said:

Like say if he says to his Mum that he wants to live with his Dad and stuff, then she might get really angry with him, and hit him and stuff, and then he'd be scared.

But he also said:

The court should let kids have their say, and like, I know it wouldn't be very good, but for the kids to be able to go to court and say what they want, so they could feel better.

4.2.3 Children's actual and perceived involvement

How much say did children have, according to them and their parents?

Sixty per cent of the children (27/45) said they had had some say (either 'a bit' or 'a fair bit') at some stage, in the arrangements about where they would live and when they would see their parents after their parents separated. For some children this was not in the immediate aftermath of their parent's separation but some years later when circumstances changed or the children wished them to; some of these children had been very young when their parents separated.[25] Two mothers also indicated that their adolescent daughters' views were influential in their final decision to leave their husbands. In the words of one:

I talked to her and I said 'Well, what would you think if I said to you I was thinking of leaving?', and she said 'I don't know why you went back in the first place', and 'I'd be relieved if you left.' So, I . . . um, that was it for me.

Eighteen children in 14 families, according to the children and their parents, were instrumental in seeking changes to their contact or residence arrangements in the years following their parents' separation. Other studies have cited similar proportions of children influencing or determining the arrangements.[26]

---

[25] Similarly, Gollop et al reported that a number of the 107 children in the 73 families in their New Zealand study who were not consulted over the arrangements at the time of separation 'subsequently had input into the way their time was divided between their parents', especially as they got older (Gollop et al, n 4 above, at 391).

[26] There is some consistency in the findings over the last decade or so across studies in various English-speaking countries although the age range of the children involved, the questions and the way these are expressed in terms of the type and level of children's involvement differ from one study to another. In their study involving 103 children aged 8 to 14 interviewed during the late 1990s in England and Wales, Butler et al reported that about 60% of children said they had had some influence over the post-divorce arrangements even though less than half of them said that they had not been consulted over the decisions about residence (44%), staying contact

Changes in residence

Changes in residence initiated by children were less common than changes in contact. In two families, adolescent girls changed residence without contest. In both cases the girls remained in or moved back to the family home with their father after the separation so that they could be close to their school and their friends but within 12 to 18 months they decided to move to their mother's home. Their relationship with their fathers remained close after the move, and one father moved from his home town to the city to be closer to his children.

In three other cases, however, the change of residence to the father was con-tested and difficult. It was the children's disclosures of abuse, calls to police or running away to the other parent that led to protracted court action resulting in orders that changed the residence arrangements. All three cases involved children who were quite young at the time of the separation and the matters returned to court on several occasions. They were finally determined in favour of the children living with their father following evidence of abuse or neglect and abduction by the mother and her partner. The other case involved allegations of abuse that were not substantiated amidst allegations of the father using undue influence to secure the children's move to the father's home.

Significantly, despite their actual involvement in the change in residence and having clearly said that they wanted that change, none of the six children in these three cases said that they thought adults listen to children. There is therefore

(42%) and seeing contact (48%) (Butler et al, n 4 above). Similarly, Gollop et al reported that about 55% of the children in their study had some influence over their current arrangements, with 16% determined by the court. They concluded that just over half (52%) of the children had little input into contact decisions and that only a minority of the children (16%) had their views prevail as the major determinant of their arrangements. Children reported that they were more likely to have been consulted about contact than residence arrangements, except those who were aged 13 and older, and the older the children at the time of the separation, the more likely they were to say that they had been consulted, except for those who were under 5 years of age at the time (Gollop et al, n 2 above, at 387–388). Similarly, the analysis by Parkinson, Cashmore and Single (2005) of data collected by the Australian Institute of Family Studies, reported that: 'Half the young people (30/60) said they had "no say" at all in where they would live after their parents separated. Not surprisingly, those who were adolescents at the time (13 and older) were more likely to report having had at least "some say" in the decision than those who were 5 or younger (5/6 of the 13+-year-old compared with 5/14 of the preschoolers). There was little dif-ference, however, between the 6- to 9-year-old and the 10- to 12-year-old, with about half of each of these two age groups saying they had a say' (Parkinson et al, n 17 above, at 432). See also Smart and Neale, n 17 above. Earlier studies indicate somewhat lower rates of consultation, which suggest that family culture in relation to consulting children may be changing. McDonald, for example, reported that only one in five of the 81 8- to 12-year-olds interviewed in an Australian city in 1988 were consulted about contact arrangements, although this figure rose to one in three if they were involved in high conflict cases (McDonald, M, *Children's Perceptions of Access and their Adjustment in the Post-Separation Period* (Research Report no. 9, Family Court of Australia, Office of the Chief Executive, 1990)). Kaltenborn also cites a 1989 German study by Felder, in which '34.9 per cent of the children were consulted by their divorcing parents concerning cus-tody decisions' (Kaltenborn, K-F, 'Individualization, Family Transitions and Children's Agency' (2001) 8 *Childhood* 463–498, at 464).

some difference for these children between their sense of agency and their actual exercise of agency or influence. To some extent, this appears to be related to their experience during protracted litigation, outlined later.

Changes in the contact arrangements

While some changes in the contact arrangements were quite common over time as circumstances changed, in about a quarter of the cases, children clearly initiated significant changes or asked for the changes to occur. In seven cases, children refused contact or refused to stay overnight. This was because they were unhappy with the arrangements, with the parent's new partner or with the parent's behaviour or inflexibility. All but one of these cases had been contested at some stage, if not in relation to the particular changes in the contact arrangements at that time. In several cases, the fathers decided not to proceed further with the dispute about contact in the light of their children's resistance which was evident in mediation sessions or in family reports and/or psychiatric reports.

As one 16-year-old whose parents separated when she was 4 said:

I didn't see the point in going there [if I was just being ignored]. And it just went on until I was 12 or 13 when I had enough guts to say 'no'. I said 'no' and just didn't go.

Another 16-year-old said she was no longer seeing her father after being unhappy with his inflexibility and his attitude to her mother:

He just sort of thought that we were the ones who were supposed to organise seeing him instead of him organising to see us. He couldn't respect that we have lives of our own and that Mum's a part of that. And I guess that he just—he doesn't understand, that's the bottom line ... when it comes to relationships, complications, people, he just doesn't understand. ... so [I said] 'I need you to just get out of my life for a while'. It wasn't 'I never want to see you again'; it was 'I just need a bit of space'.

On the other hand, three children 'pushed' for a resumption of or an increase in contact, in two cases after relocating with their mother some distance from their father and their sibling.[27] In one case, the mother took court action on behalf of an 11-year-old girl who wanted much more contact with her father; the case was unsuccessful. As her mother said:

I talked it over with Jade and said 'Look, I can go to the courts but I don't know what the outcome's going to be'. As far I was concerned, I didn't care if I saw him again. But that's my thoughts, not what Jade wanted—not that I said that to her. So she said, 'Yes, Mum, I want you to do it. I'd like to see Dad'. ... I knew that Jade would be involved and we needed to talk to him to ask him, 'Could she see him more?' but he didn't have the time. So then I decided to go through the courts, and it was only about two years ago that it was finalised.

---

[27] In addition to these cases, three mothers and two fathers took the intitiative to resume or increase contact between the child and the non-resident parent.

...the judge said he'd never come across someone like me so his decision was based on the law but there was really no precedent—which was really unfair to Jade. I wasn't legally represented either ... So we didn't win, and Jade was devastated once again. She's suffered a real loss but you can't force someone to spend more time with someone.

All the children in these cases in which there was some indication from the parent and the child that the children had had some influence over the change in arrangements were at least 10 years of age at the time of those changes. This is consistent with the fact that overall, children aged 12 and older were more likely to report having had 'some say' than younger children (19/23 of the children aged 12 and older compared with 8/20 of the under 12-year-olds) regardless of how old they were at the time their parents separated.[28] Children who were the subject of contested cases were, however, no more or less likely than those in non-contested cases to say they had some say in the arrangements.

4.2.4 How much say did children want?

When children's comments about how much say they *had* had were compared with how much say they *wanted* to have, and who they wanted to be involved in the decision-making process,[29] the main mismatch was for those who wanted more say than they said they had. Just over half the children (22/42, 52%) indicated that they had had little or no say but wanted more say[30] or to have been involved in the decision-making with their parents and siblings, and in some contested cases, with the judge and the counsellor; 15 (68%) were under the age of 12, and 12 were involved in contested matters. Some of these children had only vague memories of being told anything about the way things would be arranged. Others were simply told how it would be. Dominic, for example, who was 14 at the time, recounted what he was told and how he felt about changes his father made in the amount of time he lived with him, said:

I can't remember exactly—it's kind of like they talked about it and then Dad talked about it to me and I kind of talked about it to Mum and they spoke a bit. I was sort of like the

---

[28] The difference was statistically significant: $\chi^2 = 4.93$, 1 *df*, *p* = .024; odds ratio = 6.3. The clustering or non-independence of the children's responses associated with the inclusion of sibling groups was taken into account by using adjusted 95% confidence intervals and by calculating the size of the design effect for each outcome measure. The qualitative analyses and case studies also indicated that there was some variation in siblings' responses associated with age and their views about contact and their own participation. Some children in a family had different experiences in relation to contact and residence associated with age and gender.

[29] These questions were: Who was involved in making decisions about where you would live and how often you would see [other parent]? Who would you like to have been involved? Did you want to have more, or less say, or were you happy with the way things were arranged?

[30] This is consistent with the findings of other studies in which some children commonly wanted more say than they had had. See, for example, Gollop et al, n 4 above; Smart et al, n 2 above; Bretherton, H, ' "Because it's me the Decisions are About"—Children's Experiences of Private Law Proceedings' [2002] 32 *Family Law* 450–457; Butler et al, n 4 above.

middle. I was thinking that this is obviously not what I want to happen, and I really hated it at first and felt upset.

Hated what?

It felt like rejection 'cause Dad's like all of a sudden 'I don't want you to live with me anymore'—just like that and it was just like 'ok'. But then I understand it's just too hard 'cause he has to go to work and stuff 'cause he said he felt like we weren't being looked after and stuff 'cause he was always at work. So if we lived with Mum it would be more like we were cared for.

So did you say what you wanted to happen or were you pretty much told what was going to happen?

Yeah, basically told. He was moving and there was no other way. Obviously we were not going to go there every second weekend 'cause it was too far away but the fact that it happened right away before he actually moved, that was...

The next largest group (17, 40%), most of whom were 12 and older (13/17), were happy that they had had some say, even if for five of them that was only 'a bit'. Only three were under 12 and seven of the 17 were involved in contested matters. Only four children said they did not want to have a say; three were under 10 and said they had had no say at all, and only one was in a contested matter.

At the second interview, most children in both contested and non-contested matters said they were quite happy about the arrangements and about their involvement, especially where there had been changes in response to their earlier concerns and in cases where there had been violence or abuse. Two years also made a difference to how a number of children who had not been happy about their involvement felt about it. At the first interview, 22 children said that they wanted more say than they had had. Two years later at the second interview, only three children said they would have liked to be more involved.[31] One was Dominic; although he was happy with the way things had worked out following his father's changed living arrangements, he would still have liked to have had more say in the way it was done. An 11-year-old also still wanted more time with his father and said that he wanted to live one year with his mother and one with his father. At the first interview he said he had had no say at all and wanted a lot of say; he didn't think adults listen to children. A 10-year-old who was unhappy about relocating, partly because it involved the siblings being separated, said she had told her mother she did not want to go 'but she just put up with that'. On the other hand, most said they had been involved enough, and commented that they had learnt to accept the changes. One older adolescent who felt she had been involved reflected on the way her family had decided on the arrangements:

... you were involved in the decisions, asked what you wanted?

Yep, yep, always.

---

[31] The questions were: Do you feel any differently now about the way things were decided, compared with several years ago? Do you wish you had been more involved in the decisions?

Do you feel any differently now about the way things were decided? Nearly two years ago?
No, not really. I think it was done fairly. I can understand now why there was so much—the arguments and all that—because I can see how everyone got hurt in the first place 'cause I can look back on it now and I can just see Dad was upset, Mum thought she was doing the right thing but everybody else was in the wrong, and I can see why everything was such a mess back then. But now I can realise that they did try to do the best they could. It all worked out as far as I am concerned. (Sandi, 18, non-contested)

4.2.5 Having a say and the fairness of the arrangements

Overall, having a say in the arrangements was not associated with how happy children were with the arrangements, at either the first or second interview. Nor was there any association between the perceived fairness of the arrangements and whether or not children had wanted more say than they thought they had. The exception was for the fairness of the amount of time children had with their non-resident parent (mostly their father).

Children in non-contested cases were more likely to say the time they had with their father was fair if they felt they *had* had some say during the process ($r = .56$, $p < .01$, $n = 21$). Of those who wanted some changes in the arrangements at either the first or the second interview, the most commonly desired change was to have more time with their non-resident parent and more flexibility in the arrangements.[32] Their concern was to maintain their relationship with both parents and to increase the amount of contact or the flexibility of the arrangements, especially as they got older. Sandi, for example, related the fairness of the way she and her sister were treated by their parents to the way they managed their relationships, as well as the respect they accorded her by asking for her opinion.[33]

And the fact that they do [are ok with it] ... with the fairness is like seeing each other ... like one doesn't mind if you go out to see the other and ... it makes it easier than one being, 'I don't want you to see your father' or 'I don't want you to see your mother'. It makes it a lot easier. (Sandi, 18, at the second interview)

In talking about the fairness of the arrangements, their focus was more on the sheer logistics of the arrangements, their own resistance to the travel or particular

---

[32] Children in non-contested cases rated their relationship with their non-resident parent as significantly closer than those in contested cases (mean ratings at the second interview of 2.7 for children in non-contested matters and 1.7 for children in contested matters (on a 4-point scale from 1 = 'not close at all' to 4 = 'very close'); $t = 2.89$, 32 df, $p = .007$, eta = .455). There was no difference in their mean ratings of the closeness of their relationship with their resident parent (3.75 for children in contested matters and 3.6 for those in non-contested matters).

[33] Smart et al referred to an 'ethic of respect' in relation to children wanting to have their choices respected, including the opportunity to make the wrong choice (Smart et al, n 2 above, pp 97–100).

time involved, and their parents' relative responsibility for getting them there than how much say they had.[34] For example:

I'd make Mum drive half-way and I would see Dad every second weekend. (Skye, 11, non-contested)

On occasions, Mum would find it really hard to get us to go over there...and we'd be really struggling, we'd have fights and she was really getting worn down...just the fact that we lived so far away, and I hate travelling. So that would be the main reason...not that I wouldn't want to see Dad more, it would just be the organising, and getting to places, and stuff like that. It would also cost more...with petrol and stuff like that. And that sort of comes back on us kids, because we're not getting what we need. (Terri, 18, second interview)

Oh, it's sort of as fair as it can be. I think Mum has a very hard time. Like, Dad doesn't do enough driving around and stuff like that. He's trying to be fair but it's not really. He does a little bit of stuff for us, but not enough. It's not fair on Mum. (Emily, 15, second interview)

For children in contested matters, the fairness of the time they had with their father was not associated with the amount of say they thought they had—but with whether they wanted more say. The less fair they thought the contact arrangements were, the more say they wanted.[35] In most of these cases, the children indicated that their relationship with that parent was not close and that they were having little contact in the wake of protracted residence and contact disputes involving allegations of violence and abuse. In a number of these cases, the children had been instrumental in wanting less contact and were quite happy that the contact had been reduced or stopped.

Why the difference again between children in contested and non-contested matters? As outlined earlier, children in contested cases were more likely than children in non-contested cases to say it was appropriate for them to have some real influence over the decision, not just 'voice' but 'choice'. Similarly, being able to stop and, where they wanted to, later resume contact may therefore be seen as being fairer and more meaningful for children in contested cases. In non-contested cases, however, the father-child relationship[36] was closer, and children were wanting more contact; in this case, fairness has more to do with the relational aspects, and to be based on fairness for the parents and siblings as well as for the child. A number of these children, like those cited in other studies, do not want to make the decision but want their views to be heard and taken seriously.[37]

---

[34] For a discussion of an 'ethic of fairness' in children's views about family arrangements, see Smart et al, n 2 above, pp 90–92.

[35] $r = .47, p < .05, n = 22$.

[36] Most of the non-resident parents were fathers.

[37] Gollop et al, n 4 above; Smart and Neale, n 17 above; Butler et al, n 4 above; Douglas, G, M Murch, C Miles and L Scanlan, *Research into the Operation of Rule 9.5 of the Family Proceedings Rules 1991* (Report to the Department of Constitutional Affairs, 2006); Taylor, n 15 above, at 160.

4.3 Parents' Views

Ninety parents (43 mothers and 47 fathers) were asked a range of questions concerning children's participation, including questions about whether children had had any say in the arrangements, either within the family or in more formal court-associated processes, and whether they thought that it was appropriate for children to do so.[38] They were also asked: What do you think are the benefits? And the problems? At what age do you think children are old enough to be asked what they want to happen? Too young? If children do 'have a say', what do you think is the best way for that to happen?

4.3.1 Should children have a say?

Most parents (87%) said, with varying levels of qualification and support, that it was appropriate for children to have a say. A group of eight parents (9%) were unequivocal in their view that children should definitely have a say, and even make the decision. In most of these cases, the children involved were teenagers (aged 12 to 16) and several parents in non-contested matters had, according to their own reports and their children's, invited their children to express their views and to influence the decision. In one case, two adolescent siblings had moved between their parents' homes several times, and had not stayed together throughout the period after their parents separated:

I wanted the kids to move up here with me but it was their choice. And that's the way I tried to be all the way through. If I felt that they were making the wrong choice completely, then I'd step in. But as Sandi has pointed out to me many times—'Dad, at the age of 12, I can ask the Judge to put me wherever I want to be', disregarding what the parents may want. I said, 'Where did you find out that information?' She said, 'On the internet at school'. I mean, the old days of what the parent says, goes, has gone out the door. That's bad in some ways, but I suppose it's progress and it's good in other ways. The kids have got to make up their own mind and they've got to be happy where they are. (Father of 16- and 14-year-olds)

Another mother whose 12- and 15-year-old children were in shared care arrangements explained her position this way:

I think for sure that they should have a say … because ultimately, they're the ones who've got to do the moving around and living and they should, because if they, like for instance, if Dominic says to me now 'Oh Mum I think I want to stay with Dad because it's more convenient or whatever', well I would say 'Well yeah, I think that's OK, and I'll see you—maybe you can spend two weeks with Dad and one week with me or whatever?'

---

[38] Most of the mothers (39/43, 90.7%) were resident parents, and the majority of the fathers were non-resident parents (32/47, 68%). Seventy-one percent of the parents were involved in contested matters.

The parents in the four cases involving younger children argued the strength of their position in two ways. In several contested matters involving children under 10, non-resident parents (two fathers and one mother) strongly advocated the courts listening to their children, especially where the children's views were very strongly held:

I most certainly do. Because... it's one thing for the courts to say the children are too young to make a decision and everything else, but if the children are adamant about where they want to go and where they want to stay, well the courts should listen to them. (Non-resident father of 7- and 8-year-old children)

In two non-contested matters, a non-resident mother and a non-resident father both called on their own experience as young children whose views were not listened to or were over-ridden when their parents separated:[39]

Yes definitely, definitely, because I was—my mother and father broke up when I was 2 and I went and I lived with my father and my grandparents until I was 5 and I loved it. Mum used to come and see me. And the day I started school, Mum came and took me and I went back to Cityville and I was never, ever happy. (Non-resident mother of 5-year-old)

In my instance I'm all for it, but in my parents' instance ... I used to go to my father's, it broke my heart actually. I said to my father when I was a kid 'I want to come and live with you', and he said 'Oh you know, your Mum needs you' and at the end of the day, it absolutely broke my heart. Now, I'm old enough to know my stepmother wouldn't have had me. I wasn't in a position where the stepmother, like my wife, says 'hey you want to come and live, here the door's open, it's yours, we'd love to have you', so that really does depend even to the point if they made the kid make the decision but don't tell the parents what the child's decision was. (Non-resident father of 7-year-old)

Ten parents (seven fathers and three mothers), seven of whom were involved in contested matters, took a directly contrary position, saying they believed it was inappropriate for children, and their children in particular, all of whom were under 12, to be involved. They were mostly referring to decision-making and had several main reasons for this view: first, the inappropriate pressure and burden of responsibility this places on children; secondly, concern about the choices children might make, especially under pressure or influence from the other parent; thirdly, the 'parent knows best' argument.

Children are children. And children are the responsibility of their mothers and fathers. And mothers and fathers, um, should have an idea really of what is better, is best for their children, until they become adults. And I think if you've got a heart for your children, you will know what is best for your children, you will know that they need to be with

---

[39] Smart et al reported similar findings (Smart et al, n 2 above, p 168, citing Smart and Neale, n 2 above). They commented that 'the divorced parents they interviewed often drew on their own private experiences of being a child of divorced parents as a way to guide their own behaviour. They tended to say that they wanted to manage post-divorce life better than their parents had done, and thus turned the experiences they had had as children into a moral resource for their adult actions'.

their mother. You will know that they need to be with their father. (Non-resident father in contested matter involving 11- and 8-year-olds)

A non-resident father of three children aged 8 to 10 years involved in a contested matter explained:

How are they going to make a decision? Say the separation or divorce happens quickly and the child doesn't know which of the parents they're going to go for, it can be very hard. Especially if you love them equally which most kids do anyway. The child is really torn between the two of them. Some cases are fairly straightforward and it works out okay, but then other people are vindictive and carry on like idiots. They don't think about what's happening to the child, they just think about what's happening to me.

Another non-resident father of children aged 10 and 12 in a non-contested matter admitted:

Early on I suppose I was probably scared that they wouldn't choose to come and live with me. But I'm not sure they know... I still think they're too young to be making that decision.

The majority of parents fell between these more extreme positions. They expressed a range of views about qualified acceptance, depending on children's age and maturity and the context or the circumstances. The idea that children's views should be heard (voice) but should not be decisive or determinative (choice) was common.

You have to take the circumstances into account... and the maturity of the child, and I don't think it should be directed by the children but having their opinion [taken into account], yes. (Resident mother of three children aged from 6 to 11 years in non-contested matter)

I think they should be involved. I do, I think they should. Children, obviously, are not always mature enough to make a sound judgment, they don't always know what's best for them—no—most of the time they probably don't. But, there are occasions I think when it's justified for a child to—I don't think they should have a decisive role, but I do think if there's—if a child's wishes are different to either of the parents, then that needs to be explored. (Resident mother of 10 year old in contested matter)

Some parents emphasized the matters that needed to be decided, the options 'on offer' and the process by which children were involved. They did not believe that children should be asked to make a bad choice but could be asked what was important to them and what their preferences might be among various options.

It shouldn't be just as a straight question, you need to know what the reasons are, and that the parent they're living with is not influencing them. (Resident father of 10-year-old, contested matter)

Well if the child can have a say and say, 'Well, look I'm more than willing to do every weekend at Dad's place or Mum's place, and spend the rest of the time at the other's place', that'd be fine. But where there's a residency order where there's no contact with the other parent, that could be harmful to the child where they have to choose. (Resident father, of 8-year-old in contested matter)

Several parents advocated children having experience of the options so that their views were based on the actual experience rather than a hypothetical or imagined scenario:

I think it's difficult for children of an age of less than about 10 to actually understand what they're asking for, or being asked to choose between, until they experience the other side. So the only way that can possibly work is if you were maybe to have six months in one arrangement or six months in another arrangement, or three months or something, so that the child can actually experience it. Because while it all looks rosy from the other side, actually being here and living here in the other parent's house might not be what it's cracked up to be, particularly if contact is always on a weekend, so the contact house gets seen as a holiday house. So the grass looks greener from the other side...

   After a year of litigation we're not very good at communicating with each other. So that's the sort of thing that I think the system should try to get out of young children of 5 to 6 years of age—to try one thing and try another thing and ask them to tell the lawyer or the counsellor what they liked the most. (Non-resident father of 5-year-old in contested matter)

4.3.2 Age, maturity and parental influence

Two main themes permeated parents' responses about the appropriateness of children's participation. These were the significance of the children's age and maturity and concerns about parental influence and manipulation. These concerns were very similar to those of the lawyers, discussed in Chapter 5.

When children are old enough to have a voice

Most parents, without prompting and also when specifically asked, referred to children's age and maturity as one of the main factors that determined for them the weight that should be placed on children's views, and whether it was even worth involving children at all. Those who specified an age or an age range nominated ages ranging from 2 or 3 years through to 14, with parents, more than children, embracing both the lower and upper extremes of the age groups. On the one hand, some parents argued that very young children should be listened to:

I've seen very small children, of 3 and 4, who haven't got the communication skills, but a 3 year old can be very vocal. From 3, if the child is given enough time at the level of cognitive development that they're at, knowing that they're egocentric and all the rest of it, they will love to talk about themselves, and they can give you quite good solid information. So I'd say from 3. But that's my opinion. There are children I've known at 2 that are quite vocal. But a 3 year old can be very clear. (Resident mother of 4-year-old, contested case)

On the other hand, some parents were reluctant to allow children under 12 or even under 16 to be involved in any decision-making, referring to the development of rational thought and the turbulence of puberty. For this reason, one non-resident father of 7- and 8-year-olds was more concerned about adolescents than younger children having a say.

They're confused, at puberty their system goes way, way, way out of whack, so no, get them before that age, and then somewhere like 16 or 17, where they're probably on the verge of thinking for themselves. Yeah 15 or 16 is a right enough age, because they can start thinking on that level properly. But between 11 and, and uh 14, no. Because they're at a confusing age, a rebellious age type thing. And before that, say between the ages of 7 or 8, the kids do know what they want. They're adamant about what they want at that age.

Late primary and early teenage years were often seen as a time when children should have a right to decide:

Now she's 6 and a half, I still don't think that that's an age where they can decide. I reckon 12 or 13, I reckon that's... and when Amy is 12 or 13, if she wants to live with Theresa, well I'll let her do that, but Theresa's also got to provide that I still have good contact, not like once a week. But if both parents can agree and like sit down without going to court, then I reckon 12 or 13. (Resident father of child aged 6)

To be honest I think that at 4 and 6 and those sort of ages, I think whoever doesn't make them go to bed early will win the race there. Once they get over 13, I think they can start to make a decision. (Father of 14-year-old in shared arrangement)

For other parents, children's maturity and the context were more important than their age (15, 17%). The circumstances mentioned included the presence of violence especially involving the child, the potential or actual influence or manipulation by the parents, and the joint issues of who was asking the child and interpreting what they wanted. One non-resident father said, for example:

Of course they should have a say and they should be able to put it in their terms... but I think you need to overlay that with the broader context and contextualise the children's wishes and work out the level of maturity and understanding of what it means. (Father of children aged 7 and 11, non-contested matter)

Parents' own experience and the age of their own children and other children they knew, as well as the differences between their children and others, and between siblings, were important factors for many parents. One non-resident father of children aged 11, 7 and 5, for example, referred to the differences between his children and the different approaches they needed:

I don't claim to be an expert but what I would say is that... all of this has to be tempered on the child, the individual, and so I could even say from my three. Daniel, at age 7 is far more aware in many respects than Matthew at age 11... I think, what I remember was something about at age 13 they have a choice, and it seems to me, I'm thinking probably more of nieces and nephews here, but also where my kids are going... that's probably not too far off the mark.

Like this parent, several parents were under the impression that once children were somewhere between 12 and 14, they were able to make their own decision:

I was counting the years until my daughter turned 12, because I was told the age of 12 is when I can do this. The problem is, my daughter turns 12 my son's still 11. And they were told, 'I can't do anything until James turns 12'. Because if the courts won't give me James and you at the same time, I need you to be there for him, so I can take you both at the same time. (Non-resident father of 7- and 8-year-olds)

This idea, that there is a certain age when the law gives to children the right of choice, has no foundation in Australian law.

There were few differences in the views between mothers and fathers or between resident and non-resident parents. Those in contested matters, however, were significantly more likely to say that it was appropriate for younger children—those under 10—to have a say than those in non-contested matters.[40] One resident mother involved in a highly contested property and contact dispute said, for example:

My opinion is that from the time a child can string a few words together, and are able to articulate thoughts in relation to other matters, they've obviously got feelings and thoughts in relation to the parents, so I think they should be listened to, and certainly at least in family reports. (Non-resident father of 9-year-old in contested relocation matter)

Children as manipulable and subject to parental pressure

Well over a third of the parents expressed some concern about children being influenced or manipulated, either in general terms (16, 19%) or more specifically in relation to their own children (22, 26%). Both resident and non-resident parents referred to the influences that they or their ex-partners could use or had used in relation to their children. This included direct bribery by buying children games, toys and motorbikes, as well being the 'fun' parent and allowing children more freedom than they had in the other household. At the extreme end, several parents, like several children, were concerned about the repercussions and actual harm to children who did not say what one parent wanted them to say. Two fathers who had successfully contested residence with their violent and abusive former partners referred to threats and the children's fear of their mother:

... his mother told him 'Don't tell anyone about the drugs or they'll take Mummy away and you'll never ever see her again', you know. Or a parent might say to a kid 'You don't want to go over to Dad's because he's going to take you away for a long time' so the kids say they don't want to go. So at least talk to them in a safe environment.

Another spoke of his concern that the children were being 'programmed':

---

[40] 68% of parents in contested matters were in favour of children under 10 having a say compared with 32% in non-contested matters (χ^2 = 5.49, 1 df, p = .019, odds ratio = 4.74). There was also a trend for parents favouring younger age-appropriate involvement for children for their contested matters to have been resolved in their favour but the cell sizes were small.

So you feel they're being manipulated in the whole process?
Oh yes, they've been programmed. It's very obvious. The other kids are more being manipulated into being nasty towards me.

Several parents, however, indicated that during the heat of the dispute they had been suspicious about the other parent being manipulative but recognized later that it had not happened.

While it was younger children who were generally seen as more vulnerable to manipulation, bribery and more benign influence, adolescents were not seen as exempt, especially in relation to their wish for greater independence.

It was not just the parents who were seen as blameworthy in relation to manipulation. Eight parents also expressed some concern about children and adolescents manipulating or 'playing their parents against each other', so undermining parental authority.

Kids are very smart. Kids love to play one off against the other. At Mum's I have no rules, but at Daddy's, because I see Daddy every second weekend, we run riot, and Daddy buys us this, or Mummy buys us that. And as they get older, 'I'm a teenager and I want more freedom to go and hang with my friends, hang out in the streets until 10 or 11 at night, because I'm 13, 14, and I think I should be allowed to—I'm not living with these rules, I'm going to go and live with Dad, or with Mum.' So, yeah, why wouldn't they swap sides? (Resident father of two children, aged 8 and 7)

On the other hand, an equal number of parents explicitly challenged the idea that children are manipulative or easily 'bought off', indicating disagreement with their ex-partner over this issue. For example:

But I actually don't think children can be brainwashed. I actually think that that's thinking that children are like puppets, or like, that we can coerce them into thinking and believing whatever we want them to think or believe, and that's far from the truth. (Resident mother of children aged 8 to 19, contested matter for younger children)

Children as saying what the parent wants to hear

For another sizeable group of parents (20), the concern was less about children being pressured, bribed or manipulated than that children would say to both parents what they thought they wanted to hear. Both mothers and fathers and resident and non-resident parents expressed these concerns:

Charlotte was so worried about upsetting either of us—whoever she was talking to, she would agree with that person. So it did get to the point where I did wonder 'What the hell is in your head, child?' Like...I had a talk with her one day. We went to the beach, and went for a long walk, and she did say to me, 'Yes, I tell Daddy that I want him to live with him, basically because that's what he wants to hear.' And I said, 'But you tell me that you want to live with me?' She said, 'Yes'. And I said, 'That's because that's what I want to hear?' And she said, 'Yes'. She's a smart cookie. So I said, 'That's not going to help the situation. If somebody asks you, you've really got to tell the honest truth, so you need to think about that, and stop trying to protect our feelings. We're grown up and we can cope with it.' (Resident mother of 9-year-old in contested relocation matter)

Kids end up getting torn because it's like...the classic example is when I asked Danny where they went on the week-end after he told me last week they were going away when I was trying to arrange to see them. He wants to tell me because I'm his Dad but he doesn't want to betray any trust with his mother because that's who he's living with. And that's when it's hard when you say 'Well, what do you want to do?' and at some ages, they will feel right in the middle of this, and not want to say 'Yes, I want to see Dad' because Mum might perceive that as saying that I don't like her—taking sides in the argument. (Non-resident father of four children aged 3 to 9 years in contested matter)

For this reason, the process, including an independent mediator or counsellor, was important to a number of parents to ensure that children could have a say, and that their real wishes and views would be heard.

Divorce is not always easy for kids to understand and I'd say a lot of kids want to please Mum and they want to please Dad. When they're with Dad, they want to please Dad, when they're with Mum and vice versa. And if they've got another voice other than Mum just taking it to court and saying this is what the kids want or vice versa, then they can actually say it without being threatened. Because I mean the child's representative, the kids are on their own with him or her, so they can say how they feel, what they think. So that way, they actually get to say what they would really like to do. (Resident mother of three children aged 9 to 12 years in contested matter)

Children as being unable to make a judgment about their own interests

Some parents were also concerned that children caught in the midst of their parents' dispute would not be able to make judgments that were in their best interests, either because they lack the capacity or life experience or because they may try to be fair to their parents.

No, no, because they can't put the whole thing in context, you know, they really can't see the broader picture you know, and in this case, you know, yeah, in the general opinion, I think it takes a level of maturity to be able to contextualise the whole thing, you know, I think it's a very difficult thing to put on the kid and in an almost yes or no way, because you've got to understand the ramifications of 'yes' and you've got to understand the ramifications of 'no', and I don't know if the kids are quite up to that. I think it's a decision that they can participate in when the parents are essentially going to be near to each other. (Non-resident father of 7- and 11-year-olds)

I would be very scared if Adam was put in a position where he was asked to make a choice, or asked for his wishes...but yes, they should have an opinion. It's such a hard thing to answer because knowing the child that Adam is, and his nature, whether he's 7 or 12, I know he will be loyal to both. And I'd be scared that he could say something like, 'Well I'll just live half there and half there' just to try and keep everybody happy. That's his personal situation. (Resident mother of 7-year-old in contested matter)

Children's views as changeable

Some parents were also wary of children's judgments because they were seen to be changeable and therefore unreliable. While some children said they were keen to have a 'recovery route' and be able to change the arrangements if they made the wrong decision, some parents saw this as unchangeable.

But the down side is, if… the child gets the chance to make a decision and then they realise that it's the wrong decision… then the repercussions of that are that as the child gets older and says 'Well sorry I don't want to live with you any more, I want to live with this one', and this one says 'Well sorry, but you've already told the Court that you want to live with me and that's how it's going to be and there's nothing that will change it'. (Non-resident father of 6-year-old in contested matter)

4.3.3 Parents' views on the benefits of children having a say

For parents, like the children, there were three main themes in the reasons they gave for supporting children's involvement—at least in terms of voice, if not choice. These were first, children's need to have their feelings and opinions acknowledged and taken into account; secondly, the belief or hope that this would ensure more informed decisions, better outcomes and happier children. Thirdly, for some parents, there was the therapeutic benefit for children in being able to express and manage their feelings and the positive impact on their self-esteem and development. Unlike the children, relatively few parents referred to children's right to be heard.

Better decisions, better outcomes

The most common theme running through parents' reasons for involving children was that taking children's views into account would lead to better decisions, and therefore to better outcomes and happier children. Some parents—both resident and non-resident parents but particularly those in contested hearings—saw the real benefit as being that children would be able to be with the parent they felt most comfortable and secure with.

The benefits are that they're with who they feel comfortable with—like the one who makes them feel like more secure. And that they're going to be happy. I guess if they're with who they feel more secure with than who's a more supportive parent. (Resident mother of 5- and 7-year-olds)

For some parents, it was a combination of obtaining a better or more complete picture as well as respect and acknowledgement:

They're the only ones who are in the position to judge what their life is like under the current regime and under the possible alternate regimes, and they are the only ones who are going to be in those conditions. (Non-resident father of 13-year-old, contested matter)

The benefits would be that the court would hear what the child is feeling, where they're really [wanting to be] . . . I mean sure they can be emotive, they can be unreasoning, but I think all in all they do know what's best for them, and the fact that they're not taken into account at all I think is diminutive to their intelligence. (Non-resident father of 14-year-old, contested matter)

Being acknowledged

A second and related theme was children's need for acknowledgment and the importance of feeling that they have some control over what happens to them. For some parents, this was simply a matter of respect and recognition that children are people.

Even if you don't go the way they want, you've got to treat them as human beings and talk with them about it. They're people, they're part of the family, why would you not? I've always involved Jade, depending on her maturity and what she could understand, but you just have to do it in a way they can understand. I saw the trauma she went through in moving house but she helped choose the colour of her room and decided to stay at her school. (Resident mother of 13-year-old, contested relocation matter)

For others, it was a matter of fairness and due process, and of children feeling they have some control and 'can own the process' rather than, in the words of one father whose children were in a shared parenting arrangement, 'having Mum and Dad throwing them around like a beach ball'. One resident mother of three older children involved in a contact dispute said of the judgment:[41]

It wasn't really fair . . . because the kids didn't really have a say. It was the judge who said this is what's going to happen, and that's it. You know, the kids weren't entered into the decision at all . . . no say if they'd wanted longer, shorter or different.

Therapeutic benefits

In an extension of both the empowerment and 'happy child' themes, some parents referred to the longer term developmental benefits for children who are included. They referred variously to children's self-esteem and self-efficacy (though not necessarily in these words) and to their developing capacity to make decisions and manage their feelings.

If they're included in the decisions then . . . it's a big step in their development as a human being. They're starting to make decisions for themselves. (Resident father of 8-year-old)
    I just think that if children aren't given what they want and they're not listened to then they have so many more problems when they're teenagers, and Laurence has real problems adjusting to not being listened to. (Non-resident mother of 8- and 10-year-olds, contested)

---

[41] Two years later, at the second interview, the father had relocated and none of the children were in contact with the father.

...because they haven't got that feeling of impotence that they have been dragged from pillar to post without any say in the matter. And I think that's one of the big things about childhood—I know a number of people, and you quite often see it, and it may be a little like the hostage situation who have always being told what to do so and never had an opportunity to change that attitude. (Non-resident father of 9-year-old, contested)

Some based their views on their own experience of parental separation, either in relation to their children or when they were children themselves.

I knew at 5 what I wanted to do and I wished I'd had that choice. I think I would have been a lot more different person. I wouldn't feel so much at the mercy of life. I'd feel more in control. (Non-resident mother of 5-year-old)

4.4 Children's and Parents' Views Compared

4.4.1 Similarities and differences in children's and parents' views

Most parents, like most children, said it was appropriate for children to have a say; in fact, the proportions of parents and children who said it was *not* fair or inappropriate for children to have a say were small and similar (13% and 9%, respectively). Both parents and children also gave similar reasons for the benefits and fairness of children having a say—acknowledgement and respect, and as a contributor to better decisions and outcomes. The distinction between having a say (voice) and making the decision (choice) was also quite common among both parents and children. In particular, some parents and children referred to various aspects of their living and contact arrangements that children might feel more able and more comfortable to comment on, rather than what might be seen as a 'zero-sum game' of choosing one parent over the other.

The main difference was that parents were more likely than children to be concerned about pressure on the children—and particularly in its less benign form, manipulation and bribery by the other parent. About half the parents saw children as possible 'victims of manipulation' at the hands of the other parent or less commonly as 'potential manipulators', views that are similar to those expressed by solicitors in this study (see Chapter 5) and other studies.[42] While a minority of children were concerned about pressure from their parents, children's greater concern was divided loyalty, not being fair, and jeopardizing their relationship with either one of or both their parents. Except for the youngest, most children also said that they knew what was best for them and were generally less concerned

---

[42] Murch, M, G Douglas, L Scanlan, A Perry, C Lisles, K Bader and M Borkowski, *Safeguarding Children's Welfare in Uncontentious Divorce: A Study of S41 of the Matrimonial Causes Act* (Lord Chancellor's Department, Research Series 7/99).

than parents about their competence to have a say or to exercise a choice. Age or maturity were not the primary considerations for children in saying whether or not they should have a say, and most children nominated ages younger than their own as being appropriate for children to have a say. On the other hand, children over 10 years of age were more likely to indicate they had had a say, and this was in line with parents' views that it was more appropriate for older than younger children to be involved.

4.4.2 Differences between those who had experienced contested proceedings and those who had not

There were marked differences among both the children and the parents in their views on children's participation related to whether they had experienced contested proceedings. Children involved in contested matters, particularly those involving violence, serious conflict or abuse, were more likely than those in non-contested matters to say that it ought to be up to the children to choose their residence and contact arrangements. Indeed, only one child in a contested proceeding was against having a say. They were likely to indicate a younger age at which children's voices should be heard and were less concerned that being asked to express a view put them in a difficult position, even though some had been subjected to threats and repercussions. Children in non-contested matters, on the other hand, were mostly 'content' to have a say, to have their views taken into account. They were generally closer to their non-resident parents than children in contested cases, and were generally concerned to maintain their relationship with both parents. Their preference, where possible, was for the arrangements to be made collaboratively with their parents.[43]

Both resident and non-resident parents who had been through contested proceedings were more likely than those who had not to regard hearing children's voices—but not their choices—as an avenue to better decisions being made, and to believe that children would be able to indicate which parent they felt most comfortable with, if a preference needed to be given. Parents in contested matters were more likely to indicate that children under 10 years of age should be heard than those who did not go through contested proceedings. On the other hand, only two of the parents who supported children's choices were in contested cases and their children were adolescents. In addition, seven out of the ten parents who considered that children should *not* have a say had been involved in contested proceedings. In many of these cases, this reflected concerns about the views that children would express if they were given a say and that they could be manipulated by the other parent.

---

[43] Gollop et al, n 4 above; Neale and Smart, n 13 above; Bretherton, n 30 above; Parkinson et al, n 17 above.

4.5 Voice and Choice in Children's Participation

For children to be able to be involved in decision-making concerning the arrangements that affect them most, first and foremost they need a receptive audience. In the frontline of this audience are their parents. So an understanding of parents' views and willingness to take on board what their children have to say and affect the outcome is crucial. The parents at least in this study, despite some variability in their views, were generally receptive and could see the potential benefits of understanding their children's views and feelings in terms of better decisions, better arrangements and happier children. They were, however, much more likely to entertain their children's 'voices' than their 'choices'. For the most part, this was what children wanted too. In contested matters, however, and especially where there were issues of violence, abuse and serious conflict, children were more likely to say that they should be involved, have more influence, and to do so at a younger age. The view that children's choices should be determinative, however, was held by only a small group of parents, most of whom had resolved the arrangements with their former partner without contestation; several reflected strongly on their own experience of not being listened to as children.

The other pre-conditions for children's involvement, that they be provided with appropriate information and opportunities to have a say, were less obvious. In terms of children's actual influence, children in some families had considerable influence over the contact and residence arrangements after their parents separated, not necessarily immediately but in the years following, and especially as they got older. In some of the families in this study, children were instrumental in stopping or reducing contact with their non-resident parent where this was upsetting or causing them problems, and in several others, they initiated or resumed contact with parents they had not seen for some time. In several cases, children changed residence with or without court action. In these families, children and adolescents, mostly over the age of 12, literally 'voted with their feet' and initiated changes that they wanted. Other studies have cited similar cases and proportions of children influencing or determining the arrangements.[44]

The other preconditions for children's participation relate to children's and parent's trust in the process. For parents, it means that they wanted to be sure that the voice they heard was that of the child, not the result of influence or manipulation by the other parent. For children, this means that they were concerned about being able to express their views, either within the family or in more formal processes, without fear of jeopardizing their relationship with their parents. In contested cases, where violence and abuse, and the ongoing disputation, have

---

[44] Gollop et al, n 4 above; Smart and Neale, n 17 above; May, V and C Smart, 'Silence in Court?: Hearing Children in Residence and Contact Disputes' (2004) 16 *Child and Family Law Quarterly* 305–316.

disturbed children's trust in those relationships and concern for maintaining them, children wanted more say in the decision.[45] As Neale and Smart noted:[46]

It seems that where children are frightened of, undermined or neglected by a parent, then the standard rules of fairness about how family members should treat each other are violated and no longer apply. Inclusive ways of negotiating arrangements, those based on consensus or compromise, are simply unworkable. In these circumstances, different criteria about what is fair (or just), and alternative 'rules' of citizenship, those based on individual rights and autonomy, might come into play.

The relational model of procedural justice developed by Tyler and Lind[47] also provides some theoretical backing. According to procedural justice models, people[48] are primarily concerned, in making fairness judgements, with whether or not they have had some control over the decision-making process ('voice') and over the outcome ('choice'). Research by Tyler and Degoey[49] suggests, however, that in family and community settings in which people expect to have ongoing relationships with those involved, trust and the maintenance of the relationships are more important than 'voice' or 'choice'.[50] In essence, then, children's participation is a relational process. It is based on children's trust in the process, and bounded by parental and adult conceptions of what is appropriate for children, and on the capacity of the adults and children to communicate and facilitate the process.

---

[45] Smart and Neale, n 17 above.

[46] Neale and Smart, n 13 above, pp 16–17.

[47] Lind, E A and T R Tyler, *The Social Psychology of Procedural Justice* (Plenum Press, 1988); Tyler, T R and E A Lind, 'A Relational Model of Authority in Groups' in M Zanna (ed), *Advances in Experimental Social Psychology* (Academic Press, 1992) vol 25, pp 115–191.

[48] Unfortunately very little research in this area has concerned children and young people.

[49] Tyler, T R and P Degoey, 'Community, Family, and the Social Good: The Psychological Dynamics of Procedural Justice and Social Identification' in G B Melton (ed), *The Individual, the Family, and Social Good: Personal Fulfillment in Times of Change* (University of Nebraska Press, 1995) vol 42, pp 53–91.

[50] Similarly, Van den Bos et al found that when people lack information about the trustworthiness of those making the decisions they are more likely to need and rely on procedural fairness information; in families where people have an array of information and experience on which to base judgments about the trustworthiness of those making the decisions, it is therefore likely that children will rely on control over the process and the decision for their judgments of the perceived fairness of decision-making (Van den Bos, K, H Wilke and E A Lind 'Evaluating Outcomes by Means of the Fair Process Effect: Evidence for Different Processes in Fairness and Satisfaction Judgments' (1998) 74 *Journal of Personality and Social Psychology* 1493–1503).

5

Professional Views of Children's Participation

5.1 The Importance of Professional Perspectives

The professionals who are involved in family law disputes play an important role as advisers, gatekeepers and adjudicators.

Counsellors in the Family Court and Federal Magistrates' Court, while mainly having a role in dispute resolution and writing family reports, inevitably give advice to parents about what helps and harms children in the course of trying to help parents reach an agreement on the parenting arrangements. Community mediators may also, in some circumstances, impart that advice. Lawyers also give advice to their clients and play an important counselling role in helping clients through what, for most parents, is a time of great turmoil and conflict.

The advice of counsellors and lawyers may play an important role in how parents see the views of children and the participation of children. If they are opposed in general to the involvement of children in resolving disputes, they will advise parents against it when the issue arises, or not mention options that are theoretically possible.

Lawyers and judges are also gatekeepers of the family law system. While lawyers act on instructions, they shape those instructions in terms of the legal process, and their views on whether and how to involve children are important to the decisions that might be made about applications to the court.[1]

Counsellors and judges are also adjudicators. Counsellors of course, are not adjudicators in any formal sense; yet in their role as writers of family reports for the court, they will often have a decisive impact on the outcome of a case.[2] A

---

[1] Douglas, G, M Murch, L Scanlan and A Perry, 'Safeguarding Children's Welfare in Non-Contentious Divorce: Towards a New Conception of the Legal Process' (2000) 63 *Modern Law Review* 177–196.

[2] Several studies in the US and Canada have reported that judges generally value and make determinations that are consistent with expert custody evaluation or court welfare reports or the recommendations of guardians *ad litem* (Kunin, C, E Ebbesen and V Konecni, 'Archival Study of Decision-making in Child Custody Disputes' (1992) 48 *Journal of Clinical Psychology* 564–573; Joyal, R and A Queniart, 'Enhancing the Child's Point of View in Custody and Access Cases in Quebec: Preliminary Results of a Study Conducted in Quebec' (2002) 19 *Canadian Journal of Family Law* 173–192; Sorenson, E, J Goldman, L Sheeber, I Albanese, M Ward, L Williamson and

well-written family report which comes down strongly in favour of one outcome or another may well have so much influence on the outcome of a case if it goes to trial that it prompts settlements. Certainly, this was the experience of many lawyers who were interviewed for the purposes of this study. Judges of course, are the formal adjudicators of the cases that reach trial, unless settlement can be reached prior to or in the course of the hearing.

How then do these professionals perceive children's voices and what view do they take concerning the appropriateness or otherwise of involving children in parenting disputes? It emerged from the interviews that lawyers and counsellors had quite different rationales for listening to children. For lawyers, the focus was on competence to make decisions and workability, whereas for the counsellors, the justifications were enlightenment and empowerment. There were also substantial differences between lawyers and counsellors on the extent to which parents talked to children about the issues and whether or not they should do so. These different perspectives suggest the need for a major re-evaluation of why it is that we listen to children in family law disputes.

5.2 Family Lawyers

Forty-two lawyers, 21 men and 21 women, were asked a range of questions concerning children's participation, including such questions as: How important do you think children's views are in terms of making satisfactory parenting agreements after separation? Do you encourage parents to involve the children in the parent's own negotiations about the parenting arrangements? Do you think it should ever be up to the young person how much contact he or she has with their non-resident parent? How important do you think it is for children to have a say in the proceedings?

The lawyers were classified in two different ways for the purposes of analysis. First, their views on the importance of children's participation generally were assessed. Lawyers were categorized into three groups as follows:[3]

- strong support for children's participation (15 lawyers);
- qualified support, with lawyers generally saying it depended on the age and maturity of the child, and noting the problem of parental influences on children's views (23 lawyers); and

---

C McDanal, 'Judges' Reliance on Psychological, Sociological, and Legal Variables in Contested Custody Decisions' (1997) 27 *Journal of Divorce & Remarriage* 1–24; Waller, E M and A E Daniel, 'Purpose and Utility of Child Custody Evaluations: From the Perspective of Judges' (2004) 32 *Journal of Psychiatry and Law* 5–27.

[3] Inter-rater agreement was 95% and was resolved on the two outstanding cases by discussion. The coding now reflects agreement between the raters.

- scepticism about listening to the voices of children in parenting disputes (4 lawyers).[4]

The lawyers were also categorized in accordance with whether they had had experience as child representatives into three groups: (i) those who had (19 lawyers); (ii) those who had not (20 lawyers); and (iii) those whose experience was very limited (either having had experience many years ago, or having assisted another lawyer in the firm who had been appointed as a lawyer for the child) (3 lawyers).[5]

There were no differences between the lawyers in terms of their views on the importance of children's voices associated with either gender or experience as a child representative. Of the 19 lawyers who had experience as child representatives, 8 were classified as strongly supporting children's participation, 10 gave qualified support and one was a sceptic. There were also no differences between lawyers' views associated with their level of experience as family lawyers, the percentage of their work in family law, and the percentage of their work in children's matters.

5.2.1 Age, maturity and parental influence

The largest group of lawyers (23 respondents, 55%) considered that the significance to be attached to children's views depended on their age and factors such as the extent of parental influence in forming those views. These lawyers focused upon the issue of children's maturity and capacity to form views independently from the parents, rather than the workability of the arrangements.

When a child is probably mature enough to make the decision I think they should start to be heard. Children below 10 probably are not mature enough to make a proper determination. (Male lawyer)

It depends on the age of the child, certainly. I don't like getting younger children involved at all. Perhaps older children I'll be more willing. Mature children. Children that are able to express their opinion in a mature manner, and that comes on a case by case basis. There are some children that are really immature and yet they've attained the age of say 15, 14. (Female lawyer)

The issue of the wishes is an important one but you have to balance that against the circumstances of the family and the dynamics in the way the wish came about because invariably children get influenced by one parent against another. A child may express a

---

[4] The general support for children's participation from almost all lawyers stands in contrast to a British study in the late 1990s which reported that only 55% of solicitors thought the views of children ought to be ascertained at all, with 22.5% limiting this to 'older' children (12 year olds and upwards) (Murch, M, G Douglas, L Scanlan, A Perry, C Lisles, K Bader and M Borkowski, *Safeguarding Children's Welfare in Uncontentious Divorce: A Study of S41 of the Matrimonial Causes Act* (Lord Chancellor's Department, Research Series 7/99) pp 183–184). However, in that study, lawyers were asked their opinions on ascertaining the views of children in the divorce process whether or not there was a dispute about the parenting arrangements.

[5] There was complete agreement between the researchers on this classification.

wish that I want to live with Mum because of loyalty, for example, rather than what's in the best interests of that child. (Male lawyer, child representative)

Fairly typical of this group was this comment of a very experienced male lawyer and child representative who classified children in age bands:

In that age group, say from 10 upwards for argument's sake, where you get up to about 14 or thereabouts, then yes you should be giving some reasonable weight but it shouldn't be the thing that is uppermost in your mind. But it may be the factor that might tip the scale if everything else is balanced. There's a very strong argument you could mount to suggest that the court shouldn't make any orders about children over the age of 14 years. It's just a waste of time.

This group of lawyers acknowledged the importance of children having a say, but the weight to be placed upon those views was another matter. The common concerns of lawyers in this group were about children's age and maturity,[6] and the extent to which they can be coached and manipulated by parents to align themselves with one parent's view or the other's.

If children were to be listened to below about the age of 10, it was because children were perceived to be growing up faster these days:

I think that the law's a bit backward in realising how children are growing up so much more quickly than they were a generation ago. Because of their exposure to different stimuli, these days, I think, a five year old can come in here and say 'I really want to do this, I really want to go to swimming, I don't want to see Dad that day, I want to go swimming—I want to see my Dad, but not on Wednesday afternoon', you know. (Female lawyer)

Children as manipulable and subject to parental pressure

There was a widely held opinion that any views that children expressed could well be strongly influenced by the views of a parent. Children were also seen as open to bribery.[7] For example:

I have ... seen cases where parents have exerted enormous pressure, either deliberately, or perhaps unintentionally, on children to get them to make choices one way or the other. (Female lawyer)

---

[6] A number of studies in the UK and US have found that lawyers and judges commonly report that children are more likely to be consulted and their views given more weight as they get older; age, as well as intellectual and emotional maturity, are seen as key factors affecting the likelihood of lawyers soliciting views from children and giving them more weight (see Murch et al, n 4 above; Crosby-Currie, C A, 'Children's Involvement in Contested Custody Cases: Practices and Experiences of Legal and Mental Health Professionals' (1996) 20 *Law and Human Behavior* 289–311; Felner, R D, L Terre, A Goldfarb, S S Farber, J Primavera, T A Bishop and M S Aber, 'Party Status of Children during Marital Dissolution: Child Preference and Legal Representation in Custody Decisions' (1985) 14 *Journal of Clinical Child Psychology* 42–48).

[7] Murch et al, n 4 above.

If they've got a parent who says you'll get a shiny red motorbike if you come over here, they might have a different view. (Male lawyer)

I think that one of the things that has happened is that people are told what are the factors, then they go home and they start on the kids. And there's this process of well, you know, if I can win the children over, and quite frankly, my son would go and live with anyone who bought him an X Box and a bike, and a CD player for his bedroom. And that's what happens. (Female lawyer, child representative)

One lawyer commented on the impact of loyalty conflicts on children's views:

It's a survival issue for children, I think, that they can't afford to be disloyal to Mum—as they see it—because they're living with Mum. So if Mum has expressed a strong view that 'I don't want you to see Dad', then they feel that they might be disloyal to Mum if they say 'I do want to see Dad'. (Female lawyer, child representative)

Many other lawyers referred to parental pressure on children as being a significant problem, and this was a major argument against putting more weight on children's views. As one experienced male lawyer and child representative put it:

It would...be hard for a parent if they understood that their children's wishes were going to have a significant effect on the outcome; they would almost be saintly if they could hold themselves back from trying to influence their children in some way. Even unconsciously they would do it. There would be a group that would take it as a course to make sure their child held their point of view.

Almost all lawyers thought that parents talked to their children, in an inappropriate way, about the issues:

Incessantly. Regularly. Vast majority of cases. (Male lawyer, child representative)
Constantly and obsessively. All the time. (Female lawyer, child representative)

Estimates of the proportion of parents who talked with their children about the parenting dispute varied from 50% of parents to almost all.

Probably about 80% of the time. I think that they're inappropriate 80% of the time. (Female lawyer)

I would say probably 60 or 70% of cases. A lot do. They say they don't, but...You hear it back from the other side. So I think it happens a lot. (Male lawyer)

I think it's extremely unusual for that not to happen. (Female lawyer)

The extent of parental influence led one very experienced child representative to be quite sceptical of the value of hearing children's voices at all. He said:

Well personally, I think at times [children's views] are overvalued. At times everyone runs around and says 'what does the child say?' as though the child is suddenly the judge, and the child has sufficient maturity, and as if a child is free from influence to a degree where it can be considered, which I don't see very often. I do a lot of children's sep rep work, and generally speaking it's one parent who brings the child in to see me. And I don't think I've had a case yet where the child hasn't expressed wishes consistent with the interests of the person who brought them in.

Children as being unable to make a judgment about their own interests

Some lawyers also expressed concern that children, who are caught up in conflicts between parents, may not make the best judgments about their interests, seeking either to align with the interests of one parent or to see equal time as being best because it is 'fair' to each parent.

In my observation, children have a strong sense of what's fair, and they don't necessarily think about what's best for them but what's fair for Mum and Dad ... so, it's not fair for me to spend more time with one parent than it is the other. And sometimes I think that's misdirected... I've also seen cases where young teenage boys have been very protective of their mothers when their fathers have left, and... teenage girls, I've observed do the same thing ... and those sort of factors I think prevent children from making an objective assessment of what's best for them. (Female lawyer)

Some kids will deal with [loyalty conflicts] by aligning with one of their parents and sort of excluding the other... but other kids do the divide in half thing. (Female lawyer, child representative)

The concern that children may say they support an equal time arrangement which is not fair to themselves has also been expressed in research on children's voices in parenting proceedings.[8]

Children as saying what the parent wants to hear

Many lawyers saw children as ambivalent and considered that their views would align with what the parent wants to hear.

The child will be more inclined of course to tell Mum what they perceive Mum wants, and tell Dad what they perceive Dad wants. That's the problem. (Male lawyer)

Most kids want to please both people, so most kids will say the same thing to both of them. (Female lawyer)

Most little kids that you talk to will say, if you pose the direct question, which I don't think you ever should, you know 'What would you like?' They'll always say 'I want to live with Mum and I want to live with Dad.' Or, you know, if you say 'Do you like living with Dad?' 'Yes.' 'Do you like living with Mum?' 'Yes.' You know. So you've got to be a bit cautious about their wishes. (Male lawyer, child representative)

Children's views as changeable

Another reason given by lawyers for being cautious about children's views is that they were seen as changeable and dependent on circumstances.

Sometimes you have kids that are absolutely adamant that they never want to see their Dad again... Then they have one contact visit, you see them the next time and suddenly he's Santa. (Female lawyer, child representative)

---

[8] Smart, C, A Wade and B Neale, 'Objects of Concern'?—Children and Divorce' (1999) 11 *Child and Family Law Quarterly* 365–376; Parkinson, P, J Cashmore and J Single, 'Adolescents' Views on the Fairness of Parenting and Financial Arrangements after Separation' (2005) 43 *Family Court Review* 429–444.

The other thing is children's wishes change just as parents' wishes changes. When parents initially separate, they are very different people to what they are twelve months later. The children are as well. We have to be careful when we look at the children's wishes in terms of that. (Male lawyer, child representative)

The search for the rational decision-maker

The search for the rational decision-maker reflects lawyers' traditional understanding about childhood that children's voices matter when they are competent to make their own decisions. Discussion of children's age and maturity as a basis for taking account of their views is a common discourse in law. The mature minor, for example, may be accorded the right to make his or her own medical decision if he or she has reached a level of competence that makes it legitimate for the child to take over from the parent as the decision-maker.[9] The child who is assessed as competent to do so may give direct instructions to the solicitor.[10] The child may be able to give sworn evidence in court if capable of understanding the meaning and significance of the oath, and may otherwise be able to give unsworn evidence if he or she passes a lower threshold of competence.[11] Lawyers, in the criminal sphere, are also concerned with contamination of children's evidence,[12] and in the civil law, there is an established discourse on 'undue influence' to determine whether transactions are the result of a person's independent judgment.

The discussion of age and maturity by so many lawyers reflects the transposition of that discourse to the area of decision-making about parenting arrangements. The question about children's voices becomes interpreted as being about the stage at which children's views are treated as sufficiently rational and mature to be given weight. This is reinforced by the legislation which states that the court must consider children's views, taking account of their age and maturity.[13]

5.2.2 Workability and children's happiness

By way of contrast, the second largest group consisted of eight women and seven men who expressed strong support for children's participation and saw their views as being very important.

I think [children's views] are very important. I do and I'm really delighted that children are having more say. (Female lawyer, child representative)

---

[9] *Gillick v West Norfolk and Wisbech AHA* [1986] AC 112.
[10] Sawyer, C, 'The Competence of Children to Participate in Family Proceedings' (1995) 7 *Child and Family Law Quarterly* 180–195.
[11] Spencer, J R and R H Flin, *The Evidence of Children: The Law and the Psychology* (Blackstone, 1993; 2nd ed).
[12] Ceci, S and M Bruck, 'Suggestibility of the Child Witness: A Historical Review and Synthesis' (1993) 113 *Psychological Bulletin* 403–439.
[13] The Family Law Act 1975 (Cth), s 60CC(3)(a) provides that the court must consider any views expressed by the child and any factors (such as the child's maturity or level of understanding) that the court thinks are relevant to the weight it should give to the child's views.

I think that children's views are almost the top rung of the ladder when it comes to considerations of what should happen and are not given enough airtime or consideration . . . they need to have some ownership of a process that has such incredible outcomes for them. (Female lawyer, child representative)

I think [children's views] are really important. Yeah, I think they are absolutely important. I mean depending on their age obviously. (Male lawyer)

I think that [children's views are] absolutely essential, and by that I don't mean that you need to follow them, you just need to know what they are. (Female lawyer, child representative)

A range of reasons were given for this view, and some qualified their support for children's voices by reference to caveats about how children's views were ascertained, but a common theme was to emphasize the strength of the children's views and the impact that has on the workability of the arrangements, rather than the rationality of those views. This focus on the strength of children's views meant that age and maturity were not seen as such major issues. This was reflected, for example, in the view of one very experienced child representative when asked whether he felt that there is an age at which children's views should be taken into account more than others:

All children are different. You get extremely strong views from a 5-year-old and a 12-year-old may not have any feelings. (Male lawyer, child representative)

Others expressed a similar view:

Some children are really articulate and clear. They can be any age, I wouldn't put any age, I'm not prepared to say it should be anyone over 5 or over 10. I know some pretty strident, intelligent 6 year olds who have been brought up in a family that have encouraged that. (Female lawyer)

By far the most important reason given by lawyers in this group for paying attention to children's views was workability, and this was related to the strength of their views and how likely it is that children will be able to adapt to the decision:

I think [children's views are] very important as the kids get older because they're, you know, they're so important as to whether or not the arrangements are gonna work. A 12-year-old can torpedo arrangements pretty effectively if they haven't been listened to. (Female lawyer, child representative)

Depends on the age, but the views—no matter what the age—if the child has a view, a strong view, it's very hard to overcome it. (Female lawyer)

One lawyer in this group, for example, commented on the situation where a child has a strong view that has a false premise:

You will sometimes get the situation that . . . the kid holds a view about the other parent which is not real, which is not the truth. But regardless of that, they hold it. Sometimes you have to come to the realisation that it doesn't matter how they came to the view they got, they have that view and that is the view they hold. (Male lawyer, child representative)

There was a particular recognition of the issue of workability in relation to teenagers, and many lawyers expressed the view that making orders which go against the wishes of teenagers is futile.[14]

If you took a matter to court with a 9-year-old, the court might be inclined to dismiss those wishes in favour of arguments in the best interests. But you know, if you get 13, 14, 15, 16, 17—which we do, I don't know why we do—you just can't make an order. The court's totally aware it can't make an order against a kid's wishes, because they just won't wear it. They'll just get on a bus and do something else. (Female lawyer, child representative)

The court is hesitant to make orders for children 13, 14, 15 years of age if they are expressing strong wishes. There have been a couple of cases where the judge here has called the kids into chambers and said, 'You will obey.' But I think there is a growing reality that children would get on a bus. They will literally vote with their feet. (Female lawyer, child representative)

Other lawyers emphasized the happiness of children which was related to the durability and workability of the arrangements.

Well it's all about the kids being happy, isn't it? So if the kid's not with the parent they want to be with, they're not gonna be happy. (Male lawyer)

Any arrangement you make is more likely to work if the children feel that they've been part of the process in coming to that arrangement. And there's some level of ownership of that. If parents make decisions about older children...and the children are not happy with those arrangements, they're more likely to fail. (Female lawyer, child representative)

One lawyer expressed another rationale for the involvement of children, and this is that parents involved in litigation are often unable to see their children's needs, and the children may therefore be better than the parents at understanding what the optimal parenting arrangements would be in the circumstances:

I think the children should be involved because invariably the parents, each of them, either have an agenda to achieve or they are really not focussed on what's best for the children. They might be focussed on their emotional attachment to the other parent or their relationship or the separation and they are making decisions or they are putting forward proposals based on those issues rather than what they think is really best for their kids. So yes, I think they should become more involved. (Male lawyer, child representative)

[14] This view has been expressed by lawyers elsewhere and is not new. Siegel and Hurley in 1977, for example, commented that most US courts 'realize the futility of a custody order contrary' to the wishes of a child who 'absolutely refuses to be with a particular parent' and 'will, albeit sometimes reluctantly, give it controlling weight' (Siegel, D M and S Hurley, 'The Role of the Child's Preference in Custody Proceedings' (1977) 11 *Family Law Quarterly* 1–58, at 10). More recently, Ackerman et al reported that judges, lawyers and psychologists in the US believed that children should be allowed to determine with whom they live at 15 years of age (see Ackerman, J, M C Ackerman, L L Steffen and S Kelley-Poulos, 'Psychologists' Practices Compared to the Expectations of Family Law Judges and Attorneys in Child Custody Cases' (2004) 1 *Journal of Child Custody* 41–60).

5.2.3 Protection from participation

A consistent theme running through the lawyers' views was the importance of shielding children from harm in the litigation process. Protection was a more dominant concern for lawyers than participation. This was a major reason why lawyers thought that children should be given a voice rather than a choice. Lawyers consistently emphasized the risks of harm from children's participation rather than any benefits that might flow from it.[15]

This view of children as being in need of protection in the litigation process was, for example, expressed by one lawyer with experience as a child representative:

There has to be something about children meaning that they are vulnerable and need to be protected, and I don't think you can say necessarily because they're not at the front stalls of everything, that they're not, that they're not being served well. I mean, we don't ask children how to drive at 10, or we don't have them do other things, which they might wish to do, and which they might have a legitimate wish—there has to be some sense that the system has to protect them from what would be possibly damaging, that they don't see. (Female lawyer, child representative)

Children were seen as being in need of protection from conflict, responsibility and power.

Protection from conflict

Like the lawyers in two British studies who thought that children should be kept out of family law proceedings,[16] a major concern of lawyers was to try to protect children as far as possible from their parents' conflicts.

In terms of children's participation, it is incredibly valuable, subject to it being in a fashion that doesn't create emotional conflicts for them in the sense that it is not being aligned with one of the parties. I think that is very damaging both in terms of children's psychology and also in the future success of arrangements. (Male lawyer, child representative)

I think involvement would also result in an increase in involvement in the parties' conflict. (Female lawyer)

This concern to protect children from conflict led the great majority of lawyers to say that when acting for parents, they would not encourage their clients to discuss the issues with the children and to find out their children's views. They generally

---

[15] Chisholm, R, 'Children's Participation in Family Court Litigation' (1999) 13 *Australian Journal of Family Law* 197–218. A study by Felner et al reported similar attitudes among US judges over 20 years ago, with only 30% of judges citing possible positive effects compared with 75% citing possible negative effects such as loyalty conflicts, guilt and emotional trauma for the child (see Felner et al, n 6 above).

[16] Douglas, G and M Murch, 'Taking Account of Children's Needs in Divorce—A Study of Family Solicitors' Responses to New Policy and Practice Initiatives' (2002) 14 *Child and Family Law Quarterly* 57–75; Piper, C, 'Ascertaining the Wishes and Feelings of the Child' (1997) *Family Law* 796–800.

did not trust their clients to do this sensitively and without putting pressure on the children.

I'm sure there's thousands of cases out there where children are involved in a roundtable discussion at home around the dining table, Mum and Dad are separating, what do you guys think, you know? By the time people get to us, that's not working. They can't communicate. They can't discuss stuff. Either one of the parties or the other is totally intractable. So they're not people usually... capable of involving their children in an appropriate way. (Female lawyer, child representative)

    I actually discourage it because I have no faith that the parent can do it. I discourage it and say let them know you are sorting it out. Say something simple and encourage and soothing to the child. Don't involve them. (Female lawyer)

    Leave the kids out of it. (Male lawyer)

Indeed, lawyers typically advised parents not to talk to the children, with a few making an exception only for older teenagers. However, almost all lawyers said that parents did talk to their children about the issues, sometimes obsessively, and saw this as problematic.

    This position that children needed protection from their parents' conflicts sat uneasily with a consensus among the lawyers that it was important to allow the children to have a say. This led them to express a view of children's participation that appeared somewhat contradictory. For example, one male lawyer with more than 30 years' experience said:

I think children's views become more important as they get older. By the time they're 9 or 10, I think they're of great importance; probably once they're past 7, they're of significant importance... I would shrink from any system which did not involve drawing out the attitudes of the children, either by getting them to express them directly or by observing them.

Yet like most, he did not think the parents themselves should involve the children in negotiations:

I tend to recoil from it, from involving the children at all. Intellectually and emotionally. I tend to recoil from it as being abusive of the child.

Lawyers reconciled this somewhat contradictory position by saying that children's voices should be heard through professionals, and mostly, those lawyers who did sometimes encourage parents to listen to their children did so by encouraging a process involving a professional. For example:

[Parents should be encouraged to seek their children's views] provided it's in an environment that is properly supported such as family counselling. I think family therapy and counselling can be enormously powerful and useful. Mediation? Perhaps not the initial mediation when there's a lot of angst flying around but there's no doubt, once parties have had a successful mediation... then I would think it would be very useful. It must be... in children's best interests to see their parents acting in a mature way trying to work things out with support. It's got to send a pretty good message to kids generally. (Female lawyer, child representative)

The profound ambivalence towards involving children led most lawyers to accept the status quo in Australia as representing the best way of hearing from children—having their voices heard through a family report, and often a child representative, on the basis that this involvement would somehow shield the children from direct involvement in the parents' conflict.

Protection from responsibility

Like the family lawyers in the British study by Murch and his colleagues,[17] another major theme in many of the responses was the importance of protecting children from the responsibility to make the decisions.

To have a say I think it's important, but again to have a say in a manner which is not traumatic for them, and which is not in any way putting them in a position where they feel that what they're about to do is going to determine the rights of Mum and Dad or anything like that. So yes, have a say, but in a manner in which the child shouldn't form the perception that what they're about to say or do will determine whether Mummy and Daddy lives with them, who they see. (Male lawyer)

It would really almost put the children in the position of determining the outcome if too much weight was put on their views and that would therefore mean that the children would be put in an almost untenable position. They would be as young as 10 or 11 almost determining what happens to Mum and Dad. (Male lawyer, child representative)

For one very experienced lawyer, the difficulties involved in placing responsibility on children led her to consider that children should not be involved at all:

It is pretty tough isn't, you are 11 years old and you are asked by a court, which is a pretty scary place, and people you don't know 'at least say whether you want to go to Dad or what happens when I go to Mum'. It is just impossible for children to work out. It is just too hard. Parents can't do it; Judges can't do it, why are children going to do it?

Protection from power

Another theme in some of the responses was the importance of protecting children from the power that they may gain from being seen as the de facto decision-maker:

I suppose I'm a bit old fashioned too, and I think that kids should do what they're told, and I don't think that kids should be allowed to run things. (Male lawyer)

It is very, very easy for them to be put in a position of being absolute power broker in the relationship and having a 10-year-old child having two adults running around doing whatever they want them to do. (Male lawyer, child representative)

Yeah I think it is important [for children to have a say], but it is also important to protect them from the power they may seem to have in making that decision. (Female lawyer, child representative)

[17] Murch et al, above n 4, p 185.

5.2.4 Children as decision-makers

Lawyers were evenly divided about whether it should ever be up to the child to decide about contact visits with the non-resident parent. Half the lawyers did not think that children should be the decision-makers at any stage, however old or mature they are, or said that their views should rarely be determinative.

You'd never leave it up to the child. You'd certainly listen to the child, and it may well be that there is more contact required, say, during the winter football season if you like and Dad's prepared to take and pick the boys up and go to football training after school. (Male lawyer)

It would be a very rare case that... it should be left up to the child. (Male lawyer)

The older they get, the more input they should have. I don't ever think it should be necessarily on their shoulders, even a 14 year old child. (Female lawyer)

Male lawyers were twice as likely to say that it should *not* be left up to the child as female lawyers. Female lawyers tended to be more attuned to the issue of children's emerging autonomy and need for self-determination.

While the other half of the lawyers did countenance the possibility that it should be left up to the children in some circumstances (particularly when the children are teenagers), only a minority of respondents were unequivocal in their view about this. Many of those who indicated it should be left up to the child to make their own decisions emphasized the problem of enforcing contact arrangements against the strongly held views of a teenager.[18] Others who said that children should be allowed to make their own decisions after a certain age, emphasized that teenagers often have other interests apart from spending time with the non-resident parent and that parents need to accept this and be willing to be flexible about it.

Some child representatives, in particular, answered the question in terms of whether they would be prepared to say that the children's best interests would be served by going with whatever they wanted above a certain age. They took the view that sometimes this would be the case, and sometimes not:

It depends on the circumstances and on the consequences...In some cases that would be just actually spot on, and in other cases it means that...the kids will be an arbiter. (Female lawyer, child representative)

It's very difficult because case by case there are some children who are so alienated they don't have the freedom to make that sort of decision. (Female lawyer, child representative)

Should it be up to that child? Um, well I suppose to a degree; but I think we have an obligation to look at the broader long term ramifications and interests. I don't think wishes should be the sole criteria. (Male lawyer, child representative)

A number of child representatives gave examples of where they did not consider that adolescents' best interests would be served by adhering to their strongly held

[18] See n 14 above.

views, and found themselves in a position of some difficulty in acting as a 'best interests' advocate for the child in these circumstances.

5.2.5 Children's participation as about choices between adult positions

Lawyers generally responded to the questions on children's participation by seeing the issue in terms of children expressing choices between the competing positions of the parents. Choices were therefore seen as binary in nature, and the views that a child expressed would necessarily be a view in favour of one parent or another. Lawyers therefore tended to think of children's preferences as being about outcomes, with the available choices being defined by the parents' respective positions. Lawyers' perspectives on children's participation were therefore very task-directed, and often framed in terms of children's wishes rather than their more general views.[19] There was an implicit assumption in some of the interviews that because the parents could not find the middle ground of a dispute, and were locked in adversarial positions, there was therefore no place for the children to identify and articulate that middle ground, or to suggest the compromises that might lead to settlement.

However, there were some exceptions to this:

> I don't think children are given enough credit for understanding what goes on, their ability to understand how it can work. And I think children can have some incredibly positive inputs. I don't think you should place children in the role of mediating between parents, but they often do and they're acutely aware of the positives and the negatives of each of their parents. (Female lawyer, child representative)

A psychologist who had retrained as a lawyer also expressed a broader perspective on children's participation, which might involve finding out what the children thought about the parents:

> No. I think decision-making is too difficult a decision to put on a child. I think you have to remember, assuming that the child loves both parents and is devastated in his or her own way or at least confused by it or unsure of the future in regards to the separation, the last thing one should do or say to that child is 'Well, how much time do you want to spend

---

[19] There has been considerable critique of the distinction between children's 'wishes' and children's 'views'. New Zealand academic lawyers Taylor, Tapp and Heneghan were critical of the use of the term 'the wishes of the child' in their country's legislation and influential in having this amended in the new statutes. They saw 'wishes' as being too narrow and implying 'a futuristic orientation' rather than the 'wider range of issues and concerns important to the child' (Taylor, N, P Tapp and M Heneghan 'Respecting Children's Participation in Family Law Proceedings' (2007) 15 *International Journal of Children's Rights* 61–82). More recently, a former Australian judge, Richard Chisholm, argued that 'the word "wishes" might suggest that the only relevant thing is the child's wishes as to the outcome of the case' (Chisholm, R, 'The Family Law Amendment (Shared Parental Responsibility) Bill 2006: Putting Children at Centre Stage?' paper at the *Contact and Relocation—Focusing on the Children Conference* (Byron Bay, Australia, May 2006) p 12).

with Mum and Dad?' I don't think that is right. You find out their views about Mum and Dad. (Female lawyer)

This way of thinking about children's participation was different from asking children which outcome, being advanced by their parents, they preferred. A related theme in the responses of this small group of lawyers was about respect for children's position as important stakeholders in the decisions and having interests that needed to be taken into account:

I think parents really should hear their views and take them into consideration rather than simply impose some pattern on the children…If the parents want to impose an agreement on the children that really is disruptive to, say, sporting events, or some important aspect of their school or social life, or something like that…I think parents should take them into account and be flexible. (Male lawyer)

5.2.6 Changing the system

About 60% of the lawyers considered that the Australian legal system had got it about right in terms of its involvement of the children. The other 40% were in favour of increased participation. There was a view that when there is a child representative appointed, the children are very much involved. As one experienced female child representative working with the Legal Aid Commission said:

Well, if you've got a child rep, kids are involved quite a lot in it…we have kids in and out of this place constantly.

Those who suggested that children could be more involved tended to recommend one of three options; first, the greater involvement of children in decision-making outside the court system. A number of respondents referred to the possibility of involving children more through counsellors. For example:

I think having the children involved in a mediation session with a family and child mediator with the parents may not be a bad idea because it may give some reality to a situation for the parents as to what the children want, why they want it and it gives the parents guidance from the mediator as to perhaps why the child or children express certain views. (Male lawyer, child representative)

Using family therapy, family meetings more expansive counselling and mediation that includes kids…I think that type of process that involves them in a cooperative decision making process with their parents, I think is long overdue. (Male lawyer, child representative)

A second set of recommendations was for greater provision of resources, in particular for more child representatives to be appointed and for family reports to be available in every parenting case.

A third group recommended the earlier involvement of children in parenting proceedings as a means of promoting settlement. This also had resource implications, particularly if family reports were to be ordered at an earlier stage, in which case they would need to be ordered in many more cases.

5.3 Mediators and Counsellors

The views of family lawyers may be compared and contrasted with the views of community-based mediators and counsellors in the family courts. Mediators in community organizations engage only in confidential mediation, outside the court system. 17 mediators, 12 women and 5 men, were interviewed, from three large community-based organizations in New South Wales.

If an application is made to court, parents will at an early stage see one of the family consultants. These are psychologists and mediators employed by the court itself, who have a conciliation role in trying to help parents reach agreement, and a report writing role which includes giving an account of the children's views, perspectives and attachments to each parent. These family consultants will be termed, generically, as 'counsellors'. Twenty four counsellors working in the family court system in New South Wales were interviewed. There were 18 women and 6 men. They came from three different registries of the Court—Sydney, Parramatta and Newcastle.

The mediators and counsellors do not necessarily see the same clientele. At the time of the interviews, at least, pre-filing mediation was not compulsory, and so the parents seen by mediators were a section of the population that was committed to attempting mediation on a voluntary basis. Many of these would resolve their issues without any court involvement. Although the mediators and counsellors engaged with families at different stages of the dispute resolution continuum, with counsellors involved with children in the litigation process, they had very similar views. All of them considered that children's views were important to the process, except when the children were very young and seen as not knowing what was going on. However, they gave some different reasons from the family lawyers, and offered some different concerns about involving children.

One very experienced counsellor explained the importance of hearing from children in terms of Warshak's two justifications—enlightenment and empowerment.[20] Enlightenment comes from the information children can provide about the family situation. Warshak explained this rationale as being that children 'have something important to tell us that may change the decisions we make on their behalf and the way in which we make them'.[21] Empowerment comes from giving children a say, 'the idea that children profit by participating in decisions

---

[20] Warshak, R A, 'Payoffs and Pitfalls of Listening to Children' (2003) 52 *Family Relations* 373–384, at 373–374.
[21] Warshak, n 20 above, at 374.

that affect central aspects of their lives'.[22] Almost all the counsellors expressed support for children's participation in terms of one or both of these rationales. By way of contrast, family lawyers were mainly concerned with the 'reliability' of children's views and the workability of arrangements.

5.3.1 Enlightenment

The importance of children's views in terms of enlightenment was a constant theme of the mediators and counsellors' responses:

I think kids' views are pretty good. They know who they feel they can relate to. I mean, probably particularly sort of [from] 8 years old. Before then it's probably a bit hard for them to conceptualise. (Female counsellor)

The benefits of involving children are that you really get to assess what's going on for the child, and if they do have a view. (Female counsellor)

For both the mediators and counsellors the most important aspect of the involvement of children was to enlighten the parents. Even the court-based counsellors placed much more emphasis on enlightening the parents than providing information to the court. The assumption of these mediators and counsellors was that parents did not know what their children really thought, whereas lawyers were concerned about the extent to which parents talked with children and tried to influence them:

It's about giving feedback to the parents in terms of how they are travelling, what is happening for the children, you know, why they are saying that and what it means for them, and what would it mean for them to want more contact, etcetera, etcetera. So, it's for the parents to make more informed decisions that involve the needs of their child. So it's not about giving responsibility to the children about the decision-making. It's not about that. (Female mediator)

If the parents don't know [the children's views], then sometimes it's refreshing or educational for them to know that. Sometimes they'll go into it with an assumption of something and I've met parents who really believe this child or children really want to live with him or her. (Male counsellor)

[There are] certain situations when children do need their views heard. The parents do need to know about their children; they do need to know that they might not be realising certain things about their children, and need to be taking notice of that, to try to make better parenting arrangements for their kids. (Female counsellor)

In the majority of cases, I would like to have the child's voice heard, because I think all parents can learn about how their children are travelling. And everyone knows children have thoughts they don't express to their parents, and if the parents can be more child-aware and child-focused, that's good. (Female mediator)

Involving children was thus seen as a tool for settlement, by making parents aware of their children's needs and feelings, with the assistance of a professional to whom the children could talk about their situation.

---

[22] Warshak, n 20 above, at 374.

5.3.2 Empowerment

Empowerment, giving children a say, was another important theme for mediators and counsellors. The mediators in particular were likely to see children's participation in terms of their rights:

I think child inclusive work is very important, and to feel as though the children have got some say. My concern is those cases where the parents are so insistent about the children having their say that I have some caution about that…I think there are some children that really want their views heard, and they really feel that they need some empowerment in that process. And we have that responsibility to support the children in that, and this is sometimes the only opportunity for them to be able to do that and have it validated. (Male counsellor)

Children have the right to have a voice, and to be heard about what's happening to them, because their issues are going to be different to parents' issues. (Female mediator)

I think in every case the child's wishes should be considered. Without a doubt. Whether the children's responses are primarily emotional or not, they are no less valid. They don't have to be rational to be considered… Because we know that developmentally, they are disadvantaged and socially they are disadvantaged of course. So yes, for the sake of democracy, I think they should. (Female mediator)

They're the people that are most intimately affected, this is what this is about, and you know on a children's rights issue, they have a right to have a say. I don't mean have the casting vote necessarily, but they need to be involved in the decision making. (Female counsellor)

5.3.3 The involvement of children in mediation

Such were the perceived benefits of helping the parents to understand the needs and perspectives of children, that there was very widespread, in principle, support for the involvement of children in mediation. For example:

I would do everything short of bringing them in and sitting them down on a chair beside their parents, to see their parents' bad behaviour. Short of that, I would go as far as I could possibly go. (Female mediator)

For the most part, this was by use of a child consultant speaking with the children separately and feeding their views and perspectives back to the parents (child-inclusive mediation). However, there was some openness to involving children more directly in the mediation process. One mediator, for example, reported on the utility of setting up a meeting directly between a teenager and a non-resident parent in a controlled environment:

I've done mediations where older children have been included with parents that they have the issues with—if the children are saying, 'I don't want to go to live with Dad' or 'I do, only if this, this and this happens' and it seems pretty clear that you're not going to be able to get this across without the kids actually having this discussion with that parent themselves and in a controlled place.

Some counsellors had also involved teenage children directly in mediation.

Many of the mediators and counsellors would only use children's voices in the mediation process if they thought parents would be open to hearing the children's views:

Those times that I've involved the child in decision-making is when I feel that the parents are going to at least listen and not automatically reject a view that is not in line with their own. (Male counsellor)

One of the concerns expressed was that if parents are not willing to hear the views of the children, then children may be more damaged by the process of involving them than if their views had not been sought:

Do you think that there are benefits if you can access children's views, in terms of the arrangements?
Yes, I think so, if parents are prepared to hear it and adjust accordingly...That parents would be prepared to change what they were hoping to see happen. And...I guess a readiness in their future decision-making to bend and stretch according to what is going to be helpful for the kids. (Female mediator)
I don't think there's any point in raising kids' expectations and then nothing changing. So I have to believe that there's a chance that the parents might listen to what the other argument is; also that even if the parents won't listen and even if I think it's going to a family court, it's possible that it could help the kids before they get to the family court to be more at ease with the process. (Female counsellor)
I think it's quite destructive for parents to bring a child in with an expectation that it matters what they think and then just turn around and do the other thing. (Female counsellor)

Another concern was to ensure that children were not exposed to pressure or manipulation:

I just think it's something that needs to be carefully managed, because there are a proportion of parents, I'm talking about the extreme, who could manipulate that quite effectively and put the children in a worse position than they are in the first place. (Female mediator)

5.3.4 Workability

In contrast to the lawyers, counsellors gave very little emphasis to the issue of workability, although it was more likely to be mentioned by mediators. It was, of course, one reason why many mediators and counsellors thought that much attention should be given to the views and choices of teenagers. However, only a small number of mediators and counsellors mentioned the issue of workability across the age range of children:

If children's views are consulted, they've got a better chance of working. (Male mediator)

While understanding children's reasons for holding particular views may be related to workability, it was more often seen as part of the assessment process for counsellors.

Well, I think if you make recommendations that children clearly don't like, then you really need to have good reasons and you need to understand why children don't like what you might be recommending. Children usually have reasons for holding the views that they have, so I suppose that I would want to explore and know why it is that they are saying what they are saying at a particular time. I think that is part of the assessment process. (Female counsellor)

5.3.5 Therapeutic benefits

A few mediators and counsellors saw therapeutic benefits in involving children. One benefit was seen to be to help parents and children to communicate:

I think, ideally, and what we've all got to aim for is the children and the parents being able to express themselves among one another. And that is the whole aim: children can be helped to talk to their parents, the parents can be helped to talk to their children, and if I can do an intervention that means the next time that the children and the parents have something, children can do it by themselves or the parents can do it by themselves, then I've done something that's worthwhile. (Female counsellor)

Another benefit was in terms of giving children a chance to express their feelings to an outsider:

Someone who is experienced in getting things out of children, and in an environment where the child does not feel that he is undermining relations with either parent or turning them against one another. (Female mediator)

The chance to have a say was also seen as being of therapeutic benefit to children. Some counsellors in particular emphasized the risks of not giving children a say:

It gives them the ability to have a vote. To have a say. And to let people know what they think. That can be important later on down the track when they're developing into adults and they look back on that time. If they didn't have an opportunity to put forward a point of view, they tend to feel really angry and ripped off. This was about me, but nobody talked to me. So it's really, really important that children have an opportunity to be heard. Even if they choose not to say anything, that's fine. (Male counsellor)

All through those [high school] years, I think it benefits them to feel like they've got some control over their lives. I think anyone who feels that they're powerless in a situation, whether they're children or adolescents, could be vulnerable to feelings of depression and powerlessness. So, I think at least give them an opportunity and a sense of being heard, even if it isn't the outcome. (Female counsellor)

5.3.6 Concerns about pressure and manipulation

Given the important role that counsellors play in writing family reports for the court, the interviews with the counsellors involved a detailed exploration of the issues of determining influences upon children's views. There were significant differences between the family lawyers and the counsellors in this respect. The counsellors were much less troubled about the problem of manipulation and pressure on children, and discerning whether the children had been coached. This was for three reasons.

First, counsellors did not think parents talked to children about the parenting dispute nearly as much as lawyers did. Whereas lawyers thought that most parents talk to the children about the dispute, and considered this to be inappropriate, the counsellors thought this was much less common, and in any event, did not always think it was inappropriate, as they considered it important for parents to know what their children thought.[23] Asked whether they find that the parent has spoken to the children before they are first brought to see the counsellor, these were typical responses:

Some do and some don't. And those that do might simply say something like 'We're going to see a counsellor to help the family make a decision'. Others might say 'I want you to tell the counsellor this and that'. Others take the view that children shouldn't be involved, rather like we sometimes take that view, and keep them pretty much in the dark. (Male counsellor)

You know sometimes it is clear that they've had lots of discussions with children. But generally, no, they haven't. (Female counsellor)

Some parents don't tell the children much at all, some parents tell the children way too much and suggest things that they shouldn't say. (Male counsellor)

Only a small minority of the counsellors thought that *most* of the parents talk with their children in an attempt to influence them.

Secondly, the majority of counsellors thought they could identify the situations where the child has been told what to say or has been strongly influenced by a parent. They were particularly attuned to the situations where the children used the parent's language and illustrations:

Well, usually they use the same language as the parent that's rehearsed them. (Female counsellor)

Because they sort of tell you the same stories their father or mother has told you. (Female counsellor)

You talk to the child and then you talk to the parent and they're telling you the same history. You know, even the words that they're using are so closely aligned that, you know, the adult talk and language that the children are using, and the adult concepts can be pretty much a giveaway. (Male counsellor)

Other indications that the children had been coached and rehearsed come from the way the child spoke about the situation:

Something 'parroty' about it all. It lacks substance ... it lacks colour. (Female counsellor)

Sometimes they, before they forget, it's like they've got to wheel off this stuff that they've got to say about Dad. (Female counsellor)

---

[23] Murch et al, n 4 above, reported that 83% of mediators in their study in England and Wales suggested to parents that they should consult with their children.

Where they were least confident was where the children had been subject to such influence and pressure that they had internalized the parent's viewpoint and it had become their own, but this was not a commonly expressed concern.

The third reason that counsellors were less concerned than lawyers about coaching and manipulation was that they did not worry too much about discerning the pure, uncontaminated voice of the child. For example:

Nearly all children are going to be influenced one way or another by what their parents think. It need not be just parents sitting down the night before saying 'I want you to tell the counsellor this and that', but nearly all children if you ask them 'what do you think your Dad thinks?' or 'what do you think your Mum thinks?' they usually know. Which means that they found out somehow. You know, like the song, it's like family osmosis. Most of us in a family would know what each person thinks about a particular issue. (Female counsellor)

I think, you know, the parents colour it, and by the time they get to the court, we are dealing with parents who do that. You know, some of them don't have the capacity not to manipulate or use their children, or they wouldn't be here. They wouldn't be in the system. (Female counsellor)

Consequently, their rationale for involving children was related to enlightenment and empowerment. They saw children's participation as being a means of discerning the children's best interests and promoting those interests by giving them a voice in the process, rather than a means of discerning decision-making competence. Mediators also expressed very similar views.

5.3.7 Age, maturity and self-determination

What was the significance to mediators and counsellors of age and maturity then? Once again, the themes of enlightenment and empowerment were dominant in both mediators' and counsellors' responses. One male counsellor expressed the importance of age and maturity to enlightenment in this way:

Age, articulateness and the level of intelligence and perception has a whole lot to do with the children's ability to express their needs.

A female mediator explained the enlightenment that can come even from a 2-year-old:

Do you take a 2-year-old's view into consideration that they want a lolly? No, you don't. But do you take a 2-year-old's views into consideration that they're frightened when they sleep at Daddy's house, because he lives with three other people? You obviously would. So it's actually weighing it up to try and get something that works, that's safe for the child, and going to enhance their relationship.

Perhaps because counsellors' work involved conducting holistic family assessments in the course of writing family reports, they were not at all inclined to take children's views out of the context of the whole family dynamic, or to give those views some higher position than their assessment of the children's needs and best interests, taken as a whole. They tended to speak more broadly about children's 'voice' and their 'views', and the need to understand the underlying reasons, rather than children's 'wishes'.[24] There was also a strong reluctance, expressed by many, to specify an age at which children's views should carry particular weight.[25]

I think it's very hard to set an age on it, because I think you need to be looking at the family dynamic. Look at what the experiences of the children have been in that family, and also to look at the ages and maturity of the children to be able to deal with that. I mean, coming back from the whole area about giving the children a voice, which is fine, but what are we exposing them to? And what do they have to go back and live with? (Male counsellor)

Some children at 12, you know, have a very good idea, other children at 12, you know, are not able to really think through their situation. (Female counsellor)

A similar view was expressed by some mediators. The counsellors and mediators emphasized, rather, that each child was different, and each circumstance different. Many also explained that in their experience, children's maturity, and their ability to articulate a reasoned opinion, varied enormously.

There were nonetheless, some mediators and counsellors who took the view that at a certain age, children's choices should normally prevail. The most commonly expressed view was that this point is reached in the high school years from about 14 onwards.

I mean any child at 14 I suppose you really shouldn't go against what the child is saying. But in a case of alienation, I would still have concerns about that. (Female counsellor)

I guess it's that age, that sort of teenage bracket I'm thinking about, they can actually see for themselves, can decide for themselves what's going on. (Female mediator)

I think there's an age where, if parents are reasonable parents, they ought to be able to respect the fact that the child is individuating and...I think the child ought to—all things being equal—live where they feel they want to live, provided the parent can care for them and protect them. (Female counsellor)

The views of counsellors on this were particularly significant, as they write family reports and make recommendations to the Court. While a small number of counsellors thought that the views of children as young as 11 ought to carry a lot of weight, there was generally a reluctance to suggest that the views of a child who

---

[24] See Chisholm, n 19 above, and Taylor, Tapp and Henaghan, n 19 above, on 'wishes' versus 'views'.

[25] Similarly Cantwell and Scott, both court welfare officers in the UK, commented that 'age or intelligence are probably much more important than the emotional context' (Cantwell, B and S Scott, 'Children's Wishes, Children's Burdens' (1995) 17 *Journal of Social Welfare and Family Law* 337–354, at 343). Crosby-Currie also found that mental health workers (30%) were much less likely than judges (86%) to say that the child's age was an important factor in the weight they attached to children's 'wishes' (Crosby-Currie, n 6 above). Nearly all the judges (99%) and 92% of the mental health workers groups said, however, that the child's maturity was more important than their age.

is under 13 should be determinative. Counsellors reported that many parents came in with the perception that at 12 years' old, children get to choose.[26] They were at pains to correct this:

I mean, most parents come in here [saying], I thought my child—12 years old—is able to make a decision. I said, 'not really', I said, 'A 12-year-old is still a child'. (Female counsellor)
    A lot of kids are told when they're 12 or 13 that they really are old enough to decide, so I have to dispel that very quickly. (Female counsellor)

The most commonly expressed view of all the counsellors and mediators was that children should have a say, but not be the decision-makers.

5.3.8 The risks of involving children in the litigation process

Counsellors expressed some different concerns about involving children in the litigation process to those expressed by lawyers. They were well attuned to the problem of giving children a burdensome sense of responsibility for the decision,[27] and in the process of interviewing them for family reports, they would seek to put children at ease about this. They were also well aware of the problem of parental pressure:

I see risks in setting them up to be harassed by their parents, because they're part of the process. (Female counsellor)

Loyalty conflicts

Loyalty conflicts were also seen to be a great pressure for children, and many children responded to that pressure by refusing to participate:

I mean, most kids are torn between their parents. There's a loyalty to both and they don't want to upset one or they don't want to get one into trouble or whatever. (Female counsellor)
    Caught in the middle. I think that divided loyalty is just so hard for so many of them. I always say, always give them the option in family reports, in confidential counselling, don't say anything, you don't have to pick. And I'm always surprised by how many say they won't. (Female counsellor)

---

[26] This seems to be a common perception in England, Canada and Australia (see, for example, Williams, S, *Through the Eyes of Young People: Meaningful Child Participation in Family Court Processes* (International Institute for Child Rights and Development, 2006)).
    [27] Cantwell and Scott, n 25 above. There was similar concern about the burden of responsibility on children in Trinder's analysis of the views of social workers in England although she differentiated two frameworks: one where the focus was on working with parents in mediating solutions, and the other more focused on children's views being seen as one part of the picture in their overall assessment (see Trinder, L, 'Competing Constructions of Childhood: Children's Rights and Children's Wishes in Divorce' (1997) 19 *Journal of Social Welfare and Family Law* 291–305). The workers in Trinder's study generally preferred not to involve children directly compared with the more child-inclusive approach of the Australian counsellors and mediators in the current study.

That's an incredibly stressful thing for a child, because their perception is 'I have to choose between Mummy and Daddy' and a lot of children, they just cognitively shut down. They can't do it. They won't do it. (Male counsellor)

Repercussions

One of the other concerns that counsellors had about the involvement of children was about the repercussions for the children once they have completed their work and issued a family report which contains an account of their views:

It can be very difficult, because you know that the children have to go back to that craziness, you know, they still have to go back to that fairly dysfunctional family. (Male counsellor)

[We] have concerns about involving kids, writing down what they're saying, because we know they're going to cop it at home... and that's kind a different twist on child inclusive stuff because the kids tell us lots but we really worry what's going to happen to them. (Female counsellor)

Parenting the parent

Another concern expressed by a number of counsellors was that children's views were shaped by a concern to respond to a parent's needs rather than their own:

They often are willing to sacrifice themselves for a solution, to see themselves as responsible for a solution so they'll suggest things that are fair to their parents or keep their parents happy but are not necessarily best for them. (Female counsellor)

You know, I sometimes suspect that some parents do it without much insight into what they're actually doing. You know the non-coping, non-resident parent who goes to tears or is the victim of it all. That's a really real experience for him. He can't contain it and the kids feel sorry for him and it therefore it spills over onto the kids... and the same with the Mum. The Mum may be very limited or carrying some disturbance or whatever we want to want to label it. (Male counsellor)

5.4 Judges

Perhaps not surprisingly, the views of judges and magistrates were broadly aligned with those of the lawyers.[28] All judges considered that children's voices should be heard in parenting disputes, in contrast to a study of the views of District Court judges in England and Wales, reported in 1999, in which 20% of judges said children should not be involved at all.[29] However, judges responded to questions concerning the importance of children's views from a different standpoint to the

---

[28] For a similar finding, see Ackerman et al, n 14 above.
[29] Murch et al, n 4 above, p. 179.

lawyers. In their work, children's views were just part of a large body of evidence that needed to be weighed and assessed in reaching a decision in the case.

Like the lawyers, the dominant discourse of the judges was in terms of the age and maturity of the children, and the extent to which their views were influenced by parents:

Well it depends on all of circumstances of the case I suppose, it depends on whether the children are mature, it depends on the strength of the children's wishes, the context and the background in which they emanate: clearly the older the child, the more weight I would give to it. (Male federal magistrate)

Well you give them less weight when the child is immature, you give them less weight when you know that there's some extraneous factor that's affecting their wishes... and there's all sorts of extraneous factors, sometimes there's the promise of a motorcycle, or there's some incentive via one of the parents, other times there's an artificial idealization of one of the parents or somebody, then there's the other side of the coin where the child feels responsible for a parent and the child thinks it's their responsibility to do something that's fair. (Male Family Court judge)

5.4.1 Children's voices in the context of all the evidence

Judges were clear that the views of the child would not be determinative. They emphasized that whatever the age of the child, the decision had to be made on all the evidence available to the court, and they were alert to all the problems that lawyers were, of coaching, pressure and manipulation.

The importance of children's 'views' increased with the age of the child.[30] Like lawyers and unlike counsellors and mediators, they often referred to children's 'wishes' rather than their 'views'. Most commonly, judges who nominated an age at which they would give considerable weight to the views of children said that they would do so in relation to children from about 12 years old.[31] For example:

There are many instances where I've been happy to abide the child's wishes because all the other evidence supports it, and you know, until they get probably 12 and upwards, you'd be pretty unwise to rely only on wishes as your reason for doing something and even beyond that age of course, if there were serious factors. But in circumstances where you've got two decent parents, and you're not too troubled about which parent the child should live with because all the risks factors are absent and they could both do a good job, then I think you should be doing what the child wants to do, frankly; and I think you

---

[30] This is a common finding in studies based both on interviews with judicial officers and on analyses of court files in the US, UK and Canada (see, for example, Crosby-Currie, n 6 above; Felner et al, n 6 above; Stamps, L E, S Kunen and R Lawyer, 'Judicial Attitudes Regarding Custody and Visitation Issues' (1996) 25 *Journal of Divorce & Remarriage* 23–37; May, V and C Smart, 'Silence in Court?: Hearing Children in Residence and Contact Disputes' (2004) 16 *Child and Family Law Quarterly* 305–316).

[31] Reference to the ages of 12 or 14 as important ages at which judges are willing to attach more weight to children's preferences is also quite common: Crosby-Currie, n 6 above; Felner et al, n 6 above; Stamps et al, n 30 above.

also know with a level of comfort that when they're getting to that age, that if you got it wrong, they'll vote with their feet later, they'll go trotting back to Mum, or trotting back to Dad. (Male Family Court judge)

You're looking for a match, I think of age-appropriate maturity at least, and a reasonably freely formed desire for a particular outcome with some understanding of what that means. Now children can put that together much earlier than 12, but then there are children at 12 perhaps, who can't. (Female federal magistrate)

On this approach, there ought to be no reason why we should consult children who are not at an age where it is at all likely that they will be mature enough for their views to count. Judges answered this potential criticism by reference to the potential maturity of even very young children:

Every so often you get something from a quite young child, that they put through, and I think that's interesting. You know, truly out of the mouths of babes... (Male Family Court judge)

The wishes of very young children may also be soundly based. (Female Family Court judge)

I feel like a lot of people treat 8 to 10 year olds as though they are very young... yet I've seen even in my own children and families that I've mixed with that a lot of kids in the 8 to 10 bracket can be very perceptive about what they want and have definite views and they're certainly of an age by then that they start to have their own preferences. (Male federal magistrate)

Three judges expressed a perception that children are growing up faster these days than a generation ago, and have far more knowledge on which to form opinions, which may justify placing reliance on the views of children at a younger age than in the past. This was a view expressed also by some counsellors and mediators.

While the search for decision-making capacity and reasoned opinions was the dominant paradigm, a few judges took a much wider view of children's voices, in terms which reflected the views of the mediators and counsellors. The issue, according to one judge, was not so much what children wanted, but what insights they could provide into their family circumstances—the enlightenment rationale.

I always take into account children's wishes. Be they 5, 6, 7 or 13 or 14 because I think they are important to be listened to because they often give you an insight into relationships and all sorts of other things—not necessarily 'Oh I want to live here' or 'I want to live there'. I certainly always place very significant weight on what children say about the conflict because I think you get a real feel for what their ability to be able to cope with the orders you make will often be, how much they've been enmeshed in the conflict. So I think it's really important to listen to what they're saying and how they're reacting to things in that way. (Female Family Court judge)

Another commented on the importance of hearing children's views on the range of options available to the court, not just on the major issues dividing the parents:

I don't think kids have been given an appropriate opportunity to comment on the range of possibilities that may occur in the case. It's usually a one-liner—'Where would you like to live?'—and that's it. Whereas the dynamic of what might happen in the court is far broader than that so that the question of 'Well, if the judge decided that you would live with your mother, and have contact with your father, what sort of contact do you think you'd like to have? Where would you like to have it?' That sort of thing and vice versa. So that all too often we've got no idea at all, because the child's had no opportunity to have any input into the finer questions—you know would mid week overnight contact be something that you'd like or not like? (Male Family Court judge)

5.4.2 Evaluating children's wishes

A common theme running through most of the judges' comments was that in determining what weight to give to children's wishes, they were looking for some additional quality about those wishes that justified them in placing weight upon the children's preferences in reaching their decision.

Judges formulated this additional quality in a variety of different ways. Most commonly, they referred to whether the children's wishes were really their own. For example, one judge looked for 'whether those wishes are contaminated' while another asked himself 'can you be confident that you're getting an accurate representation of the children's wishes?'. Four judges expressed what they were looking for in terms of whether the wishes were 'genuine'. Another would ask whether the children's views appear 'impartially based'.

A second type of criterion used to assess children's views was whether the views were logical or rational. For example, judges considered whether the views were 'soundly based', or whether they indicated 'some reasoning that followed a logical path'.[32]

One judge combined elements of both these ideas by asking whether the child's views indicated 'a reasonably freely formed desire for a particular outcome with some understanding of what that means'. The same judge also emphasized the durability of children's views as a factor in determining the weight which should be given to them by asking:

Whether this is a transient response to a very difficult situation. It doesn't get harder, from the child's perspective, than the situation they're in with their parents splitting up, so getting a sense of whether this is a reaction to last night's fight between the parents, or is it a reflection of what they genuinely feel and something that really they hold. (Female federal magistrate)

When asking whether the child's view was 'genuine' or 'accurate', judges were typically searching for evidence that the views were reached independently of the

---

[32] In a 1985 study by Felner et al, judges reported that children were more likely to base their 'custody preference' on both the quality of their relationship with their parents and the general quality of life in each environment as they got older; judges also thought that children aged 12 to 14 years (26%) and those aged 15 to 18 (21%) were more likely than younger children (6 to 8 years, 7%, and 3 to 5 years, 0%) to want the most permissive home environment (Felner et al, n 6 above).

parents and were not the product of coaching, manipulation or coercion. They expressed reliance on the family report writer for this assessment. One of the criteria for assessment of the children's views, for example, was whether children were echoing parental views and ways of expressing things, rather than speaking in age appropriate language that might indicate they were expressing their own views.

The age and maturity of the children, and the extent to which their views were arrived at independently of parental pressure, were much more important factors in judges' comments than the strength of children's views or the workability of arrangements (themes which were emphasized by a substantial minority of family lawyers). Indeed, some judges gave examples of going against the wishes of young teenage children, particularly in situations where they were seeking to redress alienation of one parent by the primary caregiver. On occasions that involved changing the primary caregiver despite all the risks to workability that course of action entailed.

5.5 Lawyers v Welfare Professionals on Children's Participation

It is apparent that lawyers and judges had in most cases quite different perspectives from mediators and counsellors, about the involvement of children in family law disputes.

By contrast with the lawyers who thought that parents should not talk with their children, mediators and counsellors thought it was very important indeed for parents to know how their children were feeling. They saw children's views and perspectives as a tool for settlement, and while there was a recognition that there was not usually great value in trying to assess the views of young children, in general, the mediators and counsellors thought that children's views and perspectives were important whatever their age. Some lawyers thought so too, but even for those lawyers the issue was usually one of workability, whereas for mediators and counsellors, the value of listening to children was primarily in the enlightenment that could be gained from so doing and the possibility of maintaining and repairing family relationships.

Lawyers and judges largely approached children's views forensically, concerned with children's 'wishes' and the influences that had been brought to bear on those *wishes*. Welfare professionals approached children's *views* relationally, concerned with how children's perspectives might help the parents to resolve their dispute for the sake of the children and with attention to their children's needs. Lawyers focused on children's participation in terms of the outcome of the case, with children expressing preferences between the parents' conflicting positions in the litigation, whereas welfare professionals looked at children's participation in terms of the process of getting parents to understand their children's needs.

Lawyers tended to be preoccupied with the risks of involving children, and focused on children's age, maturity and 'competence'. Welfare professionals were not unaware of those risks, but were also concerned with the benefits to the children of having a say and feeling some sense of capacity to influence their situation. Welfare professionals approached the issue of children's perspectives by seeing the potential they had to offer. Lawyers tended to treat them with some suspicion.

A catalogue of such differences has a tendency to exaggerate and simplify the differences between these two cohorts of professionals. There were differences within the cohorts as well as between them. There were overlaps in views between the cohorts also, particularly in considering the issue of autonomy and choice for teenagers. There were welfare professionals who reflected the thought processes of lawyers and lawyers who demonstrated the thought processes of welfare professionals. That said, in the main the differences between the two professional groups were very marked and significant. When lawyers and welfare professionals talk about children's participation, they are generally not talking the same language. For lawyers and judges, children's participation is largely about the capacity for making rational uninfluenced choices and workability. For welfare professionals, it is largely about enlightenment, empowerment and conflict resolution.

5.6 Participation, Decision-making and Parental Influence

This dominant view both of lawyers and judges, that the weight to be given to children's views should depend on their capacity for making rational choices free from the influence of parents, seemed to be a search for the genuine and maturely held view of the child as a circuit-breaker in the dispute between the parents. If that mature, rational and freely formed view could be discerned, it might well be decisive in the absence of risk factors or other strong indications that the child's best interests would be served by a different outcome. Conversely, if the child's views were not the result of a mature decision-making capacity, or were not freely formed without improper pressure, influence or manipulation, then they would be discounted. While the Australian legislation refers to the age and maturity of the child in assessing children's views,[33] nothing in the legislation indicates that the purpose of considering children's maturity is to see whether they are competent to make their own choices. Age and maturity may equally be relevant to enlightenment, as the mature child may offer greater insights into the family circumstances, and his or her relationships with family members, than a less mature child.

This dominant discourse about the significance of children's views sits uneasily with the views expressed by most lawyers that children should not be put in the position of decision-makers, and that they should be free from both the power and the responsibility of that adult role. One judge commented on the desire of

---

[33] See n 13 above.

the legal profession in his city to have family reports prepared early on in a case in order to get some early independent evidence of the views of the child:

> My impression is that too much emphasis is put by the legal profession on getting their clients to ascertain the wishes of the children. Because it's sometimes seen as an easy fix, oh, let's ask little Johnny what he thinks, and then we'll accept that. You often get the parents saying that—'Oh, yes, I'll do whatever the kids want'. Now, that's passing the buck. And that's why, also for a long time in this court, the court counselling department were not keen to do early reports. The profession wanted early reports because they wanted to use them as the tool for settlement, and primarily the early reports were to address the wishes of the children. The court counselling department for a long time took the view that they wouldn't do that, because they didn't consider it was professional and that their job wasn't to settle the case. (Male Family Court judge)

If children are not meant to be the decision-makers, why then seek their views and worry so much about whether those views are mature and free from pressure and influence? When a medical decision is to be made, we may well ask, as a starting point, whether the child is mature enough to give (or refuse) their own consent to an operation. However, almost none of the professionals interviewed thought that when it comes to parenting arrangements, it ought to be the child who has the decision-making authority. Many lawyers and welfare professionals offered a realistic assessment of the likelihood of being able to enforce orders against the strongly held wishes of an adolescent, and some thought that as they move into their teenage years, young people ought to be allowed more freedom to negotiate the contact arrangements directly with the other parent. Nonetheless, there was no enthusiasm for reversing the role of parent and child, irrespective of whether the children's views were freely formed or not.

There is a further complexity about discounting children's views when they reflect the influence of one parent or the other. The fact that a child echoes the views of one parent does not mean necessarily that those views aren't shared by the child. A view expressed by an 11-year-old child that her father doesn't have a clue about the needs of pre-teenage girls may be just what her mother thinks, or it may, in addition to being what her mother thinks, be true.

Suppose the view is incorrect. Does it actually matter whether that untrue, unfair or exaggerated view has been influenced by the negative attitudes of her mother towards her father, or has been formed by a rather critical and rebellious 11-year-old, independently of some adult influence? Even if it is not true, or the criticism of her father is exaggerated or unfair, it may still be the child's genuine view.

The view of a child may also be genuinely held, but may be the product of having to find a way through the parental conflict. As both lawyers and judges pointed out, children may sometimes say they want what they perceive as fair between the parents, or align themselves to one parent or the other.[34] One judge,

---

[34] For a discussion of children's views about the fairness of the arrangements, see Parkinson et al, n 8 above.

for example, commented on how children might form their own views based upon the exigencies of their situation:

Let's assume there is high conflict between the two parents and that's the sort of case that usually comes here—so the child recognises mother provides security, food, transport, warmth, love—presumably not too many beltings—and the child hears the parents fighting on the telephone or face to face so the child has to exhibit loyalty to keep all those secure things continuing. So that's a wish or a view expressed, but it may not be very accurate. (Male federal magistrate)

A view might be no less the child's view from being borne out of emotional necessity. It may be an 'accurate' view of the child but not a view that necessarily accords with the child's best interests.

What then is the importance of a child's view being 'genuinely' his or hers rather than being the product of coaching, pressure, manipulation or a survival response to parental conflict, if no one actually believes the child should be the decision-maker in any event?

There is another paradox contained in lawyers' views about involving children in parenting disputes. Almost all were in favour of consulting children about their views, but almost all, in turn, were strongly opposed to parents consulting their children and were very critical of clients who did so. There was widespread acknowledgement that when children came to talk to child representatives or to experts preparing a family report, they had been subject to a lot of influence and pressure from parents, whether consciously or unconsciously applied. This made it somewhat illusory to imagine that the child's voice could be heard, untainted by influence and freely formed, or that just because a professional was involved in talking with the children, that would in some way protect them from parental pressure and manipulation in the weeks and days before that meeting.

The search for the rational child decision-maker is as problematic as the search for the uninfluenced decision-maker. That a child is capable of making a logical and rational decision does not mean, per se, that his or her logical and rational decision, albeit impaired by limited experience or short-term perspectives, should take precedence over professional adult decision-makers. Is the 10-year-old child's rational and logical choice to prefer living with Dad rather than Mum, to be given greater weight than that of the psychologist employed by the court who can take account of the child's views, but also a range of issues that are beyond the child's knowledge and experience?

There is then a need for a new rationale for talking with and involving children, one that does not rely on finding the authentic voice of the mature child, free from parental manipulation and pressure or the search for the logical and rational child decision-maker. The basis for such a new paradigm is offered to some extent by the welfare professionals with their emphasis on enlightenment and empowerment, and it will be discussed in Chapter 8.

6

Children's Involvement in the Litigation Process

As noted in Chapter 3, children's voices could be heard in litigation in a variety of ways. The main ways are through family report writers and through independent legal representation. Lawyers reported no use of affidavits by children and, as will be seen in Chapter 7, the practice of interviewing children in chambers is quite unusual in Australia, although some judges see it as an option.

In this chapter, we examine how counsellors, who write family reports, and independent children's lawyers, go about their work, and the extent to which counsellors and report writers in Australia work together in seeking to promote the best interests of children.

6.1 The Voice of the Child in Family Reports

Counsellors reported a variety of different techniques for ascertaining the views and perspectives of children. All said that their approach depended on the age and maturity of the children. With children of upper primary age and upwards, they tended to talk with the children directly about home, school and family;[1] with younger children, they used a variety of other methods to ascertain their perspectives. These were mostly projective techniques, such as asking them their three wishes, or asking if they were on an island, and they could take one person with them, who would it be? They also used pictures and sentence or story completion exercises.

---

[1] This difference in approach for younger and older children has been advocated in the literature. For example, see Clark who opined 'that children under the age of 11, unless they volunteer it, should not be asked directly about their preference by the evaluator. A good evaluation will allow the evaluator to acquire enough information to assess this issue without having to ask the child directly. After the age of 11, most children have cognitive ability to understand their role in the proceedings may often be asked directly without the fear of confusing or alarming the child unduly.' (Clark, B K, 'Acting in the Best Interest of the Child: Essential Components of the Child Custody Evaluation' (1995) 29 *Family Law Quarterly* 19–38, at 33).

6.1.1 Entering the child's world

Most counsellors engaged in a broad-ranging assessment of the child's situation, rather than focusing on the parenting arrangements. One experienced female counsellor, for example, would begin talking to children by asking such questions as the following:

'What's the nicest dream you've ever had? What's the worst nightmare you've ever had?' And ask them to draw something there or write something and then sometimes use that to say 'Oh okay, if you put yourself in the centre, maybe you could give me an idea of who else is in your family and you can draw them as if it was a map of who's who'.

Another explained her technique in this way:

I'll interview a child fairly broadly, really looking at how the child is, and sees themselves as functioning in those sorts of areas. And how things are going with school and with friends, with their life, generally. And we'll gradually move on to their parents and their parents' separation and how they make sense of that—what they were told about it. And I would ask fairly detailed questions about how they perceive their parents interacting with one another. Also, how they felt living in that situation.

In interviewing the children, counsellors sought to build a picture of the children's experience of family life, rather than their views on the parenting dispute:

I think it really is a process of talking to the child about their experience—what they do, what's their experience of contact, what was their experience before their parents separated. It really is about finding out what the child likes, and what experiences work for them and what doesn't work for them. So it's just a process of talking to the child, and they tell you things. Sometimes they might sit down and do some drawings for you, but I think basically just trying to understand their experience and...you draw inferences from that. (Female counsellor)

You start off with, 'Tell me about school, their teachers, their friends, if they like school, what do they like best?' Just talk about their normal everyday lives and then I say and 'what sorts of things do you do with Mum and Dad?' and 'how is that going?, what are you doing?' and so you'll get activities that they might do, and then I just go with their answers... it's like meandering almost, rather than questioning them. (Female counsellor)

I try to focus on likes and dislikes in each household. And when they talk about likes or dislikes, if something sounds interesting, I encourage them to expand on it. (Female counsellor)

Generally, counsellors preferred to avoid any questions which were too direct or involved forced choices. One counsellor, for example, did not like sentence completion exercises because they were too confrontational:

My Mum becomes the most angry when...I think that that automatically triggers a defensive anxiety thing and it's kind of quite explicit, I guess, and is maybe forcing them into that sense of having to elect preferences.

However, one female counsellor did use a particular forced choice question to gain an understanding of children's worlds:

I've got another question that I always ask children and no one else uses this, but I find it really helpful and it's 'Which parent do you worry about most?'. It's a forced choice, and they'll tell you if they don't worry about either, but mostly they'll nominate someone, and then I explore with them which parent it is. (Female counsellor)

Counsellors also tried to be clear that children did not need to express a view-point on the parenting arrangements:

I always try and give them the message that the Family Court is really about decisions that have to be made by the parents, not decisions that have to be made by the children. And I guess that's a message I try and get across to the children I see here anyhow, whether it's in mediation or family reports. (Male counsellor)

In contrast to all the female counsellors, two male counsellors took a much more direct approach to eliciting children's views from the beginning:

After an early banter about school and food and TV, I'd ask them why are they in here?...And then I would explore with them, sometimes I'll ask them a question you know about residence or contact and I would often give them the options and say, 'What would it be like if this was the decision? How would you feel if the judge said this, that, or the other?'

I explain why we're having a chat, explain that it's an opportunity for them to say what they would like or to say what sorts of things worry them or concern them or upset them. Most children, at least above the age of 8 or 9, have a pretty good idea of what's going on and either they are quite keen to have a say, or don't have a say at all.

6.1.2 Assessing the child's views

An important part of the family report writing process is to assess the child's views and perspectives in the context of all the information available. The focus on children's experiences rather than their views was seen as important to contextualize whatever preferences they might express, and to evaluate it within the broader framework of the child's relationship with both parents and his or her needs at that time. Counsellors were alert to the fact that expressions of opinion about the parenting arrangements may be reactions to the moment, and subject to change:

I try and assess the reasons and the logic behind their point of view. Quite often it's an emotional point of view. Or it could have to do with the fact that they've just had a great weekend with Daddy, and Mummy yelled at them and won't let them have a new mobile phone...Dad promised them a mobile phone and they had a good weekend, and 'Oh I want to live with Dad'; whereas the next week it might be a different response. So I guess we're used to [the fact that] children change their minds frequently and tend to be emotional. (Male counsellor)

Sometimes, you can take what a child says on face value... [but] we ask other questions to ascertain whether the child really thinks that way... [and] whether their reasoning is sound. What is their reasoning based on? (Female counsellor)

I contextualize [children's wishes] in terms of pretty major things. What have the parents been saying about one another? And what do the parents want? And how do they think the parents feel? Which gives you an idea. If the child's saying, 'I actually want to live with Daddy, because Daddy's really sad and every time I leave Daddy, he bursts into tears'. That gives you an idea about what the voice means. (Female counsellor)

It followed that expressions of 'wishes' were much less important than a holistic assessment of children's worlds—their experiences of parenting in the two households, and their needs. Indeed, one counsellor was very critical of a practice of seeking brief family reports confined to an assessment of children's wishes:

A 'wishes' report is the same sort of format as a family report, but really it doesn't involve interviews with the parent... it just involves getting the wishes of this child. Magistrates often like us to do wishes reports but we try to say that it's very hard to distil the wishes of the children, and we'd normally always do interviews with both parents and children... I wouldn't do a wishes report of a child brought only by a mother or a wishes report [brought only] by a father.

Another counsellor emphasized the importance of context in evaluating the basis for children's expressed preferences. She gave the example of relocation disputes:

Do they really appreciate what it's going to be like to change the situation that they're in now to the situation that they're going to be in? Do they think it's going to be like an extended holiday? So it's weighing up their ability to predict themselves what the situation is going to be like. And I suppose the older the child, the more realistic their expectations are going to be. (Female counsellor)

One important aspect of the assessment was how children would react to different decisions that the judge might make.[2] Asking about this was seen to be a way of determining the strength of the child's feelings about issues:

If they're very determined about something, it's quite telling. If you say to the kids, 'I'm going to write everybody's story in this. Mum and Dad have written their stories. All of this information is going to go before the judge and the judge will decide. Right? So, it's not Mum and Dad deciding and it's not me deciding, the judge will decide. If the judge decides that you spend a bit more time at Dad's place, how would that be?' Now sometimes that's enough for them. It's not their choice, they'll say 'oh, that will be okay'. So, it gives them an out... [But] if the judge says that you need to go mainly with your Dad, live mainly with your Dad, then some kids will say then I'll run away. Right? Or I will kill myself. They're that determined. (Female counsellor)

In a recent case with a 12-year-old, how violently the child reacted was quite a demonstration to me of how strongly the child felt about that. (Female counsellor)

---

[2] This was required by an appellate decision, where a child has expressed a particular preference (*R and R* (2000) FLC 93-000).

Most said they approached this issue in a direct way, but the male counsellors tended to want to explore the issue more indirectly:

I'll sometimes write on the whiteboard all their options especially if it is a residence issue and ask them to rank them in preference. (Male counsellor)

I might ask exactly that question, but I think it usually comes out in other ways more in the context of the family. (Male counsellor)

One other way of assessing the significance of the child's views in the preparation of a family report is through observation. Counsellors reported different practices in terms of this. Some used observation only with children up to about 9 or 10 years old. Others were prepared to use it with teenagers. Each parent's interactions with the child are viewed by the counsellor either being in the same room with them, or through a one-way mirror. Counsellors expressed different preferences about that.

The main purpose of observations is to assess the interactions of the parent and child, the level of comfort the child has with each parent, and how the parent relates to the child. Counsellors generally acknowledged the artificiality of the observation process and that it was only seeing parents and children in a particular moment in time, and in a situation of some stress. They reported that sometimes nothing could be gained from an observation, but that at other times, a great deal was learnt.

Now, you might think people are on their very, very best behaviour. But it doesn't work that way. But what comes naturally, actually naturally tends to happen. They don't tend to have sensed that there's much wrong with it, or even the tone of voice they might use when the other parent comes up. (Female counsellor)

If children are afraid of their parents or don't feel close to their parents, it's usually able to be picked up. (Male counsellor)

Counsellors did report, however, that observations are also one way of assessing the views of the child, and comparing them with other information about the child and family situation:

[What] I'm looking for is the consistencies between what the child has said and how the child behaves with that parent. And that's a hugely important factor, because sometimes the two are very different. (Female counsellor)

A female counsellor gave a rather graphic example of how an observation indicated that a teenager's needs might be discordant with his wishes about his living arrangements:

I had a 15-year-old some years ago, who had lived most of his life with his father, he'd gone to live with his mother, stepfather and little siblings. His natural sister, his full sister, was still with Dad, and while he was with the Mum, he'd done all sorts of things, throwing paint out of the school bus onto the roof of cars. He'd been a bit of a problem and Dad had put on an application wanting him back. Now in the interview, he said to me that he wanted to stay with his mother. He was very clear, very adamant. He didn't want to go back to his Dad; he wanted to stay with his Mum. He was 15 years old, a young 15, but 15 years nevertheless.

In the observation session, he took his mother's handbag, he took some money out of it against her wishes, he went downstairs and got a can of Coke, against her wishes, against the specific instructions, he came back with a full can of Coke, he didn't buy any for his siblings, he banged one of his sisters about 6 on the head with the can of Coke... His father came in to the observation session. He sat next to his father and burst into tears. He hadn't seen his father for quite some time, had a little talk with his Dad, and then quite unprompted, said to his sister, I think we'd better clean up this room.

6.1.3 Family reports and children's secrets

Counsellors in the court system at the time of these interviews engaged with children both on a confidential and non-confidential basis. When they were involved in privileged mediation with the parents at an earlier stage in the litigation process, they would sometimes talk with the children separately, and contract with the children and the parents about what would be fed back to the parents:

I make it clear to them that I will have a confidentiality agreement with the children, particularly children who are about 9 onwards. And the only feedback the parents would get is what the children allow me to feedback. However I explain to the children that I give parents a general overview without giving them any (detailed) information. And the parents (seem to) accept that. (Female counsellor)

When it comes to confidential counselling, I say to them, look they're free to talk to me and that it's confidential and that after we've had a talk, I will then review with them what they want me to tell Mum and Dad. So that it is under their control what Mum and Dad are told. (Female counsellor)

However, in preparing a family report, then the process of talking to children was not confidential. A different counsellor would, however, be involved in preparing the family report.[3] The counsellors endeavoured to make it very clear to the children that in preparing the family report, they would be writing something for the judge and there could be no secrets.

In a report it's different than in a mediation because, you know, it's really hard to have confidentiality because everything's reportable...I'll talk about writing it down. If they're young, I'll say 'look I'll tell you why I'm writing things down'. I'll start to write and then I'll say, 'excuse me that I'm not looking at you all the time, but I've got to write some things down because I'm writing a story for the judge'. (Female counsellor)

In a somewhat confusing message,[4] one counsellor said:

---

[3] Now, because of changes to the family law system (as described in Chapter 3), privileged mediation occurs in the community, and mediation during the course of the litigation process is reportable.

[4] This explanation could be quite misleading and confusing for children because whispering implies 'telling secrets'; yet the counsellor is telling the child 'there are no secrets'.

I've told them there are no secrets, and that this is their chance to lift up the wig of the judge and whisper in his ear. They tell me, and that will get to the judge. (Male counsellor)

One female counsellor explained also that she might have to give evidence and reveal more information on the witness stand:

I've said, 'It is important that you understand that whatever you tell me could go into the report. And even if it doesn't go into the report, if I'm being cross-examined I have to tell the truth, I have to tell them what you said'. And I also tell them that it is important that, if they feel that they, you know, anything they say, could get them into trouble, it's better for them not to say it. (Female counsellor)

How then did counsellors deal with situations where, in the course of writing a family report, the child indicated that there were certain things he or she did not want the counsellor to reveal? There were many different approaches to this question. Some said they dealt with the problem by being so clear at the beginning that there could be no secrets that the issue did not arise at all. It was common, for example, for counsellors to explain to the children that they didn't need to express a view at all, or to instruct the children not to tell them things that they did not want to get out:

If they don't want the judge or Mum and Dad to know anything, don't tell me. (Male counsellor)

I guess it's for me to assess their reaction in how they answer that question, you know, 'Do you have any concerns?' 'In telling me what you want, will there be any trouble?' Some children have said, 'No', some children have said, 'Oh, I'm a bit worried', and I've said, 'Well it's important for you not to say it then'. (Female counsellor)

Others left more room for children to say things that they might not want reported, dealing with the problem by exercising some discretion about what goes into the report and how it is expressed:[5]

I'd explain that their Mum and Dad would both be seeing the report and the judge would see the report and we'd have to be really careful what we wrote in the report. That we could, if there are things that they really, really didn't want their Mum and Dad to know, then they should tell me that, [and] we can work out, if there's some way of getting that

[5] Family court practitioners were reported in a British study to be more likely to interpret what child said than to include it verbatim in their written reports (see McNamee, S, A L James and A James, 'Can Children's Voices be Heard in Family Law Proceedings? Family Law and the Construction of Childhood in England and Wales' (2003) 16 *Representing Children* 168–178). Mantle et al in the UK also commented on the unavoidability of interpretation in conducting and writing an evaluation report (Mantle, G, T Moules, K Johnson, J Leslie, S Parsons and R Shaffer, 'Establishing Children's Wishes and Feelings for Family Court Reports' (2007) 37 *British Journal of Social Work* 785–805). They stated:

Interpretation is unavoidable and meanings are likely to be contested. What goes into the welfare report is a representation, constructed by the author and reflecting a process that touches different stakeholders, purposes and interests. (at 792)

across... I think you can interview them in such a way that you don't make them say anything that they don't want to say. (Female counsellor)

Another counsellor explained that her approach was to say to the children that if they needed to say something (as opposed to merely wanting to do so), then they should do so and she would work out how to handle it:

I say 'If you need to tell me something... tell me, and let me know that you're worried about it, and I'll try and handle it in a way that will be the least problem'. (Female counsellor)

She gave the example of having to report on the wishes of boys who wanted to live with their father rather than their mother because of what the mother had said and done. She reported accurately what they had said about the mother and what their views were, but without attributing the information to any child by name. When pressed on the witness stand who had said what, she turned to the judge seeking permission not to answer in order to protect the children from repercussions. The lawyer withdrew the question.

Another male counsellor explained that he would try to resolve the problem by persuasion:

Okay, they've told me something and I thank them for trusting me with the information. Because they've certainly made a big step and I think that they would have been desperate... so, I go back over what they want to achieve and I let them know that it's not their choice. A judge decides. So if Mum or Dad are going to get angry, they're going to get angry at the judge. I come back to the fact that I'm helping the judge, they're helping me. But also it would help Mum and Dad to let them know what the child thinks. After all Mum and Dad are giving up a lot of time and money in pursuit of their respective claims. So I try to let the child know from the point of view of the parents.

Would counsellors ever leave out of family reports matters which were clearly relevant, out of respect for the child's wish for confidentiality or to protect them from any repercussions from their parents? On this issue, there were sharply different views. One male counsellor was particularly clear about where his obligations lay:

We have a difficult role. We have to report what children say to us, yet quite often children will say things that if their parents know that the children have said that, they could be in danger or at risk. So my bottom line is that I will protect the child at all costs. So there are some times, well there are lots of things that people say to us that we don't use in reports. (Male counsellor)

Many others would leave out even important things if they felt that they had to do so or the children asked them not to say something:

You really have to use a lot of discretion because you've got to protect the children but still get the message across to the court. (Female counsellor)

We try everything to protect kids, we talk about them as groups, don't individualize them. We try and be careful, we probably only give half the story... you've got to get

across that the child has either very strong views, or the evidence is really strong and compelling, that there either needs to be no contact, change of residence, you know …
*And if they say they don't want you to say some things? This is what I want but I don't want you
to say that to the judge?*
Well I'll say that gets a bit delicate. I'll say I won't. (Female counsellor)

Two counsellors allowed children to withdraw things:

I do give them permission to say look if they've said something—at the end, when I've
spoken to them, I say 'Look is there anything that you've said that you wish you hadn't
have said, or you don't want me to talk about, well let me know'. Depending on their age
of course, but there's that notion that they can sort of backtrack and make corrections if
they so wish. (Male counsellor)
   They may sometimes say things that afterwards they feel they don't want to be in a
report and I personally want to protect them from that. If they tell me something, we
might go through the report again and they might sometimes say 'I don't want you to
write about this', so I have to find a way of writing around it but because it's sometimes
important for us to really understand where they're coming from. I don't mind if they let
their guard down as long as they are not betrayed afterwards. (Female counsellor)

However, other counsellors appeared to take the view that their obligation was
one of full disclosure to the court, albeit mediated by discretion and careful judgment about how information should be imparted in the report:

I'd probably say, 'Look, it's got to go in the report. I've told you before that the judge
needs to see it, but I'll try to raise it in such a way that Mum and Dad won't get upset, and
that's the best I can do, the best I can promise'. (Female counsellor)
   It isn't confidential. It's a document that will go to court … I am trying to get information that will be useful for the court to make a good decision for these kids … I want to
use what I can use, but I'm clear about it. (Female counsellor)
   I just have to say, 'I'm really sorry, but you've said that now, I explained at the beginning of the report writing process that everything they say is, I can include that in the
report and I must'. And I say 'Look … the reason there is a trial, is you. And the judge
needs to know what you think. I would hate the judge to make a decision without the
judge knowing that.' (Male counsellor)

6.1.4 Following up on outcomes

Report writers invest considerable time and effort seeing families and preparing
reports, and in some cases being cross-examined on the content of the report during a court hearing. Finding out how the case was determined and whether the
orders were consistent with their report's recommendations provides some feedback to counsellors about the standing of their report in relation to the evidence
before the court.
   Most counsellors were keen to follow up on the outcome and the orders in
cases for which they had prepared a report, especially for those they remembered

as particularly difficult or involving child protection issues. Some referred explicitly to the educational value of this follow-up or the curiosity value.

I think most family reports are often included in great chunks in the judgment. I suppose that for my self-reflection I find that's a really positive way of understanding what is having an effect in the system. (Female counsellor)

My ego is sufficient to want to know what they did with my opinion. (Female counsellor)

They were rarely surprised by the orders, which were generally consistent with their recommendations. But where they were not consistent, there was generally evidence that was not available to them, with their report providing one part of the picture.

Because I think sometimes that there is other evidence that you don't know about. And—I think that because we worked in the system for so long, you are aware that what you see here is, you know, only a part of what's out there, you know, what, and also what the parents tell you. So you're seeing a small part of what happened. So, I always go into cross-examination with a fairly open mind. (Female counsellor)

Part of what we need to be like in this job is to be okay if judges go against our recommendations, but the things is we realize that we're—that our role is circumscribed: we're looking at family dynamics and children's wishes and so on. The judge has got more information on which to base a decision, so no I'm not often surprised. (Female counsellor)

Only three counsellors said they never follow up on the outcomes, because they need to close the door on a case once they have completed the report, either because of the continuing work load or because they need to do so psychologically.

No, once I have finished the family report and done the cross examination, that's it. Other people do. I don't. I have to shut the door. It's something about just finishing it off at that point, partially because I am juggling a whole lot of other cases at the same time. And I just need to shut the door without actually knowing because I've got no control over it—whether it's the right thing or not. (Female counsellor)

Rarely did they have any further follow-up with the families involved unless they returned during further contestation.

6.2 The Role of Child Representatives

The voice of the child also comes through child representatives. While child representatives do not give evidence about their conversations with children, since they are advocates for children, they are expected to put the children's views to the court by way of submissions, whether or not they consider that those views align with the child's best interests.[6] Consequently, their understanding of the

---

[6] This may vary according to jurisdiction and which lawyers are involved. In some US states and in Canada (Quebec), for example, some lawyers are more likely than others to interview children

child's views and their means of ascertaining and representing those views are important in determining what submissions they make to the court about the outcome of the case.

6.2.1 Meeting with the child

The guidelines for child representation in New South Wales, where the interviews with lawyers for this study took place, are clear that child representatives should meet with a child who is verbal.[7] That has not been the uniform position around Australia. A lack of uniformity of approach may also be seen in other countries.[8] Lawyers varied as to whether they ever made exceptions to the normal practice of meeting with a verbal child. The majority of lawyers at least wanted to see verbal children even if they were not doing so for the purpose of ascertaining their views but 'to get a sense of who they are' and to introduce themselves.[9] Four child representatives indicated that they would not see children under 5, or school-age, unless it was a meet and greet occasion when seeing the siblings. For example, one female child representative said:

I wouldn't meet a child who was not yet school age on the basis that there wasn't much point having a conversation with that person since I'm a lawyer, not a psychologist. My ability to engage with someone who is not yet of school age is limited.

In one case with very young children, the lawyer was concerned to meet the children and to see them in their home environment.

I went recently up to Town X to meet two children who are living with their father. There have been a lot of allegations made about him. Both the parents are Aboriginal and there are two very small children who were 2 and 4, little girls. I thought it was the only way that I could really satisfy myself about their father's situation. He seemed like a nice enough

---

and more likely to be expected by the court to put forward the child's view as well as their view of their 'best interests'. See Crosby-Currie, C A, 'Children's Involvement in Contested Custody Cases: Practices and Experiences of Legal and Mental Health Professionals' (1996) 20 *Law and Human Behavior* 289–311; Joyal, R and A Queniart, 'Enhancing the Child's Point of View in Custody and Access Cases in Quebec: Preliminary Results of a Study Conducted in Quebec' (2002) 19 *Canadian Journal of Family Law* 173–192.

[7] Law Society of New South Wales *Representation Principles—A Guide for Children's Lawyers, 2002.*

[8] Family Law Council, *Pathways for Children: A Review of Children's Representation in Family Law* (2004) p 19. These lawyers are not alone in not always meeting with children. For commentary and research in the UK and New Zealand, see Gray, A and P Martin, *The Role of Counsel for the Child: Research Report* (Department for Courts, Wellington, 1998) p 63; Taylor, N J, M Gollop, A B Smith and P F Tapp, *The Role of Counsel for the Child—Perspectives of Children, Young People and their Lawyers: Research Report* (Department for Courts, Wellington, 1999); Piper, C, 'Assumptions about Children's Best Interests' (2000) 22 *Journal of Social Welfare and Family Law* 261–276, at 265.

[9] Their views are remarkably similar in many repects to those of US lawyers in 1977 (Landsman, K J and M L Minow, 'Lawyering for the Child: Principles of Representation in Custody and Visitation Disputes Arising from Divorce' (1978) 87 *Yale Law Review* 1126–1190).

guy, a bit rough but solid. So I went up there and I visited his home twice. And I visited the oldest child at pre-school and I was much more satisfied in my mind in telling the court the kids were ok there than just by reading his affidavits, because the mother was making a lot of allegations, and I'm very relieved I did that. And I saw the care that he'd taken in the way their rooms were presented and that there were so many appropriate books and toys and it was a tiny, tiny little house on a main road and it was all of that, but that wasn't it. The stuff I could pick up about the day care, the transport driver about the lunch that was prepared, their presentation—all of that was what I needed to be confirmed.

Another exception, expressed by two male lawyers, was if the child had already been subjected to multiple interviews by child protection workers, police, psychiatrists, doctors, or other such professionals.

6.2.2 Ascertaining the views of the child

There were some significant differences between the lawyers in how they went about ascertaining the views of children. Whereas counsellors generally sought to understand children's worlds, lawyers tended to want to understand children's views. They were thus much more focused on getting from the children their views about the dispute, and their preferences, if the children had any that they were willing to express.

Two major strategies emerged from the interviews. Most lawyers did this by finding out something about the child before exploring the issues in dispute, thereby being able to gain some picture of the child's life. This initial exploration tended however, to be largely an exercise in building up some rapport before getting to the 'real business' of finding out what if anything, the child would like the judge to know.

You just have a chat to them, it really is getting to know them, 'Where do you go to school, what are your favourite subjects, what sport do you do? What did you get for your last birthday?' After you have done all that, you say to them, 'If at some stage your Mum and Dad can't agree the judge is going to make a decision, are there things you want to tell the judge?' And you find most of them are forthcoming. (Male child representative)

We chat a lot about other things first, and then I ask questions about who's in Mummy's house, who lives in Daddy's house, if they have their own room in Mummy's house and Daddy's house, how often they see one or the other, are you happy with that particular person, you know, are you comfortable with that, do you play sport, does it interfere, just get around, but make it really clear that I'm asking whether they're comfortable with the current arrangement. Do they know what Daddy's asking? Do they know that Mummy and Daddy aren't particularly happy with the current arrangement and they want something different? If they want something different, what would you like 'different' to be? (Female child representative)

The male lawyers, like two of the male counsellors, tended to be quite direct in talking with the children about the issues in dispute:[10]

---

[10] For similar views about the directness of lawyers in their questioning of children, see Landsman and Minow, n 9 above, at 1163.

If they're old enough that you can have a serious conversation with them, you might just say 'Well look, you understand what the dispute's about. It's X and Y. And I understand that you're now living with Dad or Mum or whoever'. You know, you'd ask them 'How's that working out? Is it okay? Would you like any changes in that? Could that work better for you? Is there some way that we can make that work better for you?' or whatever. So you'd talk to them reasonably. (Male child representative)

Initially I ask them why they're here and they may say 'Well, because Mummy said we have to come here and talk to you about seeing Dad' and you may follow that up and say 'Well what do you think about that?' or 'How do you feel about seeing Dad?' and talk about them in terms of the judge is going to make a decision in court and would they be happy with the decision of the judge? And if they are not happy what would they do? And then say 'Well, how do you feel if the judge says that you have to see Dad say every second weekend?' and the child might say 'Oh no', or 'Yes that's alright'. (Male child representative)

This direct approach was characteristic of the male lawyers but not confined to them. For example, one female child representative explained her technique:

I always ask them their understanding of what's going on—what the problem is and what the argument is and what it is that Mummy wants and what it is that Daddy wants and then I ask them. I ask them pretty straightforwardly 'Do they know what they would like?' And then if they're able to tell me, I make absolutely sure I've heard it right with them.

By way of contrast, other lawyers, all of them women, engaged in a much broader process of assessment of children's views and experiences of family life. This involved quite indirect means of finding out about children's worlds:

Almost never do I say, 'What are your views?' Almost always I'll say, 'Can you just tell me the story of your family, who are you with now, how long?' and then I'll let them tell the story. I ask as few questions as possible and then, just tell me the story, and I might say, 'When did that happen?' or 'What do you think about that?' And you let them, I say now, and sometimes I even call it chapters, I might say, 'Now what's the next chapter, when your Mum and Dad stopped living together?' And sometimes that emerges, it's pretty obvious where a kid's going with that and so what you might ask later depends on all of that.

I tell them I want to draw a family tree with them, so that I can learn all about their family…You know they just become involved with that process, and you do both sides of the family and as you're doing that I ask them about what the nature of the relationship is with that person…and we draw all them in, and how often do you see them?…that will basically give me a fuller picture of what all their family relationships are, and I ask them about pets…and then after that, I'll talk to them about what their arrangements are currently, about how much time they have with each parent, talk to them about what arrangements were in the past, if that's changed, and then that will lead into well, how do you feel about it? If the court made a decision this way, or that way, or if your parents agreed to this, or if your parents agreed to that?

Women lawyers who interviewed children in this way would use drawings and genograms and other devices to understand more of children's worlds and their preferences. One described in detail how she engages with children through talking about school and friends and drawing a genogram of the family:

And then I say, tell me some good things, what do you like best about Mum? What don't you like about Mum? What do you like best about Dad? What don't you like about Dad?...So then, if it's just a contact issue, then I might just move straight to that. Say, you know, when did you last see Dad? And you know, would you like to see him again? So that's how I'd find out about their contact. Then another thing...I do is that you can do the numbers ten to one, and kids have indicated to me that they like that. On one side is that they really want to stay with Dad overnight, they want to go and sleep at his place—that's ten. And one is don't do it. And I ask them to indicate a number, about where they want, how much they want to stay at Dad's, or how much they don't want to go. So they'll circle that.

It was a minority of child representatives who engaged in this kind of structured process of engaging with children.

Another approach was to talk with the children directly, but without actually asking them about the issues in dispute:

I just ask the questions about the things they like to do. The good things they like to do at each of the parent's houses and the bad things they think about their parent's houses. And that gives me an idea of wishes, mostly. (Female child representative)

I usually start chatting about what school they go to, who their teacher is, what their teacher is like. You sort of joke about it, who's always in trouble, who is the best in the class, all that sort of stuff and you let it unfold and see what comes out. (Male child representative)

6.2.3 Representing the child

The children's lawyers were quite clear that they had a responsibility both to present the child's wishes to the court and to represent their best interests in accordance with the guidelines. How they went about doing this and how they communicated this to the children varied, however. This was particularly evident in the way they managed divergence between what children wanted and what they thought was in their best interests.

Most lawyers indicated that they explain to children that the role of the court is to make a decision, based on all the evidence, that may not necessarily be what the children want or like. This serves several functions. It allows them to see how the children might react to orders that are contrary to their wishes, and this provides useful information that informs their submission to the court.[11] It also helps them to manage children's expectations so, for example, the children don't

---

[11] Seven of the 21 child representatives mentioned concerns about children threatening to 'run away' if the orders were contrary to their wishes but one saw this as a ploy with parents telling children to say this.

'walk out thinking that I have led them to believe that coming in and expressing an opinion means that that's what's going to happen'. Beyond that, lawyers differ in their approach. The majority were clear that they would tell the child, and that they had an obligation under the guidelines to do so.

Yeah, and again the guidelines require that you do that, and I think sensibly. Discuss it with them: you said that is your wish but I'm concerned about that... These are the reasons why, how do you feel about that?...I think if you are going to tell them that you are going to express a contrary view, you at least owe it to them to tell them why. (Male child representative)

　　Well, you've got to be honest. You've got to say, 'Well, you and I have got a difference of opinion on that, and I'm going to run my case along this way'. It happens, the kid doesn't like it, but they probably respect you more if you make that clear to them. (Male child representative)

A minority said they laid the responsibility with the court and do not tell children before or after the hearing that they were advocating a position that differed from the child's wishes or viewpoint.

Um, they're the hard ones, you know. Ah, I don't know—I haven't got an immediate answer for that. I mean I guess ultimately leave it up to the judge—it's not my problem, is it? (Male child representative)

　　Oh, that's really hard...I find that very difficult to do...but sometimes that happens. Sometimes you can have two siblings in a family where one child will have one view, another child will have another view, they're both not particularly mature so I wouldn't put a lot of weight on their wishes...and...I don't think I'd tell those kids what I was going to do. (Female child representative)

6.2.4　Respecting confidentiality

Child representatives were quite transparent, according to their accounts, in the way they explained and managed confidentiality with children. Most approached it under the rubric of legal privilege. Some applied a very strict interpretation of confidentiality or made an exception only in circumstances where they perceived a risk to children's safety, and then preferably with the child's knowledge and assent.

I explain the issue of privilege and that anything that happens during our conferences—it's a privileged conference and if the client does not wish for me to reveal anything about his or her wishes to the judge even, I will not reveal it. It's part of my role as his or her representative and otherwise anything that we discuss during the conference is confidential. (Male child representative)

　　I explain my role and the confidential nature of my role and I will only disclose what they want disclosed to who they want it disclosed to. And if they don't want anything disclosed, it won't be disclosed. (Female child representative)

For others there were particular limitations with children to the formal client-solicitor relationship. In the same way that some child representatives said they presented views contrary to the child's wishes to the court, some also indicated that they may decide to tell others, including their parents, what children have said after explaining to children that this is what they intend to do.

> I would tell the kids if they are capable of understanding that whatever they tell me I won't tell anyone else until, unless I tell them I am going to. So I might get them in a second time and say, 'Look I think we should do this, and it means I have to tell Mum and Dad what you told me. That is what I am going to do'. (Male child representative)

One lawyer explained that children were accustomed to adults not necessarily listening to children.

> I explain that they can talk to me, and if they tell me not to say anything to anybody else, then I have to decide whether I think that's a good idea for them and that there are some things that I can't *not* tell anybody else and most kids are happy with that. This sounds terrible, but they are used to people not necessarily listening to what they want anyway. (Male child representative)

Others were respectful of the children's confidence and indicated that they check with children what they want them to say, and seek their agreement about the way to do that.

> I tell them that it is confidential. I say that I will be speaking to their Mum and their Dad or your Mum's and Dad's solicitors and I'm going to try and settle it. 'Can I tell them this; do you want them to know this?' You go through it with them and you find out what they don't want Mum and Dad to know. (Male child representative)
>
> I will say I won't tell your parents that you told me this, it will just be something between the two of us. If it is a wish that is really quite important to come out, I might talk to them about how else they can do, and I might say I could suggest this to them and make it clear it wasn't something you said. (Female child representative)

6.2.5 Advising the child

In addition to representing children's wishes to the court and making submissions about their best interests, child representatives may also play a role in advising children about the options, the likely outcome, and in explaining the orders to them. Indeed some indicated that some judges insist that they have an interview with the child and explain the orders to them.

While some lawyers talked about negotiating with older children about how to present their views to the court, it is clear that some also provide explicit advice to children, particularly when children are resisting contact with a parent.

> You know I think the common one is that the kids are saying I don't want to go and see dad because I would rather play soccer on Saturday and so on. You also have an obligation to say maybe you should try and see your dad. It is a bit of a difficult role to play. (Male child representative)

Others indicated that they explained the need for the children to obey the orders, even if it was not what they wanted to do. One lawyer referred to the risk that the child's mother would go to jail if the orders were not obeyed.

> I explain to them that their parents have to obey orders, and I have to obey orders, and so do they. (Female child representative)
> Yes, I think you have to explain that to them, otherwise Mum goes to jail. (Male child representative)

Several child representatives admitted that in their submissions, and in their advice to children who did not want contact, they may have got it wrong. In one case, a lawyer said she had advocated that a child, aged 8, should have supervised contact with her father against the child's wishes. She thought the child 'deserved the opportunity to meet him since she hadn't seen him for a very long time'. She believed there was no physical risk, and weighed what she judged to be the 'slight psychological risk' against the comment in the expert report about the 'greater psychological risk to her of being denied the relationship with her father'. Six months later, when the matter came back to court after the child 'found it very traumatic', the lawyer changed her view.

6.3 Counsellors, Lawyers and the Interpretation of Children's Voices

Professionals often have different approaches and styles, but these differences between lawyers were much more than matters of personal style and preference. As indicated in the last chapter, many lawyers expressed concerns about involving children in family law disputes because of the dangers of parental pressure, coaching and manipulation and the difficulties for the child of being caught up in loyalty conflicts or being given too much responsibility. The interviewing style of the lawyer acting as child representative may well make a difference in this respect. The lawyers who asked children directly what they wanted as the outcome of the parenting dispute were more likely to be placing children in the middle of the dispute than those who engaged in a more contextual assessment of children's worlds. They were also most vulnerable to prepared speeches:

> Very often kids will tell you, especially older kids. They are versed in why they are there. They've been told [Simon] is your lawyer—you tell him this is what you want and so they will tell you.[12] (Male child representative)

This may not matter where there has been a more expert assessment of children's views through a family report and children have had a chance to say what is important to them. However, such reports tend to be prepared late on in the

---

[12] The name of the lawyer has been changed to preserve anonymity.

litigation process, and many child representatives will appear at interim hearings or will help negotiate settlements to that dispute without the benefit of a family report. A number of child representatives spoke of how they did try to assess the basis for the child's expressed views rather than taking them necessarily at face value:

For myself, I find being able to observe the children's demeanour, how they say it, the emotion when they talk about things, being able to observe all of those things, I think is important. Although I am no expert, I have to form views. (Male child representative)

  I explore with children the difference between their wishes and Mummy's wishes or Daddy's wishes. So the advantage is if you get the sense that these children are speaking on their own autonomy. (Female child representative)

Nonetheless, they recognized the difficulty of so doing without the relevant training.

I'm not a child psychologist so the disadvantages are that sometimes I hear a child's wishes but I don't have the kind of level of understanding of what is going on. Then I might place too much weight on the wishes. (Female child representative)

  I suppose the disadvantages are that when they come in, they might have been coached by the time they get to my office. I'm not seeing dynamics in terms of their interactions with their family members so therefore perhaps what they are telling me is something that they've been asked to tell me or they've been influenced to tell me. So that's a disadvantage then because I'm going to court and saying 'Well the child said X...' (Male child representative)

Some lawyers reported that they communicate with the report writer in preparing a case, especially where the report was at odds with their own assessment of the matter. Some counsellors too reported that they typically worked closely with the child representative in a collaborative way but others reported a much greater amount of distance and differentiation with much less cooperation between them. An experienced child representative pointed to the tension between working in partnership and maintaining some distance and independence.

If you're a child rep, you'd really want to talk it through and find out the base of any difference, you want the court to have the best evidence it can. To that extent, it's still a partnership thing, because, you know, we're meant to be independent, we could form a different view for any reason, and we might want to cross-examine that counsellor, so we have to... while we want to co-operate, you still have to be a little bit at arm's length. (Female child representative)

Lawyers reported, however, that on most occasions their submissions would be in accordance with the thrust of the family report. Where they took a contrary line, it would frequently be because of new information that had come to light in the preparation for, or in the course of, the trial. A number of lawyers cited cases in which further evidence had revealed drug and alcohol issues, mental illness or the violence of a parent or a parent's new partner that had not been known to the report writer. When these issues were raised with a report writer during cross-examination, their standing in the eyes of the lawyers was influenced by their capacity and willingness to revise their opinion in the light of new information.

And the really, really good experts, whether they're mediators, counsellors or private experts, the really good ones will take on more information and say, 'Well, yeah, I can also look at this now I know this'. They won't be at all defensive. They're the best ones. The ones that form a view and then feel that their ego's involved and won't shift a bar, well... (Female child representative)

6.4 Parents' Views

In just over three-quarters of the contested cases (78%), there was at least one family report, or an expert report[13] by an independent psychiatrist, prepared during the course of the proceedings, as outlined in Chapters 3 and 5. Less than a third of contested cases (29%), however, involved the appointment of an independent children's lawyer, and this was generally where there had been allegations of abuse or violence or long-standing conflict and continuing disputes about contact or residence.[14] The parents in these contested cases were asked for their views about these processes—the family report process, the role of the independent children's lawyer, and the extent to which they believed the involvement of these professionals was useful in presenting relevant evidence to the court and in allowing their children's views to be heard. Their views were based on their involvement in the assessment process and their reading of the family report, the feedback they received from their children, and from their evaluation of the influence that the report and the child's independent lawyer had in the court proceedings and the resolution of the dispute.

6.4.1 What did parents think of the family report process?

Parents were fairly evenly divided in terms of their reaction to the family report process, with just over half being happy with the report and its recommendations, and the outcome of the matter. In most cases, the outcome was consistent

---

[13] In about one in five contested cases, there was more than one family report and in several cases three or four reports, including expert reports.

[14] English, Canadian and US studies have reported similar criteria and 'selection processes' for children's involvement with court professionals for specialist reports and legal representation (Felner, R D, L Terre, A Goldfarb, S S Farber, J Primavera, T A Bishop and M S Aber, 'Party Status of Children during Marital Dissolution: Child Preference and Legal Representation in Custody Decisions' (1985) 14 *Journal of Clinical Child Psychology* 42–48; Crosby-Currie, n 6 above; Joyal and Queniart, n 6 above; May, V and C Smart, 'Silence in Court?: Hearing Children in Residence and Contact Disputes' (2004) 16 *Child and Family Law Quarterly* 305–316).

with the report writer's recommendation.[15] In three cases, however, the judge's decision did not follow the report's recommendation, either at the initial hearing or on a subsequent hearing or appeal.[16]

Not surprisingly, the parents who were unhappy with the report and the associated processes disagreed with the report's recommendations which were generally unfavourable to their case.[17] It was mostly these parents who were critical of the process, including, in five cases, the failure of the report writer to listen to the children's views.[18] Two mothers were particularly upset that the strongly expressed wishes of their 10- and 12-year-old daughters not to have contact or overnight contact with their father were over-ridden in both the report's recommendation and the judicial decision. In one case, the father had a history of violence and instability, and in the other, the child had had little or no contact for years. In a further case, in which an 11-year-old girl was objecting to overnight contact with her father, the mother felt that she had let her daughter down by not standing up to the bargaining process at court between the two sets of barristers.

In the end, after 18 months of court, we were shoved together—and all the argey-bargey that went on with, with a lawyer, his barrister trying to derail me with what evidence he could bring in or not, but where was the child in any of this? The child's wishes weren't even looked at. And then the barristers draw up these orders at the very last minute, shove

[15] Six parents were unhappy with the conservative status quo nature of the report and the decision in maintaining the residence and contact arrangements, when they were seeking shared care or reduced contact. Several fathers saw this as biased against them, failing to take account of the circumstances surrounding the dispute.

What did she say in the report about Sam's wishes?
She didn't mention that but she did mention that it was obvious that Sam considered his mother the primary care giver, which was of course quite true because from the time he could remember his mother was there. The fact that he was taken from me was totally irrelevant. Of course, he's going to look at it as though she is the primary giver of the care because that's the way it was.

[16] In one relocation matter, an appeal judge overturned the earlier judgment refusing the mother permission to move from one state to another, although two family reports, an updated report and an expert report recommended against the move because of the importance of the father's relationship with the child who was then nearly 4 years old. While the father was happy with the reports, he was clearly shocked and upset about the final decision to allow the child to move.

[17] There was little difference between resident and non-resident parents or between mothers and fathers. Six cases involved applications for the resident parent to relocate with the children, with the parent respondents' reaction to the report being in line with the success or otherwise of their application or opposition to it.

[18] Another seven parents involved in cases in which there had been no family report said that they thought there should have been a report to assess and report on the children's views as well as, in some cases, the influence that the other parent had brought to bear on what the children were saying. In two cases, the children involved were interviewed and voiced the same view as their parents about being excluded from the process. For example, one mother said:

I think she should have had some involvement there because nobody really cared about what Jade wanted. She didn't speak to anybody, she wasn't involved whatsoever! Other than what she was saying to me, but for all they know, I could have been lying. No, she had no contact with any of the counsellors, nothing. I don't think she took Jade into consideration at all apart from saying she sounds like a well-adjusted child, why would you want to change it?

these [under your nose] 'here, you happy for me to show them to them?' And you're like, 'Hang on, give them back, let me read them properly'. Because it was the first time I've ever been in court and—well, been in a hearing. Um, so the family report, I think, probably played a very small role in what actually came out with all the pressure we were put under to agree at any cost. The judge said to us he wanted to have this case wrapped up before lunch. So we had to make a decision, and we hadn't seen those orders before, and in the end we had to agree on it. We were trying to do the right thing by Sarah, what her wishes were, but in the end, you know, I don't think the family report was even...came into it. Because the judge didn't make a decision, and the two barristers—certainly his barrister didn't care less what Sarah's wishes were. He was trying to get what his client wanted. And his client has no capacity to take on board what Sarah wants, because he thinks it's all brainwashed what she wants anyway. To a large extent Sarah's wishes were ignored by the court process. Even though it was set up to try and incorporate her wishes, because of the way it unfolded in the end...

She was devastated to think we had betrayed her, basically. Because she didn't get what she wanted. Which was not to stay down there overnight. And that's why I think she's keen to participate [in this study], because she thinks she can tell someone.

Only two parents spoke openly about being upset by what was revealed about their children's views. One, a non-resident father directly confronted his daughter, wrongly believing the child's views to have been incorrectly reported. Another, a non-resident mother of two children under 10, decided 'to let the children go', hoping they would come back to her later, after hearing from the family report that the children wanted to live with their father. Several other parents were positively surprised and even concerned about how upset and hurt they expected their former partner would have been about the report.

Apart from the parents' unhappiness with the report's recommendations, the main criticisms concerned the time-poor superficiality of the process and the failure of report writers to 'see through' the lies or the misleading picture the other parent presented. The most common complaint was that the report was incomplete and did not reflect all the issues and concerns they had about the other parent and the proposed arrangements. One resident mother of a 10 year old involved in a complex and difficult dispute, for example, was distressed about the mistakes she said that the expert report writer had made in the report, failing to ask her former partner about his violence and criminal involvement, and his denial of paternity. She was upset too that the report writer inferred that the child was simply echoing her mother's concerns.

He can be very charming and very nice when he wants to be but it's all a big act. He's very much a conman, I believe, and um, he was, she was taken in by him, you know, definitely. She didn't get out of him, she didn't address anything about the suicide attempt, his criminal history, his saying that Tamzin wasn't his daughter, she didn't ask him about that and why did he say those things, and he lied about several things. When we finally got the family report back, I brought all these issues up, you know, with Dr X, like why were these things not addressed and there's many discrepancies here, you know, things that you documented incorrectly. This is actually what the facts are, not what you had.

And I said that I felt that Tamzin wasn't heard at all, and you know, she said that she felt that Tamzin was probably kind of 'toeing the line of the mother'.

Like a number of other parents, she believed the report writer did not have the time to make an accurate assessment, and had misjudged her daughter. The report writer had described her as 'shy and reserved' whereas according to her mother, she had been 'a bit intimidated by Dr X, knowing that this lady had to do with the law'. Her mother commented that Tamzin was, 'as you would expect, a bit unsure about what it was all about', and needed time to get to know 'this stranger' before she was willing to talk to her more freely.

Similarly, another mother of a 10 year old said that it was difficult for children to be heard through the report writing process:

I think what little chance she has had, which was talking with that counsellor, I think that was biased, and I don't think that's enough of an opportunity or a guide for the judge to make a decision on that one little talk and that one little vision he had of her. It's not enough for him to judge.

Ten parents also indicated their concern about the capacity of the report writer to assess the influence the other parent had on the children and to detect outright manipulation and bribery. But several parents were complimentary about the report writer's alertness to the pressure children were under, and one father who had initiated court action because he had not been able to see his children for some time said:

Anyway it came out in court under cross-examination that Leanne had said to Sally and her grandfather and her grandmother 'You go in there and we want you to say this, this and this, and we'll take you to America again, back to Disneyland'. And we had RW [the report writer] under cross-examination and she admitted she believed that both the children had been 'nobbled', but because Matt was at such a young age, he didn't understand what he was supposed to do and didn't want to.

Other parents, and especially those who were happy with the content of the report, were also positive, despite feeling that the observation process was artificial and the court context not optimal for children, and difficult for parents. As one mother said:

The only thing I thought which might have been a bit of an act, as far as the adults went, was the role play. I've been around children for a long time and I know that in that one room, in that one instant, it might be very different to how it might appear at home. It would have been difficult for James [former partner] to interact with his children when he hadn't done that much before. So I thought in a way it was a bit artificial. But I think from reading the family report too, it's amazing what they pick up on. I think they can pick up what's put on and what's not.

One father who was quite happy with the report's recommendation nevertheless believed that it was important for the assessment to be repeated after the child had spent a week living with each parent.

I think if you have to do it at all, the child should go down there with her mother without the other parent there, and then come down with the father at a separate time, especially after the child has spent a week with each parent.

In another case where there were allegations of abuse against the father, he was determined to have a family report done against legal advice:

Because they said 'If it goes against you, that is really going to count against you' and I said 'Well, I've got really nothing to hide', so … but that's the way lawyers think. I think because it's an unknown 'don't get a family report' and I said 'Well I'm getting it done, and these accusations are just vile and done totally maliciously and I want the truth out'.

He was impressed with the comprehensiveness and content of the report, including the calls and visit to his son's school, and believes that the report was the primary factor that 'forced' his former wife's lawyers to negotiate over the arrangements. The child's reported view was that he 'wanted to live equally with each of us': with his father when he was not away for work, and with his mother when his father was away. The father said 'that would have worked quite well if we'd lived nearby each other but that wasn't to be'.

6.4.2 What did parents think of the children's lawyers?

Independent lawyers were appointed for the children in less than a third of the contested cases, those that involved allegations of abuse and violence or were long-standing and particularly contentious. Several parents explained that there was no lawyer for the child in their case because the children were too young (all under 6), and several others said they could not afford it. Two other parents had supported the idea of their children having 'their own lawyer' but none was appointed. According to one mother, her lawyer had advised against it on the grounds that it was an unnecessary and unpredictable complication.

He didn't want a children's representative—he said from his perspective, a Children's Rep, was not advantageous, to help us get what we want. Because it just throws a third person into the realm who may or may not agree with what we were doing. And if we were truly representative of Sally's wishes, then having a third person who's separated from us, that may not help our case.

Most of the 17 parents in cases in which an independent children's lawyer was appointed were negative about their performance. They were generally supportive of their role, expecting them to represent their children and present their views to the court. But in their view, the lawyers' performance did not meet their expectations of a direct instructions representative. A non-resident father who was fighting allegations of abuse explained what he expected of the lawyer:

I thought the job of a child rep would have been to, to represent Polly and to find out her wishes and to, to see both parents and tell them exactly what Polly would like to happen. And um, for the sake of the child, to do what, what she wishes.

Similarly a resident mother of children aged between 10 and 13 years said:

To fulfil what the kids think, what they feel, you know; um, they're there for the kids, they're not there for him and they're not there for me, yeah. Wholly and solely for the kids.

For most, however, their expectations were clearly not met or they were unaware of what the children's lawyer did. The most common comment was that they 'did not do anything', and in several cases they said they did not even speak to the children although various guidelines for children's lawyers make it clear that they should do so.[19]

I don't think she did anything for Tamzin really, apart from being there on the day. She didn't ask her how she felt, she told her what the process would be, but she didn't really ask her how she felt, or what she wanted. (Resident mother)

A father who fought for residence over several years had experience of several children's lawyers, one of whom had been helpful when he was self-represented. Later, however, this father was critical of the lawyer in the subsequent proceedings for not even talking to his son, then aged 10.

Do you think it is appropriate for lawyer to ask the child what they want to happen?
Yes, I think so.

Do you think the lawyer should say what the child wants to happen or what he thinks is best for the child?
I think that they should at least talk to the kids and find out what the kids think and then, even if they do the same thing and watch what happens, what the mum's sides doing and the dad's side, and then go with what they think from there. To me, they should be representing the child and at least putting the child's point across, you know.

Several parents distrusted the lawyer's allegiance, suggesting that they were 'on the side' of the other party.

He didn't really say or do anything. I don't know how he could represent the children. He basically sat with the mother. He seemed to be some kind of ally for the mother. He didn't speak to me. I think he would have been better off being the mother's solicitor, or the mother's solicitor being with the kids. He should have been looking after the children's best interests. (Non-resident father)

---

[19] Similar concerns about the legal representation of children in family law matters, including criticisms of not speaking to the children they were representing, were reported in 1997 in a comprehensive review of children's involvement in legal processes by the Australian Law Reform Commission and the Human Rights and Equal Opportunity Commission (Australian Law Reform Commission and the Human Rights and Equal Opportunity Commission, *Seen and Heard: Priority for Children in the Legal Process* (ALRC Report 84) (1997) ch 13, pp 272–278. Available at: http://www.austlii.edu.au/au/other/alrc/publications/reports/84/13.html (accessed 10 June 2008)). A former Family Court judge referred to these statements as 'startling' (Chisholm, R, 'Children's Participation in Family Court Litigation' (1999) 13 *Australian Journal of Family Law* 197–218). See also the guidelines and critique of legal representation for children outlined by the Law Society of New South Wales, see n 7 above, and Blackman, L, *Representing Children and Young People: A Lawyers' Practice Guide* (Victoria Law Foundation, 2002).

Others were critical of their competence and level of preparation, and their willingness to simply accept the recommendation of the family report and not seek further evidence. In some cases, their view appears to have been based on what the children had said about the lawyers being 'interfering' and 'not helping at all',[20] and in others it was based on the parents' observations. In one case, a resident mother of 6-year-old Michael recounted her experience of a poorly prepared lawyer and the child's anger about being misinterpreted.

So you don't think she did her job properly?
She was not impartial. She told me that she was not prepared and she knew nothing about the case. She started by talking with me and said that she came before to look through the files but said 'I haven't really read anything, so can you tell me what this is about?' And so I tell her. Then she interviewed his father. Then she comes back to me and says, 'Look the man's turned over a new leaf, what's your problem?' Then her interview with Michael—she then stood up and said that she recommends Tuesday nights and the weekend!

What do you think her job was?
Well, it was never explained to me but I thought she would have read through all of the documents, interviewed both the parents and the child, and basically found out what was in the best interests of Michael.

Did she ask Michael what he wanted?
I asked Michael that. She said, from what Michael said, she asked him about staying overnight and he said, 'I'm not sure'. And Michael said to me, she asked me 'did I want to sleep at Daddy's?' and I said, 'I'm not sure'. And when I came home and said, they've decided you have to stay at dad's overnight, he was really angry with me. He said, 'I told her I didn't want to'. I said, 'No, you told her you weren't sure'. So he was very angry about that. I got in trouble—I copped it.

Another parent, a non-resident father in a complex relocation matter, also commented on what he expected of a children's lawyer in being able to communicate with the children they represent. He was suspicious of lawyers and damning in his report of the lawyer's communication with him.

Well, I think they should get to know the child a lot better and not just be a lawyer and go in there and ask them all these stupid questions because they can word it that way and trick the child. You know, legal jargon and that. And the child wouldn't understand it and I think basically they're like most lawyers—they're only there for the monetary gain, like they get $1500 a child. Well, I watched this bloke on the day and he did six cases. I think there was probably one or two children from every case. That's $1500—he got three grand from me for two children.

[20] Comments about legal and counselling professionals being interfering and unhelpful were also made by children in several studies in England and Wales and Canada (Neale, B, 'Dialogues with Children: Children, Divorce and Citizenship' (2002) 9 *Childhood* 455–475; Williams, S, *Through the Eyes of Young People: Meaningful Child Participation in Family Court Processes* (International Institute for Child Rights and Development, 2008).

So what did he actually do in court then?
He walked in and spoke for the rights of the children and what he thought was the best option.

What was that?
That I have no contact with Simone. He even told me before we went into court—he says 'I'll tell you now—you can forget about having any contact with Simone. She hates your guts.' His exact words were 'She hates your guts and you won't ever see her again'. And I said 'What?' And he said 'Here's a copy of what I'm presenting to the court'.

On the other hand, three parents were quite positive about the children's lawyers involved in their case because they said what their children wanted. In one case, this meant a change of residence to the father. In another case, the mother of several older children who did not want contact with their violent father explained that she was pleased the lawyer was able to present their views to the court.

Yeah, I did think it was a good thing for them, it saved them the um, agony of going into court themselves and facing their father.
So what do you think the job of a children's lawyer is?
Um...from my experience, she listened to the boys, what they wanted. Like, she asked them—I don't ask them the sort of questions she did—where they would like to live? Who they would like to live with? Why don't you stay with the other parent? And from that she deduced, and presented it to the judge.
And you heard that? You were in court when she presented that?
Yes, yes. And she just said in court what the boys had told her, which was that they wanted to live here with me, and they didn't want anything to do with their dad.
Did you ever speak to the children about what they spoke to the lawyer about?
Um, they usually tell me themselves, I usually don't ask them very much.

The orders in this case reflected the children's views, allowing them to get in touch with their father again later when they were ready to do so.[21]

  Overall the parents were quite negative about the way the children's lawyers represented their children's views and interests. There is little research on parents' perspectives of their children's lawyers but clearly the lawyer's performance and interaction with their children did not meet the expectations of the parents in this study, as far as they were able to judge that from the reports of the children and their observations of what they did in court.

6.5 Children's Views

Just over half the children (25/47, 53%) had experienced contested proceedings, and in all except one of these matters, a family report or an expert report was prepared at some stage in the process. About half of these matters also involved the

[21] The children in this case expressed similar views to their mother.

appointment of an independent legal representative for the children. These were the most contentious or long-standing of the disputed matters. Like the children in English and New Zealand studies, however, children did not necessarily remember or had limited understanding about who the professionals were and exactly what their role was.[22] Those who did had mixed views about the helpfulness of their involvement.

6.5.1 What did children think of the family report process?

The children who remembered and understood why they spoke with a 'counsellor' or another person in relation to the preparation of a family or expert report were fairly evenly divided about their experience. Like the parents, most of those who were positive had outcomes that were more in line with what they wanted. But the outcome was not the deciding factor for those who were unhappy with the process. For these children, the main issues were their discomfort with the process and their unwillingness to say what they thought, their feeling that their views had not been understood or taken seriously, and distress about the consequences of the lack of confidentiality of what they said. A number of children said they did not know who would be told what they said and were concerned that their parents might find out. Four children were upset that they had. One girl suffered the consequences of this and was upset, saying that she had not been told about the lack of confidentiality.

If they are going to put it in a family report, they should at least tell you, so you know not to say 'I hate my dad' because then he's going to see it and get mad at you.
Is that what you said?
Yes. And then he got mad at me and I got no dessert and he yelled at me and we had to have a family discussion, and then I argued that it wasn't a family because Margaret [father's new partner] wasn't part of the family. And then I got into even more trouble for saying that because I made Margaret cry.

Another girl expressed her anger about the effect on her relationship with her father in these terms:

'cause the stupid lady wrote a family report and sent it to them and both my parents and now Dad uses the things I said against me all the time.

Her mother also referred to the repercussions[23] and her daughter's distressed state after the father questioned her about what she said to the report writer and why she had done so. This turned into a 'screaming match' with her father and his partner.

---

[22] Taylor, N J, M M Gollop and A B Smith, 'Children and Young People's Perspectives on their Legal Representation' in A B Smith, N J Taylor and M Gollop (eds), *Children's Voices: Research, Policy and Practice* (Pearson Education, 2000) pp 110–133; Neale, n 20 above.

[23] See also Neale for her description of the repercussions for 'Caroline' who was involved in a long-running dispute between her parents (Neale, n 20 above, pp 465–466).

Four children who were aware of how what they said was reported were unhappy about this, with the older children saying they had been misinterpreted[24] and the younger children saying that they had not been listened to.

A 6-year-old who had seen the report writer several times said, for example:

I just don't like her any more 'cos she never listened to us. I didn't know what to say because she wasn't ever listening and no one else ever listened.
Do you think Jessica[25] [report writer] told the court what was best for you?
She told the court what was best for us but she was always saying the wonky kids were lying.

A 14-year-old said:

She took some of my quotes out of context. She asked me. This is how the question went—'If it was ordered by a judge that you had to have overnight contact, would it make it easier that your friends were there—like if you invited your friends for a sleepover?' And I said 'Oh, if a judge ordered that, then yeah, maybe having my friends there would make it easier'. In the family report, she wrote that I wouldn't be completely averse to the idea if I had my friends with me, which really... She's sort of missed the essence of what I said, the rest of what I said before.

She went on to comment on the restrictive and patronizing nature of the questioning:

I found it very patronizing and the questions weren't very appropriate. There wasn't really any time for me to just talk. It always had to be a response to a question that she was asking, and so a lot of things just didn't get touched upon because I was restricted by the questions she asked.

The other children who were happy with the process were less vocal in their comments. They indicated they had been comfortable talking with the report writer and understood that this was an opportunity to say what life had been like for them and to say what they wanted. Several children involved in contested residence disputes who had been abused, like 11-year-old Michael and 9-year-old Bianca, were keen to do so.

Do you know why he was talking to you?
Because my mum kept hitting me and I told my dad and he took it to court.

[24] It was not only children who were unhappy about being misinterpreted. Several parents made similar comments. A resident mother said:

He made me out to be an idiot—a mother who didn't care about her child. And things I said to him, he totally misunderstood what I meant or purposely twisted it, so that it was the opposite of what I meant.

A non-resident father complained about the family court counsellor getting it wrong:

I said to the counsellor, 'I didn't want to get into a custody battle'. What she wrote in her report was I didn't want custody and therefore I didn't get custody. And I kept on objecting but I had no come back because 'she's a counsellor and she tells the truth. I mean, they're the most honest people in the world, Family Court counsellors'.

[25] As for the children, all names have been changed to preserve confidentiality.

Do you remember whether he said what his job was?
It was sort of a counsellor but he also said . . . he was sort of like you a bit. So his job was to talk to you? Yes, and he asked me questions like with a piece of paper like you do.
Did you want to talk to the counsellor?
Yes.
Why was that?
So he could listen to me and what I was going on and stuff. I had someone to talk to. The only other person I talked to was my dad, and Gran.

Similarly, Bianca said:

Why do you think you spoke to the counsellor?
Because . . . so they could tell the judge, what I thought.
What do you the think the counsellor's job was?
To help children that needed help . . . To help and tell the court what they want.
Did you want to talk to the counsellor?
Yes.
What did the counsellor say?
Tell me the truth, and everything will be okay. Yep.
What did you say?
Okay, I'll tell you the truth but only if my dad can be in the room.
What did the counsellor talk to you about?
What happened at my mum's. And where I wanted to live.
You want to tell me a little bit about what happened at your mum's, or not?
Yes. At my Mum's, Tom [mother's partner] punished me and Mum didn't do anything about it. He was an alcoholic—when he got drunk, he lost control. That's it.
So would he hit you?
No, he'd smack me.
Okay.
And call me bad names.
So did you tell her what you wanted?
Yep. I want to live with my dad.
Did you think your parents would be told what you said?
I didn't know.
Were you worried about that?
No.
Did you think the counsellor understood what you wanted?
Yes.
Do you think your views were taking seriously?
Yes, she did, because she went back to court and said that.

These children met the criteria that May and Smart concluded were as central to children's involvement from their analysis of a large random sample of 430 case files from three courts in England and Wales.[26] Children over seven, involved in matters in which there was a high level of conflict, were much more likely to

---

[26] See May and Smart, n 14 above.

have been consulted than other children, and their views were more influential where there was 'a degree of congruence between the child's wishes and the court welfare officer's assessment'.

6.5.2 What did children think of their legal representative?

Only 13 children in nine families had independent children's lawyers.[27] There were allegations of abuse or violence in most of these cases, and five fathers were contesting residence on these grounds. The children's expectations were that the lawyer should say what they wanted[28] and perhaps offer some advice but generally they were unsure what the lawyer had said or done in court. Rani, 14, said of one of the lawyers she dealt with:

And do you think she listened to you about what you said, and what you wanted to happen?
I think so. She did make pretty copious notes of what I was saying. So I'm not sure what she would have done in court...because I didn't meet her for that long, and...I've only met her once. But I did feel like at least she was taking in a bit of what I was saying and at least she had heard my voice and my opinion.

She was much less impressed with the next lawyer:

I felt like that if this person is going to represent me in court and he'd spent the last half hour just telling me I was wrong, then I wouldn't really stand a good chance and that's very frustrating because...children...they depend solely on those representatives and the little paragraph on the family report. And I felt I could have done a better job at the witness box myself being examined and cross-examined. Yeah, I think that's probably the main reason that it upset me so much; because it was very frustrating to have the person that's supposed to be representing you, argue with you...and I was so sure that's what he was going to put to the court as 'this is what I recommend'.

Judging by the outcome for their case, several other children thought the lawyer probably did not say what they wanted and one child was under the impression that the lawyer had wanted to 'put his Dad in gaol'.

---

[27] The numbers of children in studies of children's views on their legal representation in family law matters have generally been small, largely because of the small percentage of children in family law disputes who have a legal representative, but also because of parents' understandable protectiveness of children in these circumstances. For example, Taylor et al in one of the most comprehensive studies in this area, obtained the views of 20 children who had some ongoing consultation with their lawyers (Taylor et al, n 22 above). In Neale's study, only about 20% of the 117 children involved 'had had direct experience of legal, mediation or therapeutic services' and in most cases they had only vague recollections of the process (see Neale, n 20 above, at 464). In Butler et al's study, only five of the 104 children had directly been the subject of legal proceedings, and children and parents agreed that there had been little discussion between them about the legal formalities (Butler, I, L Scanlan, M Robinson, G Douglas and M Murch, *Divorcing Children: Children's Experience of their Parents' Divorce* (Jessica Kingsley, 2003)).

[28] Similarly, children in care and protection matters have also voiced the same expectations (Cashmore, J and K Bussey, 'Perceptions of Children and Lawyers in Care and Protection Proceedings' (1994) 8 *International Journal of Law and the Family* 319–336).

Communication was an issue for another child who did not think the lawyer really felt comfortable talking with children.

Did you feel OK talking to him/her?
It was pretty silly really. Because he took a long time to answer, I mean, like talk. And he kept going 'Um, er, er...' like he didn't know what to say... and he only asked about one question.
Do you think he felt comfortable talking with kids?
No, not really.

Like the children in a New Zealand study,[29] about half the children were quite positive about the lawyer, saying that he or she had listened to them and taken them seriously. In the five cases in which fathers were contesting residence citing abuse or violence, all the children except two young children were comfortable talking with the lawyer and were not worried that what they said would be presented to the court. Indeed that is what they hoped would happen. Nine-year-old Harriet, for example, commented on her interactions with her lawyer:

What did the lawyer talk to you about?
Who I wanted to go with.
How did you feel about him asking you: did you feel free to say anything?
Yes, it was good because then the court would know what I wanted.

In another family, in which the children were resisting contact with their father because they were scared of him following his violence against their mother, one of the older children said:

She did everything that we asked her to, so it was good, everything went our way, the way that we wanted it to.

Another child indicated that he was happy with the way the lawyer had handled a similar dispute about contact:

What do you think the job of the children's lawyer was?
To see, to like defend us and then if we want to change the orders we could and it was her job to change it for us.
And what did you tell her?
We told her that we didn't want to see him anymore, and then she said how about I put the order where if you feel like seeing him again, you can see him instead of changing it and talk to him and stuff, but only if you make the arrangement—your dad doesn't.
And that was what you wanted then? You were happy with that?
Yeah, it was good.

In summary, children's views about the professionals they dealt with in the court process were somewhat mixed, and more so than those of the parents who were generally more negative about the child representative and influenced by the

---

[29] Taylor et al, n 22 above.

outcome of the matter. While the small numbers involved mean that it is necessary to be cautious about any definitive conclusions, it appears that children's negative views were based more on the quality of their interactions than on the outcomes, though of course the outcome also had an effect. Children's comments tended to focus on the extent to which they felt they had been listened to and accurately represented, as far as they were able to judge that, and also on the extent to which their trust in the invitation to participate had been borne out. Breaches of confidentiality, as they understood it, and being misinterpreted were clearly very upsetting and were seen as a betrayal of their trust by some children. On the other hand, children appreciated being listened to and having their views taken seriously.

These children's views are very similar to those of children reported in studies from England and Wales,[30] New Zealand[31] and Canada.[32] Speaking in an Australian voice, they are critical—and complimentary also—about the way they believed they were treated by court professionals. The Australian children, like the New Zealand children cited by Taylor and colleagues,[33] were not as strongly critical as the English children cited by Neale. In Neale's terms, professionals were described as 'bossy, inflexible, unfair, dismissive, intrusive, intimidating, interrogatory, critical, patronizing, judgemental, condescending, coercive, deceitful, secretive and untrustworthy'.[34] In essence, what children wanted was to be treated with respect, and to have their views taken seriously, not ignored, misinterpreted or filtered through others.

6.6 Filtering, Confidentiality and Feedback Mechanisms

For children and parents, contact with the professionals at court is a last resort measure in attempts to resolve the dispute, and they are likely to face these contacts with considerable stress. These are not optimum conditions for a high level of performance or for taking in important but confusing information. For children

---

[30] O'Quigley, A, *Listening to Children's Views: The Findings and Recommendations of Recent Research* (Joseph Rowntree Foundation, 2000); Buchanan, A, J Hunt, H Bretherton and V Bream, *Families in Conflict: The Perspectives of Children and Parents on the Family Court Welfare Service* (The Policy Press, 2001); Neale, B and C Smart, *Good to Talk: Conversations with Children after Divorce* (Report for the Nuffield Foundation, 2001); Bretherton, H, ' "Because it's me the Decisions are About"—Children's Experiences of Private Law Proceedings' [2002] 32 *Family Law* 450–457; Butler et al, n 27 above.
[31] Taylor, N, 'What Do We Know about Involving Children and Young People in Family Law Decision Making? A Research Update' (2006) 20 *Australian Journal of Family Law* 154–178; Taylor et al, n 22 above.
[32] Williams, n 20 above.
[33] Taylor, n 31 above, at 170–171.
[34] See Neale, n 20 above, at 467. See also Neale, B and C Smart, 'Agents or Dependants? Struggling to Listen to Children in Family Law and Family Research' (Working Paper 3, Centre for Research on Family, Kinship and Childhood, University of Leeds, 1998).

in particular, talking with people outside their family about such matters is often difficult, and research indicates that they are often not well informed about the purpose and what is likely to come out of such interactions. The way children—and parents—are treated by the professionals involved is therefore critical to their perceptions of the process. Engaging with professionals who are 'friendly, trusting, and respectful'[35] and who can communicate effectively is therefore very important.

Two aspects of that communication appear to be problematic, both for the professionals and for the children and their parents. These are the interpretation and filtering by professionals of what children say, and the related issue of how they make assessments of what is in the children's best interests and how they manage confidentiality. By definition, what is presented to the court by the professionals is a representation and interpretation of what children have said, and perhaps what they want said, together with a judgment about what the professionals think is in the best interests of the children. These judgments are made on the basis of limited interactions over quite short time periods in relation to the problems and potential 'solutions' as defined by the adults involved. It takes time and some skill to determine how children see them, time that the professionals rarely have. In these circumstances, it is therefore 'all too easy for the child's view to come to the court in contested proceedings "as a narrative that has been edited and shaped by parents, counsellors and legal representatives"'.[36] This concern about filtering and the misinterpretation of children's views has also been expressed by a number of judicial and legal commentators.[37]

The second aspect, confidentiality, was a tricky one for counsellors, perhaps more so than for lawyers who often relied on their general understanding of legal privilege. Although counsellors reported that they explain the limits or lack of confidentiality to children at the beginning of their interaction with them in preparing a family report, it is likely that children may not have heard this or may not fully understand what this means in practice. If pressed to give a view, they may also say more than they intended and then wish to withdraw it. Clearly, children in this study and in others said that they were not aware who might be told what they had said or were worried after talking with the counsellor or lawyer what might be revealed to their parents.[38]

---

[35] See Taylor, n 31 above, at 170; Taylor et al, n 22 above.

[36] See Taylor, n 31 above, at 167, citing Fitzgerald, R, 'How are Children Heard In Family Law Proceedings in Australia?' (2002) 6 *Southern Cross University Law Review* 177–203.

[37] Roche, J, 'Children's Rights: In the Name of the Child' (1995) 17 *Journal of Social Welfare and Family Law* 281–300; L'Heureux-Dubé, C, 'A Response to Remarks by Dr. Judith Wallerstein on the Long-term Impact of Divorce on Children' (1998) 36 *Family and Conciliation Courts Review* 384–391; Hale, B, 'Children's Participation in Family Law Decision-Making: Lessons from Abroad' (2006) 20 *Australian Journal of Family Law* 119–126.

[38] Piper, C, 'The Wishes and Feelings of the Child' in S Sclater and C Piper (eds), *Undercurrents of Divorce* (Ashgate, 1999); Roche, n 37 above; Gollop, M, A B Smith and N J Taylor, 'Children's Involvement in Custody and Access Arrangements after Parental Separation' (2000) 12 *Child and Family Law Quarterly* 383–399; Bretherton, n 30 above.

The difficulty for both lawyers and counsellors is their lack of time to build up a trusting relationship with a child in these circumstances. So it is easy for adults who are comfortable within a legal context to fall back on traditional notions about the capacities of children of various ages to contribute meaningfully to the process. When communication between children and adults fails, adults often attribute this to a lack of competence or maturity on the part of the child rather than their own. Various legal and judicial commentators have been particularly critical of these assumptions in the underlying models of childhood in legal and professional thinking.[39]

One approach to deal with the concerns about misinterpretation and breaches of confidentiality would be to incorporate various feedback mechanisms in the process. At various stages, such feedback mechanisms have the potential to improve the effectiveness of communication between children and professionals and to over-ride some of the assumptions they may make about children.[40] Instead professionals might approach children in a 'position of uncertainty, respecting the complexity and ambiguity of their lives' as Trinder suggested.[41]

For example:[42]

- Not only could report writers be clear with children about the limits of confidentiality, they could also check that children really understand what this means. This should help the preparation and presentation of a family report to be a more transparent process and one that is respectful of children's right to be informed about the way information they provide may be used.
- Report writers should also check with children about what they are willing to have reported about what their views are. Some consideration could be given to children being told what is said about them in a family report, if they wish to know. Whereas parents can challenge the contents and recommendations of a report in court, children rarely see them or know what is in them.[43]

---

[39] See, for example, Fox Harding for an analysis of the value perspectives underlying legal and policy approaches to children (Fox Harding, L, *Perspectives in Child Care Policy* (Longman, 1997; 2nd ed)). See also Piper, n 38 above.

[40] Mantle, G, J Leslie, S Parsons and R Shaffer, 'Establishing Children's Wishes and Feelings for Family Court Reports: The Significance Attached to the Age of the Child' (2006) 13 *Childhood* 499–518.

[41] Trinder, L 'Competing Constructions of Childhood: Children's Rights and Children's Wishes in Divorce' (1997) 19 *Journal of Social Welfare and Family Law* 291–305.

[42] Cashmore, J, 'Children's Participation in Family Law Matters' in C Hallett and A Prout (eds), *Hearing the Voices of Children: Social Policy for a New Century* (Routledge Falmer, 2003) pp 158–176.

[43] See Masson for similar issues in relation to public law matters (Masson, J, 'Participation, Placation and Paternalism: Young People's Experiences of Representation in Child Protection Proceedings in England and Wales' paper at the *International Society of Family Law 10th World Conference* (Brisbane, 9–13 July 2000). Available at: http://www.gu.edu.au/centre/flru/masson.doc (accessed September 2000); Masson, J, 'Paternalism, Participation and Placation: Young People's Experiences of Representation in Child Protection Proceedings in England and Wales' in J Dewar and S Parker (eds), *Family Law: Processes, Practices, Pressures* (Hart Publishing, 2003).

- Similarly, as a number of the child representatives say they do, legal representatives for children should explain to their clients what they will say in court, how they will say it, and ask whether that is what they expect them to say.

- After the hearing, child representatives should explain to the child what they had said and, if that was different from what the child had expected, what their reasons were. There are good reasons why the Court's decision might not be in accord with the child's wishes in some cases,[44] and children should be made aware of this both before and after the determination. It would also be valuable for them to be told why this was the case, in the same way that local authorities are required to do in relation to care plans for children in public law matters in the UK.[45]

- Adult clients generally have avenues of complaint if they are unhappy about the way they are treated. This is more difficult for children but quality assurance processes could provide for some follow-up with children after their matters are finalized, asking them how happy they were with the way their legal representative treated them and took account of their views. Research seems to provide the only avenue for this in most systems. While it can have educational value, this is a limited, indirect and irregular means of providing feedback to those involved.

Finally, of course, it is important for professionals dealing with children, and particularly those in stressful and difficult circumstances,[46] to be skilled in communication (especially with children) and to know something about the way children understand issues such as confidentiality and how they are likely to respond when they are reluctant to divulge personal information.[47] As Taylor stated:

The onus is now on the adult to understand, support, have positive expectations, and, when appropriate, guide and assist the child, whereas in the past it has been the child's cognitive capacity and level of development that has been regarded as determining their competence.[48]

---

[44] See, for example, Jones, E and P Parkinson, 'Child Sexual Abuse, Access and the Wishes of Children' (1995) 9 *International Journal of Law and the Family* 54–85.

[45] Schofield, G, 'Making Sense of the Ascertainable Wishes and Feelings of Insecurely Attached Children (1998) 10 *Child and Family Law Quarterly* 363–375.

[46] For an argument strongly advocating the need for lawyers to improve their internvewing and communication skills with people in stressful circumstances, see Sternlight, J R and J K Robbennolt, 'Good Lawyers Should Be Good Psychologists: Insights for Interviewing and Counseling Clients' (2008) 23 *Ohio State Journal on Dispute Resolution* 437–548.

[47] Michael, the child cited earlier who said 'I'm not sure' when asked by a lawyer whether he wanted to stay overnight with his father provides a classic example of children not committing themselves but being upset when they are misinterpreted and it is assumed they are not objecting.

[48] Taylor, n 31 above, at 161.

7

Judicial Conversations with Children

As noted in Chapter 3, practices vary considerably between jurisdictions on the issue of whether judges should talk with children in the course of determining parenting cases.

While the merits of seeing children in chambers has been the subject of considerable discussion and debate in Australia and elsewhere, little is known about the views of children, their parents, lawyers and counsellors on this issue. A little more is known about the views of judges.[1] If children do not want to see the judge, there seems little point in them doing so and it is very unlikely that judges would insist in most jurisdictions. Parents' views are also important; if they see such interviews as unfair or inappropriate, it may well affect their perceptions of the fairness of the process and the decision. The views of the professionals about the process are also important. In particular, if lawyers are opposed to the process, then they are unlikely to propose this option to the court. If judges are reluctant to talk to children then only a legislative or appellate court instruction to do so is likely to overcome their resistance.[2]

7.1 The Views of the Children

We explored children's views on talking with judges in two ways. First, in our initial discussions with the children, we asked them an open-ended question about

[1] In a survey of 160 judges in Arizona whose responsibilities could include parenting disputes, Atwood found that a quarter of the respondents reported that they never conducted such interviews while 19% did so regularly and more than half did so occasionally (Atwood, B, 'The Child's Voice in Custody Litigation: An Empirical Survey and Suggestions for Reform' (2003) 45 *Arizona Law Review* 629–690, at 636–637). She found that judges in her survey 'profoundly disagree about the utility and advisability of *in camera* interviews with children' (at 637). For other surveys of judges see Murch, M, G Douglas, L Scanlan, A Perry, C Lisles, K Bader and M Borkowski, *Safeguarding Children's Welfare in Uncontentious Divorce: A Study of S41 of the Matrimonial Causes Act* (Lord Chancellor's Department, Research Series 7/99) pp 179–181; Raitt, F, 'Hearing Children in Family Law Proceedings: Can Judges Make a Difference?' (2007) 19 *Child and Family Law Quarterly* 204–224.

[2] Murch et al, in England and Wales, reporting in 1999, found that only six (17%) of the 35 District Court judges interviewed would ever agree to talk with children, and only usually in exceptional circumstances (Murch et al, n 1 above, p 181). By way of contrast, in Scotland, the majority of judges interviewed in a recent study said they were happy to speak with children (Raitt, n 1 above).

how they would like to be heard in the resolution of parenting disputes. Secondly, in our subsequent meeting with them we asked them specifically about whether they thought it would be a good idea for children to be able to talk with the judge in chambers.

7.1.1 Who would be the best person to talk with?

In our first meeting with the children, they were asked who they thought the best person would be to talk with if they wanted a say in what was happening in relation to residence and contact arrangements. They were given a number of options, which included 'telling the judge directly and in private', 'telling a lawyer who can say what you want', 'telling someone who can help but without telling your parents', 'telling a counsellor who can put it in a report to the court', and 'telling your parents/one of your parents'.[3]

The largest group of children and young people (*n* = 12) said that they thought that one or both of the parents would be the best people to talk with. Only three of these children were involved in contested cases. These children and young people, like the young people in other studies,[4] expected that they had a right to be consulted by their parents, even if this had not happened in their case.

The second largest group (*n* = 10) said that they thought it would be best to tell the judge directly or, more ambiguously, they referred to 'telling the court'. Seven of the ten were teenagers, and three were aged 9, 10 and 11. All were involved in contested matters. Generally, these children had very clear and strong views that were seemingly a reflection of their experience. For several of these children, their choices—to live with one parent rather than the other, or to have little or no contact with a parent—were influenced by incidents of violence that they had experienced or witnessed.

The other children and young people referred variously to counsellors (*n* = 6), family friends (*n* = 3) or said they did not know (*n* = 6). Another group (*n* = 6) gave answers that were decidedly ambivalent.

In summary, all the children who indicated that it would be best to tell the judge or who otherwise indicated a willingness to speak to the court were involved in contested matters. Not all the children in contested matters, however, wanted to speak with the judge: some referred to counsellors or said they did not know.

---

[3] The children could respond to any or all of these options. They did not have to choose between them. Children could answer 'don't know' or 'maybe' if they were uncertain. Children and young people who were not interviewed with the assistance of the computer program were asked a similar question and prompted with similar options.

[4] Smart, C and B Neale, '"It's My Life Too"—Children's Perspectives on Post-Divorce Parenting' (2000) 30 *Family Law* 163–169; Bretherton, H, '"Because it's me the Decisions are About"—Children's Experiences of Private Law Proceedings' (2002) 32 *Family Law* 450–457; Neale, B, 'Dialogues with Children: Children, Divorce and Citizenship' (2002) 9 *Childhood* 455–475; Smith, A B, N Taylor and P Tapp, 'Rethinking Children's Involvement in Decision-Making after Parental Separation' (2003) 10 *Childhood* 203–218.

In contrast, most of the children or young people who said it was best to speak to parents or with someone else such as a trusted family friend were involved in non-contested matters.

7.1.2 Specific questions on talking with judges in chambers

The emergence of the Children's Cases Program (see Chapter 3) between our first and second meetings with the children allowed us to describe to the children how some judges were beginning to have conversations with the children concerned in a trial and to ask our interviewees specifically what they thought about this option. Most children (85%) in the second interview said that children should have the opportunity to talk to the judge in chambers if they wished to do so. All who indicated in the first interview that they wanted to talk to a judge still wanted to do so or thought it was the best means of having their say. Others whose earlier preference was to talk with their parents or a counsellor indicated their acceptance of the idea of talking with the judge. Some specifically referred to their own circumstances whereas others responded in more general terms, indicating that talking with a judge might be 'scary' and that not everyone would want the opportunity but should have the option to do so.

Only five children in the second interview—four of whom were involved in non-contested matters—were against the idea of talking to the judge and maintained their preference across both interviews for talking with someone they knew or with a counsellor.

7.1.3 Children's reasons for wanting to talk with the judge

While not all the children gave reasons for their choice, there were several consistent themes in the answers of those who did. Their reasons for wanting to talk with the judge were consistent with their reasons for wanting to have a say generally.[5] First, they wanted their views to be heard by the person making the decision because they wanted to have a say and to be acknowledged. They also thought that this would result in a better decision. Secondly, they wanted it to be private so that they could say things to the judge without their parents knowing. Thirdly, they wanted the judge to know exactly how they felt without any mixed messages or misinterpretation.

Having a say and being acknowledged

The main reason children wanted to talk with the judge was that they wanted to have a say in the decision or at least have their views heard by the ultimate decision-maker. Some children just wanted a say in the decision-making process even if the judge did not make the decision that accorded with their views. For example:

[5] See Chapter 4.

Because they should have a say in what happens in their life. (Jack, 11, non-contested)

It's going to affect them, and so they should have a say in it, I think. (Emily, 15, non-contested)

Because the children should have a say in what they want and who they want to live with...it's pretty much all about the child when you go there. It's not really about the divorce or anything. (Alex, 11, non-contested)

Some children also thought it was important for the judge to meet them to know how they felt and whose futures they were deciding:

I think maybe they should because then the judge knows how the children would feel about the decisions so yes. (Sarah 11, contested)

I think that's a good idea. I think that if the judge is going to be determining something that's going to affect the child directly, then the judge should at least know the person they're going to be making a decision on and have spoken to them. (Rani, 16, contested)

A minority of children wanted to talk with the judge because they assumed that if they did so, their wishes would prevail.

Because they should have the right to do what they want to do. (Aaron, 15, contested)

Because they might want to go with their Dad, but if they don't want to go with the Dad and they want to go with the Mum, they can. (Eli, 9, non-contested)

Yeah. So you can do what you want. Live where you want. Where you think it's safe...stuff like that. (Darren, 18, contested)

Making better decisions

Some children also thought that they might be better able to make a judgment about their own interests than their parents, and the judge might also see it their way as well:

I think it's important because no matter how much the parents think the kids don't know what's good for them, they can see a lot of what's happening around them and they do understand. And I think a judge is mature enough to understand what a kid's trying to say. (Sandi, 18, non-contested)

Because sometimes the parents might make the wrong decision and the judge agrees sometimes with the kids more. (Harry, 11, contested)

Sometimes, lots of people don't listen to a kid because they are just a kid you know? But I think if there's a proper court where you go to court for the children's say, I think it would be much better. Then people would see it from the children's side, you know the other story. (Nick, 11, non-contested)

Speaking confidentially

A relatively common reason children gave for wanting to talk to the judge in private was so that they could say things without their parents knowing, mainly to avoid hurting them but in certain cases to avoid being punished. Two siblings, who were the subject of a contested case, were keen to avoid hurting their parents and gave very similar responses in separate interviews:

Because then the judge can see what they think and not hurt their parents. (Skye, 13)
    So you don't hurt the other parent's feelings by what you say. (Karina, 14)

Similarly, Kirsten, 17, said in relation to her own situation:

You'd just be scared of hurting your parents. You wouldn't want to say certain things in front of your parents. There's certain things I wouldn't want to say in front of Mum.

And speaking about her younger step-brother's situation, Kirsten referred to him as being too scared to say what he wanted, and being prevented from seeing a counsellor:

Because then the kids can get across what they can't say in front of the parents because they might be scared of their parents and they can just say what they want to say, which is really good, because if that had happened with Jeremy, Barry wouldn't have let it happen, because he wouldn't want—he won't let Jeremy go to a counsellor. Because he just doesn't know what Jeremy's going to say. And Jeremy was so scared of him at the time; he didn't really want to go either.

Hilary, 14, also involved in a contested case, wanted to speak to the judge without her parents knowing:

Put me on the stand or for me to write a letter or something like that to the judge telling him how I felt and then he could read it—that way I wouldn't feel imbaresed [sic] in saying it in front of my parents or he could have taken me to another room and talked.

Speaking directly

The final reason that children wanted to talk directly with the judge was so that their views might be heard above the conflict between their parents, without being filtered or misinterpreted by others.

Because the parents might be trying to make the other one look bad, so the children will be better. (Imran, 17, contested)
    I think that when it comes to court cases, a lot of the time all parents do is pick on each other. It's very much just the negatives of each side and the judge would rarely hear how the child would be affected because it's just a parent's opinion. (Hilary, 17, contested)

Several cited examples of younger children in their extended families where the children were being pressured to give particular answers. For example:

...it's really bad for them...their Mum talks to them and tells them what to say, and their Dad talks to them and tells them what to say, so they're all just confused...I think if they did talk to the judge and the judge found out that was happening, then that would be a good thing. (Terri, 16)

A number of children who considered that it would be best to speak with the judge or to the court directly had had experiences either of not being heard or of those who heard them making recommendations that went against their wishes. For example, when Helen was 11, she was the subject of a residence dispute between her parents. The court ordered that Helen should live with her mother and have contact with her father every other weekend and half the school holidays. Helen did not want to live with her mother because she had grown up where her father lived and moving meant changing schools and losing friends. According to her father, Helen had no child representative or 'family report'. Helen also indicated that no one asked her about her views and that she had no say at all in the decision although she had wanted to.

Michael, aged 10, had a very clear view that he wanted to live with his father. His mother, who had problems with substance abuse, was physically abusive towards him, hitting him with a cane and a baseball bat on occasions and causing him a number of injuries. On the first occasion that his father took the matter to court, the court awarded the mother residence. Subsequently, the father was awarded interim residence following an incident when Michael was too scared to go home to his mother. His mother later did not contest the award of residence to the father. Michael had a lawyer representing him on the first occasion (when he was 6 years old), but according to his father, the lawyer did not speak to him. Michael thought it would be best to speak to the judge in private in order to avoid a 'Chinese whispers' effect:

Because he's the judge and he is the one that has the overall say and it's straight to him, instead of like it might change a bit, say, from the people to him and like through all the people. Like the counsellors when they send it, like the judge might not get the proper message. But direct, he'd get the proper message.

Jack, 11, also thought it would be best to be able to tell the judge directly. He had spoken with a counsellor, who prepared a family report, and had a legal representative, but he was unclear what role either of them had, and whether they had conveyed his views to the court. He expressed a clear wish to live with his father, and had experienced violence from his mother's new partner.

Neither Ranjit, aged 13, nor his older brothers wanted to see their father because he had been violent towards them and their mother, and the court made orders to the effect that contact should only occur if the children chose to initiate it. They had a family report and a children's representative, and both of these conveyed the boys' views. Even still, Ranjit's response to the question of how to have a say, given a choice of the judge, the lawyer, a counsellor or a family friend, was to speak with the judge directly. His older brothers, however, expressed satisfaction with having their views conveyed by the lawyer and counsellor.

7.1.4 Children's reasons for not wanting to talk with the judge

Children who said they did not want to talk to the judge gave several reasons. First, a number of children involved in non-contested matters saw it as unnecessary or inappropriate in their case. Carly, for example, explicitly rejected the idea of talking to a judge, particularly because she thought that it would cause more problems:

No. I think that's a stupid idea. Because, at the time, you sort of feel like you want them back together—and that's the only thing you feel like—so your head's all mucked up. So going up in front of the judge and saying what you want, is sort of, not really what you want. It might be in the short-term, but in the long-term it's not. And also, it just creates a bigger mess. I think it would. Having a kid get up there and say, I want to be with Mum; that would be like, very controversial and it would make the father feel absolutely horrible. I just think it's a lot easier to let the adults sort it out, because then it's done properly. (Carly, 14, non-contested)

Others preferred to keep matters within the family rather than talking to outsiders. This was mostly a view expressed by those in non-contested matters, where the decisions were made within the family and the children had little awareness of any decision-making process outside the family. Emma, for example, was not keen on the idea of talking to 'outsiders', and did not understand the process.

I think with children, lawyers and court people and all of that, I think it's a bit too much. Talking to people you don't know is also hard I think as a child. I didn't like to tell them things, and I didn't understand and all that. (Emma, 13, non-contested)

Secondly, some like Terri, saw the idea of talking with the judge as too formal or 'scary'.

Oh, probably not. Someone like a counsellor or something I'd want to talk to first, because they understand—like a judge is sort of like a person who—I don't know, they look all formal and stuff. I'd be bit put off by that. Feel a bit funny. But with a counsellor you can like relax and stuff. (Terri, 16, non-contested)

Some, like Joshua, nevertheless thought it was an option that others might like.

I think it would be scary. Well, it depends on your age. Like, I would find it still scary now ... sitting in a courtroom having to talk to a judge about it. I don't know—it's different for everyone I guess. (Joshua, 10, non-contested)

As noted earlier, most children thought that they should be given the option of talking to the judge whether or not they would have taken up the opportunity themselves.

7.2 Parents' Views

Just under half of the parents (37, 47%) who responded to this question (n = 79) indicated that the most appropriate and preferred person for children to talk with were counsellors or some independent and trusted person (including family friends or lawyers). The next largest group of parents indicated that the judge, either alone or together with a counsellor, would be the best option (n = 32, 40.5%). About half of this group qualified their support with comments about appropriate processes and how this might be done. Two-thirds of these parents (21/32, 65%) also indicated that it would be a good idea for children to talk with counsellors or other independent people as well as judges.

The main difference between parents who favoured and those who were opposed to judges talking with children was whether they were resident or non-resident parents. Resident parents were twice as likely as non-resident parents to be in favour of children being able to talk with the judge, either alone or together with a counsellor or 'interpreter'.

The parents of the children in the contested matters who clearly indicated in either interview that they wanted to talk with the judge all supported the idea of their children doing so—with the exception of two non-resident fathers.[6] For some of these parents, it is clear that their views, like those of their children, reflected their own experience and the children's feeling that they had not been properly heard in the process. A number of these cases involved protracted disputes and problems relating to substance abuse and violence. These parents generally expressed confidence in what their children would have said and their capacity to handle such a process. Some focused more on the possible contribution that directly hearing children's views could have made to the decision-making process. Others focused more on the therapeutic benefits, saying that it would have helped their children to have been able to see the person who was making the decisions and feel that they were being heard.

7.2.1 Parents' reasons for favouring judges talking with children

Parents' reasons for supporting the option of children talking with the judge were similar to those given by children, with the exception of children's interest in being able to say things confidentially to the judge. Parents' reasons were related to children's right to be heard and acknowledged, the value of direct communication and the likely beneficial effect on the decision. These views were similar to the justifications for children's participation generally.[7]

Having a say and being acknowledged

Some parents considered that children need to be heard and have a say in the decision.

I think the kids need to be heard, on what they want and what affects them. (Resident mother, contested)

The days that we believed because a child can't vote yet, they've got no right, have gone. That's the rights of the child, isn't it. (Resident mother, contested)

---

[6] The only other non-resident parent (also a father) in this group of parents was in favour of the practice.

[7] See Chapter 4.

For some parents, this was a matter of respect and acknowledgement—so the children would feel that they have been heard and could see the person who was making the decision about their life.

I think that if children can voice an opinion, or even feel like they're being heard, it makes a big difference. (Resident mother, contested)

For others, it was important that the judge could actually see the child whose life they were affecting by their decision.

I'd say the Judge. They're the ones who have the final decision on the outcome. They sit there and read the papers and then try to make sense of the papers. I think if they actually heard a child's opinion and then read the papers, they might take a different reason into account. (Non-resident father, contested)

If you're asking someone to make a decision, think about the person between the two parties. Talk to the children. Sit down and have a cup of coffee or a milk shake and take the cap off, and sit down and talk to the kids. Half of them don't even see the children. (Non-resident father, contested)

Hearing first-hand and making better decisions

A number of parents expressed confidence that judges would be able to get a more complete understanding and perhaps the 'real picture' from hearing directly from children. Like some children, some parents believed that children can provide a better perspective than their parents can and that this information could assist the judge to come to better and more workable decisions. For example:

I believe children are more perceptive about those parents and realistic about those parents and a judge would be able to make a sound decision, based on talking to a child, because persons aren't portrayed in a courtroom with reality, and a child can give a judge that reality. So yes, if it was well controlled and in the interests of the child, most definitely. If they're perceptive enough. (Resident mother, non-contested)

I think, because you've gotta get a feel for what the kids want and also kids are pretty honest from 7 to 10 with that type of thing, they'll speak from the heart, I think, rather than anything else. And I think that it is good because I think they can get a better feel for where the kids should be. (Non-resident father, non-contested)

In particular, some parents were keen for children's views to be heard unfiltered by others in the process.

So, in relation to children being interviewed by judges, the more people you have involved in the process before it gets to the judiciary, the real decision-maker, the more distortion you have. So children's views are distorted, the more intermediaries you have. (Resident father, contested)

To have a chat with the children. I think that would be the most beneficial, and the easiest. And that way the judge or the registrar aren't getting the wrong idea from a written report. They're not getting their information second hand. They're getting it first hand. (Resident father, contested)

Several parents, all fathers, had another reason for being in favour of judges talking with children and hearing from children first-hand: an efficiency argument in relation to saving time and money.

The judge. Get it over and done with quicker. (Resident father, contested)

[It] would be incredibly beneficial to be able to allow them to take all the money-grabbing crap out of the whole thing and find out first-hand. (Non-resident father, contested)

Underlying the views of parents who supported judicial interviews was a general confidence in their children's views and capacities to resist pressure or in the system's capacity to detect it. Some of these parents directly challenged the view that children could be so easily manipulated. For example:

In my opinion the judge really has to take 95% of what the kids say. The kids aren't stupid. They know who they need to live with. They're not gonna be conned by a parent who'll say, oh yeah, here we'll give you 50 bucks if you say you want to come and live with Dad. They're not stupid. They'll pick the right person. (Resident father, contested)

Similarly, a resident mother said:

Well people would say that children can be coerced by the other parent into saying things or be brainwashed. But I actually don't think children can be brainwashed. I actually think that that's thinking that children are like puppets, or like, that we can coerce them into thinking and believing whatever we want them to think or believe, and that's far from the truth. Because we can't coerce a child into thinking, believing, that they should behave in certain ways if they really don't want to, no matter how old they are—they're gonna throw a tantrum and they're gonna muck up, and they're gonna do anything that they believe, and what they want. (Resident mother, contested)

7.2.2 Parents' reasons for not favouring judges talking with children

About one in four parents (21, 26.5%) clearly articulated a view that it was not appropriate for children to talk directly with the judge. They gave several reasons for their opposition. The first and most common reason was that it would be too intimidating for children particularly in the court environment.

No it's too scary for them. To a counsellor yes, never on the stand. (Resident father, contested)

I think in a court situation, it would be intimidating. Probably in your own home would be the best bet I think and a counsellor over two or three sessions. (Non-resident father, contested)

Secondly, some parents believed that judges do not have the appropriate background or training to communicate effectively with children or the time to build up trust with the child, discern the child's views and ensure that those views are really the child's own views.

I think that would vary from child to child. But I do think that there should be some effort made to build up some trust with the children, so that you are actually getting the children's views. And probably a counsellor is a better way to go. I don't really believe that the legal profession should have any more involvement in these issues than they do. (Resident mother, contested)

I don't think a judge has enough information on board in the short time they see them. (Non-resident father, non-contested)

They're so overloaded with their own work that it's a different area of expertise...I would think someone who's trained in that area, because they'd know what to look out for. (Resident mother, contested)

Thirdly, and related to this, some parents, and particularly non-resident parents, were concerned about the danger of children being manipulated, of children playing their parents off against each other or, in one case, lying. Underlying these parents' concerns is a model of children as manipulable and, in some cases, manipulating, and a lack of faith in judges or the system more generally to be able to detect this.

One non-resident father in a contested matter involving relocation and a history of violence was quite pragmatic in his opposition to the children talking with the judge because he did not see that it would benefit him at all, given the mother's greater capacity to influence their view.

I'd say 'It won't do me any good cause they spend all their time with their mother', so the mother has got them all tuned out that their life, security and safety is with her, and if you want you'll have no life and no security with your father.

7.2.3 The preferred process

Among parents who were in favour of judges talking with children, there were various views about how this should be done. There was very little support for children being in a courtroom but some support for judges seeing children in chambers or in a more child-friendly space.

A number of parents (21, 26.6%) also indicated their support for a counsellor or someone with special training to be present with the judge. There were various reasons for this—to interpret what the child said, to record the process, and to provide support particularly if the child had already met this person. The other concern was that such a talk or interview should be part of a process rather than a 'one-off event'.

I think if that [talking with the judge] was the only thing, that probably wouldn't be sufficient because you know, talking to someone for half an hour, or an hour, you don't get a good view of it. But if it was part of a process, then certainly I think that would be good. The way the system was, when we went through the system, it was very adversarial and it just depended on who had the better lawyers at the time, and it was probably one of the most stressful experiences from my perspective, because I didn't think I was performing well enough for my daughter. (Resident mother, contested)

While the child is talking to the judge, there should be a trained counsellor that can just sit there and see if that is really what the child—you know try and analyse is that what the child really wants or is the child getting put up to it and then another session a day or two later with just the counsellor and the child to talk through the different problems that are going on and find out whether that is the real thing the child wants and if that's what's best for the child. (Resident father, non-contested)

I think at the very least they should view a videotaped interaction between the child and the interviewer, and possibly the child and the parents. It should happen over more than one half-hour session, or whatever, you know? Because that doesn't tell you anything really. (Resident mother, contested)

7.3 Professionals in the Family Law System

Most professionals working in the family law system, the practising lawyers, the judges, and the court-based counsellors were against the practice of judges interviewing children.[8] A minority in each group considered it appropriate for judges to speak with children directly.

There was a consensus among all the professionals that judicial interviews with children prior to making a decision were rare events. Only four of the 20 judges interviewed had met with the child or children prior to reaching a decision. All of the judicial officers who indicated in this study that they had interviewed children were judges of the Family Court. None had done so in more than three cases at the time of interview. The lawyers who were interviewed in this study painted a similar picture. Only four out of 42 reported that they had ever known a judge to interview a child for the purposes of assisting him or her to make a parenting decision.

One explanation for why the long-standing provisions in the legislation to allow judges to talk to children in chambers are so rarely used is that lawyers do not make applications to judges to consider the matter. Two reasons for this emerged from these interviews. One was the view held by a substantial majority of the respondents that it was a bad idea for judges to interview children directly. Lawyers who expressed strong convictions that it was not appropriate for judges to talk directly with children, or who believed that the system was set up to hear their voices through other channels, would not want to make an application that the judge hear from the children directly. They would be unlikely to do so except on the instructions of an adult client, and probably only after attempting to dissuade the client.

One lawyer reported that a child had asked him if he could speak with the judge when he was acting as the child's separate representative. The lawyer replied

---

[8] Hunter, in her evaluation of the Children's Cases Program in New South Wales, found similar opposition among professionals, and for similar reasons. See Hunter, R, 'Close Encounters of a Judicial Kind: "Hearing" Children's "Voices"' in Family Law Proceedings' (2007) 19 *Child and Family Law Quarterly* 283–303.

that he was there as the child's representative, so it was his job to tell the judge what the child had told him. It was not appropriate for the child to tell the judge himself. The same lawyer had been involved in a case where an application was made by a parent for the judge to talk to the children. The lawyer was acting as a separate representative for the child and opposed the application on the basis that the child's views were already represented in the family report. The judge declined to talk to the children directly.

The second reason was a belief that judges were reluctant to talk directly with children and therefore there was little point in making such an application. This was almost entirely an untested assumption. While many of the lawyers had experience as separate representatives for children, only one had ever made an application to the judge to speak directly with the children. He had done so twice, and both times the application was declined.

It was not at all apparent from this study that judges were as reluctant to talk with children as the lawyers thought. Three quarters of the judges interviewed (15/20) indicated either that they would never talk with children for a forensic purpose before reaching a final decision in a case, or were extremely reluctant to do so. This included all six federal magistrates. At least in the Family Court, more than a third of judges would be prepared to talk with children in some circumstances or already make it a practice to do so in appropriate cases.

7.3.1 Areas of agreement

While there were some sharp disagreements between judges on whether or not it is ever appropriate to talk directly with children, there was universal agreement on three aspects, and these views were shared with other professionals. First, no judicial officer held the view that judicial conversations with children should displace the assessments of social scientists, only that judges should talk to children where appropriate as an *addition to* hearing children's voices through the reports of expert assessors.[9]

Secondly, no judicial officer held the view that a judge could talk with a child in chambers without the parties to the dispute receiving an account of what was said. There was universal acceptance among judges about the fundamental principles of due process, that the parties have a right to know the basis on which judges are making their decisions and should have the opportunity to lead evidence, conduct cross-examination and make submissions on all matters that might be germane to the judge's final decision.

---

[9] The vast majority of the judges in Lombard's study who were experienced and confident that their interviews with children were successful nevertheless 'recommended that other experts do the interviewing, either in addition to or in lieu of the judges' (Lombard, F, 'Judicial Interviewing of Children in Custody Cases: An Empirical and Analytical Study' (1984) 17 *UC Davis Law Review* 807–851, at 816).

Thirdly, there was also acceptance that a judge could not accept anything said by a child on a confidential basis. The principle that there should be no secret communications was seen as fundamental.[10]

7.3.2 Objections to judicial conversations with children

Most professionals, including 15 of the 20 judges, said they were against judges conducting conversations with children for forensic purposes.

The objections to judicial interviews were many and various. However, they fall into three main categories. These relate to the risks to the quality of decision-making, the risks to the decision-making process, and the risks to the child.

The risks to the quality of decision-making

There was a widespread view, shared by the judges themselves, that judges do not have the skill to interview children and that their lack of skill could lead them to make poor decisions about what was in the best interests of the child.[11] One judge, for example, explained his diffidence in this way:

Some of our court counsellors are just so good at it and not only can they tell you the children have expressed these wishes, but they can also give you an insight as to whether those wishes are contaminated. What concerns me, if I'm ever asked to interview children is that I just don't have that skill. (Male Family Court judge)

Others indicated their lack of training or skills in this area:

I would take a lot of persuading that it's a good idea—I'm a lawyer, I'm not a psychologist, I'm not trained to do this. (Female Family Court judge)

I think there are times when a psychologist is able to extract the information in a much more astute way than I would be able to. (Male federal magistrate)

This view was shared by the court counsellors, who universally showed a great deal of respect for the capacities of the judiciary but did not see this as an area

---

[10] This was not always the position in Australia. See, for example, Herring CJ in *Priest v Priest* (1963) 9 FLR 384 at 392, who wrote: 'it has been regarded as proper for the judge to see the infant in private and to act upon what he learned from the child without disclosing such information to the litigants'. In *ZN and YH and the Child Representative* (2002) FLC 93–101, Nicholson CJ conducted interviews with the children in an international relocation case in accordance with the Family Law Rules at the time. Order 23 Rule 4 of the Family Law Rules 1984 stipulated that nothing from the conversation was admissible. However, as issues emerged about the wishes of the children in the course of that interview, the judge ordered a new family report for the purposes of providing updated evidence on their views.

[11] Judges in Michigan in Lombard's study who regularly interviewed children in line with accepted practice 'expressed confidence in their ability to achieve rapport with the children' they interviewed and 'were similarly confident in their efforts to discover the child's preference' (Lombard, n 9 above, at 816). Most (19/26), however, recommended that 'other experts do the interviewing, either in addition to or in lieu of the judges' (at 816). Several expressed reservations about the utility of interviewing younger children.

in which the judges were either qualified or skilled. As one male counsellor put it:

Judges are highly trained experienced legal practitioners, but they need child psychologists. Some of them would intuitively have very good skills at talking to children, but some of them probably wouldn't be that good. The other thing is that they're not university trained in child development and their cognitive development in issues like perception and alienation. I have 30 years experience in those areas. A judge would have second-hand a whole lot of experience, but they wouldn't be trained. They're incredibly learned men and women, but they don't have that behavioural science background or expertise. Simple as that.

The difficulty of interpreting children's views and assessing the influences on them was a particular problem:

Seeing a child is the easy part, assessing the quality of what they tell you is the difficult part. I think that the only other possibility might be, the judge sees the child with the expert, but then both will have to be alive to all the external influences that potentially have been there and be able to assess it and having made the assessment, be able to be tested on that assessment, which could be wrong. (Male Family Court judge)

One experienced counsellor echoed this view, indicating that one of the dangers of judicial interviews is that judges may be too inclined to take at face value the expressed wishes of the children without understanding the family situation:

I think some of the judges who might be more open to the idea of talking to children are likely to be the ones that put more focus on children's wishes and they then wouldn't have the benefit of doing an assessment about what's formed those wishes. Like, to understand the whole family's psychological dynamics. So it could be problematic. (Female counsellor)

Family lawyers echoed similar concerns:

I think the difficulty with that is our judges as a rule are incredibly competent, sensitive and intelligent people but they are not necessarily skilled in interviewing children and I think you can learn so much by asking questions but it is about understanding the context in which kids are giving their answers. (Male family lawyer, child representative)

A Family Court judge illustrated the dangers, as she saw it, of relying on her own observations of children rather than those of the counselling team. She told of a case that she had heard very shortly before the interview. The father had residence, and the mother failed to return the two children, a 9-year-old girl and a 12-year-old boy, after a contact visit. The matter came before the court again as a recovery application.[12] The judge required the children to be brought to the court the following day, and ordered their return to the father. After this

---

[12] This is an application for the return of a child who has been improperly removed from the care of the other parent or not returned to his or her care.

order was made, the father went to the children who were outside the court. A few moments later, the 9-year-old girl burst into the courtroom and yelled at the judge: 'Why don't you listen to me? I don't want to go home, I don't want to go home.' She ran over to her mother and threw herself at the mother, screaming. The judge called in the Director of Court Counselling, who spoke to the girl and her mother. Within about 15 minutes, after the girl had calmed down, she was saying everything will be alright, if she could just go home with her Dad. The judge commented on the incident: 'If I'd taken note of that, as a piece of evidence, I would have had to say she had very strong wishes at least at this time, not to return to her father.' However, in the hands of skilled counsellors, the crisis was managed and the child was able to return home with the father, with her anxieties resolved.

The Director of Court Counselling for this registry confirmed the judge's impression that this was a case where a judicial interview would not have been appropriate. The family were very well known to the counselling staff of the registry and had multiple problems which required very careful case management over a period of time.

Another concern that was expressed, apart from lack of experience, was the lack of time to properly assess what children's views were. One judge contrasted the time available for a judge with best practice for child representatives:

I guess I hark back to my years and years and years of doing child rep work. You didn't see the children once; you saw them on a number of occasions, over a period of time—brought in by Mum, brought in by Dad. You had very different outcomes at times, depending on who brought them in; you had different views expressed over periods of time; and at best, I just thought you get a superficial gloss of a child's circumstances and views on a half hour interview or something—it's trivial. (Female federal magistrate)

One experienced family lawyer questioned in any event that the judge could resolve a case by a brief conversation with a child in chambers:

Well it is a brave judge who takes a small child into their chambers and comes back and says I reached this view over a cup of tea and biscuits. If the case is that difficult, it is not going to be solved by that method. It is hard enough for a separate representative getting kids to open up. (Male family lawyer, child representative)

Another experienced female family lawyer also expressed concerns about the quality of information that could be derived from a brief interview in chambers:

To my observation, the best way of ascertaining a child's wishes and getting down to what the child's wishes really are, as freely expressed—is once they've had a number of sessions with an expert who's been able to form a relationship or gain the confidence of the child and the child has then expressed a view, otherwise for a child to go to court and speak to a judge—often they're either primed or they express the view they think is expected of them, rather than what their true view is and it may again, not be a properly reasoned view.

The risks to the process of decision-making

A second group of concerns among judges was that talking with a child in chambers would damage at least the perception of fairness and due process. The judge would no longer be a neutral decision-maker assessing all the evidence presented by the parties, but a participant in the evidence-gathering process. As one judge put it:

What is it that you are doing with this child—evidence gathering? Well, you shouldn't be. (Female federal magistrate)

One concern was that it might undermine the parties' confidence in the judicial process:

It could lead to suspicion on the part of the parents, you know—what happened in the judge's chambers? (Male federal magistrate)

If I interviewed the child, what could I add to the proceeding in doing that? It would be disadvantageous, like justice is not seen to be done, for the parents...I think there is a transparency problem. I can't see that it adds, but that it takes away. (Female federal magistrate)

A particular concern for a number of judges was that if they talked with children in chambers, then their conversation may become an issue in the case:

You'll have to tell the child that what you're about to discuss is going to be recorded and will be used in evidence in the case, and potentially in my view, questions can then be raised as to the quality of the interview process, why certain questions were asked instead of other questions, why certain questions were not asked at all, or indeed why certain questions were asked which seemed to be irrelevant. (Male Family Court judge)

Well, who do you cross examine? The Judge? Your Honour, you said...what was the basis upon which you put that proposition to my child? You can ask a counsellor that, that's no problem. (Female Family Court judge)

I'm not going to have someone cross-examine me about how I came to that conclusion, and yet they're entitled to know that. And if I say well, in my reasons for judgment, I took into account what the child told me, I either spell it out, so that they know what's being said, and then you know, they might want to know—well, did you take into account that he'd just come from his mother's house and he got a beating from his father last week?...Was that in the forefront of your mind when you were listening to this child? (Male federal magistrate)

A third concern was that children will say something which they do not want the parents to know, and then there is a problem about how the judge should respond.

I am worried about the situation where you see a child, and a child says to you 'I won't tell you unless you promise not to tell my parents'. (Male Family Court judge)

Where the conversation with a child takes place after the judge has made the decision, the concerns about procedural fairness do not apply. The conversation can be non-forensic, and a means of the judge explaining the reasons for their decision and acknowledging the child, as requested by a number of children and their parents.[13] One judge of the Family Court reported that he has made it a regular practice to invite older children in to his chambers before handing down a judgment in order to explain it to them.[14] The judge explained the rationale for such meetings:

It really embarrasses me to see a 14-year-old child in a court making a decision about them, and for them to find out from one of the parents who's partisan... I think it's also a sign of some respect that it's their life you're interfering in.

The risks to the child

A third group of concerns was that the process of judges interviewing children might actually be harmful to the child. This was another aspect of the concern about judges' lack of skills and training:

My sense of it is that I don't have the skills to do it. I would be really concerned that I could do irreparable damage. (Female Family Court judge)
    We're lawyers. We have to be really careful that we don't start doing more damage than good. (Male federal magistrate)

Another concern was that for a child to go and see a judge in chambers would be such an artificial environment. This was a concern expressed particularly by family lawyers, although surprisingly, not by counsellors.

Kids could be overawed by that sort of a process. (Male lawyer)
    If you're ever invited into morning tea into chambers—I think I've only ever been part of a legal team once, because it doesn't happen often to go into the judge's chambers—I mean it's just nerve wracking... I think it would just be intimidating. Just even the court buildings, the buildings themselves, some buildings are better than others as you know. (Female lawyer, child representative)

A particular concern for judges was that a judicial interview would be a source of pressure and stress for the children:

No I wouldn't because I think it's stressful for kids and it would be worse that it's a judge, than if it's a counsellor. It's bad enough, somebody from the court. (Male Family Court judge)
    I mean we say courtrooms are scary places for adults; a private conference, with someone, you know, 50 years older than you, they've got your life in their hands, I think it's a pretty daunting prospect for any child, or any person. (Female federal magistrate)

---

[13] Parkinson, P, J Cashmore and J Single, 'Parents' and Children's Views on Talking to Judges in Parenting Disputes in Australia' (2007) 21 *International Journal of Law, Policy and the Family* 84–107.
[14] This judge's reasons for the practice, and the legal basis for so doing, are given in *N and N* (2000) FLC 93-059.

It seems easier to me being at the much younger end of the range, and still with a young family, but what do you do about the judges that are 65 and haven't seen young children for 20 years—they're lovely people and very capable, but I can think of many that are in that 60s age bracket who even as a lawyer appearing in front of them, they seem fairly gruff and a bit forbidding. (Male federal magistrate)

Few judges, like those surveyed by Felner et al, expressed suspicion of children's motives to 'choose a more permissive home environment' but they were concerned about their own capacity to elicit and interpret children's views and the possible pressure that children might feel if they were asked to express a preference.[15]

No perceived purpose in judicial conversations with children

Another theme in the objections expressed by some judges was that there was no forensic purpose to talking with children, and therefore it was beyond the scope of the judicial role to do so. For example, one judge commented:

A judge is not a social worker, a psychologist, an uncle confessor, or anything like that. The Judge's role is to hear a case, determine the issues from a legal viewpoint, and having made the decision, that's the end of his or her role. (Male Family Court judge)

Many expressed the view that because the court has social scientists to interview children, there was no need for judges to do so:

I don't see the need for it, where we have the ability to obtain evidence about the children's wishes through other means. (Male Family Court judge)

Two judges suggested that if the conversation was conducted in the presence of a welfare professional who took notes for the purposes of a report, then that person might as well do the interview:

If there's an expert there to take notes, then I don't see any reason why the expert shouldn't be doing the interview. (Male Family Court judge)
    Well then I can't see the point of me being there. Because I'm going to see the report anyway, and the mediator is going to be cross-examined. (Female Family Court judge)

Indeed, the option of the welfare professional doing the interview in the presence of the judge was more acceptable to some judges than the judge questioning personally:

I mean I'd rather have the judge sitting there and listen to the psychologist ask the questions, and he or she could stick their bit in if they really had to but I don't think the judge has to ask the questions for the child to know that their views are being heard. (Male federal magistrate)

---

[15] Felner, R D, L Terre, S Farber, J Primavera and T A Bishop, 'Child Custody: Practices and Perspectives of Legal Professionals' (1985) 14 *Journal of Clinical Child Psychology* 27–34.

7.3.3 Judges' experiences of talking with children in parenting disputes

The judges who had seen children countered a number of the concerns that had been expressed by their colleagues. For example, in contrast to the concerns of those who thought that judicial interviews could lead to poor decision-making were the experiences of judges who felt that talking with the children had led to better decision-making.

The father who had a brain injury

One male Family Court judge told of a case which he had decided after a very long trial concerning contact between a father and his three children, aged 15, 12 and 11. The father had suffered a very serious brain injury and this had affected the way in which he related to his children. The evidence at trial was that the children did not want to see their father. The judge concluded on the evidence that the mother was influencing the children against having contact with the father. The judge decided to order limited contact.

However, months later the case came back to the judge on a contravention application because contact was still not occurring. The judge proposed to the parents that, subject to the children's consent, he would see them in chambers. A counsellor would be present and would make a short form report on the interview, but could not be cross-examined on this. This would subsequently be released to the parents and placed on the court file. The parents agreed to this. The children also agreed to meet with the judge.

The counsellor reported in detail on the interview, describing not only what the children had said but offering observations on how the children presented. She reported that all three children showed a mature understanding of the issues, and offered other observations about their demeanour and how they expressed their views to the judge. All of the children said that they did not wish to see their father at the present time. They each recounted past events when they had been very upset by what their father had said and done. They said they had really tried to have a positive relationship with their father, but had been let down when he did not attend planned visits. They also indicated they did not feel safe with him. The counsellor concluded that:[16]

The children's wishes were expressed with resoluteness and calm and were assessed to have been formed as a result of their personal experiences and not through any influence by their mother or other adult.

She reported also that the oldest boy wanted to reconnect with his father in future and that he would help his sisters to do so as well.

---

[16] The quotation is taken from the judge's judgment which incorporated the counsellor's report in full. The *ex tempore* judgment is unreported.

The judge was persuaded by meeting the children that his original decision was wrong. The children clearly loved their father but found it too difficult to be with him because of the way in which his injuries had affected his behaviour towards them. The judge concluded:

I just wish that before the case I had seen them. The case would have ended in a way that could have been seen with honour and respect, but it didn't. It went through to a bitter fight with judicial findings.

The child whose choice was not on the agenda

Another male Family Court judge told of how his decision to talk with the child had led to a settlement of the case on a basis that could not have been anticipated on the evidence. The judge was on circuit in a town in a remote part of Australia. At the end of the list was one parenting case that it was estimated would take three to four days. It involved a dispute between the father of a 10-year-old girl and her maternal grandparents. The mother had been involved with drugs and prostitution, and allowed her parents to take care of the daughter. The father agreed to this, and for a time had regular contact with his daughter. After she expressed the wish to live with her Dad, he brought his application to the Court.

The judge had a dilemma. If he began the hearing on the one day that remained, and the case did not run to completion, then it would have to be continued in the capital city where the judge normally sat, at significant expense to the parties and witnesses. The alternative would be an unacceptably long delay before that judge came on circuit to that town again. The alternative was to adjourn the matter to the next trial list before the next judge to come on circuit. That would have meant a further six-month wait for a hearing.

The mother was present and was going to give evidence in support of the father's case as she had had a falling out with her parents. Having talked to the parties and the mother, the judge proposed that he should talk to the girl as long as the parties would agree to this and would be prepared to accept his account of what the girl tells him. They all readily agreed. There had been a family report, and it reported that she wanted to live with her father.

It was settled that the judge, accompanied by his female associate, would meet the girl in a park near the court. The judge described the encounter:

I met the young girl and she strolled straight over. She was confident, articulate and knew exactly what she wanted. She basically sat me down and she said 'Now you're the judge, and you're going to decide who I live with' and she said 'I want to live with my Mum'.

This presented a problem for the judge as the mother didn't have an application before the court. However, he explored all the reasons why she wanted to be with her mother, and after about half an hour, he was absolutely convinced that she knew exactly what she wanted, that it was all properly based, and that it was a serious possibility if everybody else agreed that Mum had turned her life around.

When they reconvened in the courtroom, the judge gently explained to the grandparents and the father what the girl had told him. He said that she wanted him to convey that she loved her grandparents dearly and that the decision that she'd reached was nothing to do with how much she loved them 'but, the surprise is, she wants to live with Mum'.

The judge then explained all the options to the parties. They were entitled to have a trial if they wanted it. However the grandparents agreed that their daughter had rehabilitated herself. After talking with them further about what it might need to restore the broken relationships within the family, the judge indicated that if the parties agreed, he could accept an oral application for residence from the mother if that is what she wanted. He then sent them away to think about it for a couple of hours. They came back with an agreement that the mother would have residence and that both the father and the grandparents would have contact. They also agreed that they would have family gatherings to try and mend the broken relationships. The judge commented:

> So you know, listening to a child on that one occasion had an amazing therapeutic effect on the entire family, and I felt so good. I mean, my associate was in tears, my wife who'd come on circuit with me walked into the back of the court, and she was in tears, I was holding back tears. It was a very fulfilling experience.

7.3.4 The benefits of talking with children in chambers

This chapter has focused so far mainly on the objections to judicial conversations with children because the majority of professionals expressed these concerns. However, the judges who had talked with children prior to reaching a decision were all enthusiastic about the benefits of so doing.[17] Some of these benefits emerge from the stories given above. The benefits that judges identified from talking directly to children fall into three broad categories: those that assist the judge's decision-making, those that assist the process, and those that may directly assist children. Other professionals who expressed support for judges interviewing children echoed some of these reasons.

The benefits for judicial decision-making

There were two explicit benefits that judges who had been involved in conversations with children perceived had come from this practice. These were the benefits of hearing at first-hand from children, and of canvassing the options with them.

---

[17] Lombard found also that judges who were experienced in interviewing children were positive about the benefits, both in terms of 'giving them a "feel" for the case that they would not otherwise have' and in giving children the opportunity to 'vent their feelings' (Lombard, n 9 above, at 810).

Hearing at first-hand from children

Judges commented on the great benefits they found from talking directly to children rather than relying only on the expert report. Two judges indicated that it had given them a much better sense of the children's views than if they were reliant only on the report writer's account. One gave an example of a case where he had spoken to a child:

The other thing that I've found incredibly important arising from speaking to the children is that it gave 'colour' to the family report. In one case, for example, the family report had said that it could be anticipated that the youngest child would not welcome a change of residence but might experience some trauma in the initial stages—that sort of thing. So I mean when you read those things, you get a picture of what that might be, but having seen that child, the picture changed and it changed dramatically for me because I'm sure she was saying exactly the same things as she did to the reporter but the way she was saying it to me convinced me that there was no way she would tolerate it. That for whatever reason she would feel constrained to make life miserable in the other household, would probably run away—that sort of thing. Now that was a 'colour' that I didn't get from reading the report. (Male Family Court judge)

Another commented on hearing the account of the court mediator to the court after he and the mediator had spoken with the child:

It was a very good experience to sit in on an interview and then to hear it being reported back. The report back to the parties by the mediator lacked colour and the flavour of the actual interview. In many ways, it is reflective of the reason Appeal Courts rarely overturn judges on questions of assessment of witnesses. Seeing, hearing and observing evidence, particularly in this respect, is far more complete than a report from a mediator. (Male Family Court judge)

Talking with children in chambers is of course not the only way that children may be heard directly. With the permission of the court, they may give evidence in open court. On one occasion, a boy indicated that he wanted to speak to the judge. The boy's father had killed his mother. The boy was adamant that he did not wish to see his father. This request to speak to the judge was met by making a videotape which was shown in court. The child answered questions that had been formulated in court and which were put to him by a counsellor.[18]

Canvassing the options with the child

Another advantage is in being able to explore the finer details of the options that the judge is contemplating, based on the evidence as it has emerged by the time of the trial:

I don't think kids have been given an appropriate opportunity to comment on the range of possibilities that may occur in the case. It's usually a one-liner—'Where would you like

---

[18] See Chisholm, R, 'Children's Participation in Family Court Litigation' (1999) 13 *Australian Journal of Family Law* 197–218, at 209.

to live?'—and that's it. Whereas the dynamic of what might happen in the court is far broader than that...So that all too often we've got no idea at all, because the child's had no opportunity to have any input into the finer questions—you know would mid-week overnight contact be something that you'd like or not like—what do you think about that? (Male Family Court judge)

Benefits for the process

The judges also commented on the possibility that hearing children's views directly might expedite the process by providing input that would not otherwise be available in urgent cases and enforcement matters, by allowing for an update on a child's views where the information available to the judge was quite old, and by encouraging settlement.

Utility in cases where a family report is not available or justified

A judicial conversation with the child may be a useful option in urgent matters or where the normal processes of having child representatives and family reports are not available. For the judge on circuit in a country town with limited resources, it was not possible to call on a court welfare professional to conduct an interview with the girl involved in the dispute between her father and her grandparents. This is a particularly relevant consideration in other jurisdictions where the option of a specialist report from an experienced psychologist or other such professional on the family situation and the views of the children is not available to the courts. Here the choice is between judicial interviews and the child having no voice at all in the proceedings.

Judges in Australia do not have the benefit of family reports in every decision. They do not have this in contravention cases, for example, nor in most interim matters. In enforcement matters where the opposition of a reasonably mature child to contact is put forward as a reason for the failure to comply with orders, some means of hearing the voice of the child is likely to be essential and a direct conversation between the judge and the child, in the presence of a welfare professional, may well get to the heart of the issues far more quickly than if a new process is ordered with a family report leading to another hearing. In enforcement cases and other matters where there is ongoing conflict, a quick resolution of the presenting issue is likely to be important in providing justice and achieving resolution.

Another situation where it may be appropriate for a judge to talk directly with the children is where the issues are limited and it is not worth the time and expense of having a full family report. One female Family Court judge recounted such a case involving three children aged 16, 14 and 8. The case was heard in the Children's Cases Program. The parents had been separated for about two and a half years, and the three children lived with the mother. The mother allowed the 16 year old to see his father whenever he wanted to. However, she imposed strict limits on the father's contact with the two younger children. The basic arrangement was that the father saw the children every other weekend and in the school holidays. However, the mother did not allow them to sleep overnight at the father's house, insisting that they come home from their father's on Saturday afternoon and sleep at the mother's place and that they could not have friends go to their father's place. The father's explanation was that she wanted to control him and the children. The children had a good relationship with both parents, and there was no complaint by either parent about the parental capacity of the other.

The mediator advised the judge that the circumstances that she had heard did not justify a full-blown reporting process, and that it might be appropriate to discuss the situation generally, particularly with the 14-year-old girl. The parents were agreeable to the children discussing their circumstances with the judge in the presence of the mediator. The meeting took place in the mediation rooms of the court. All three children came. The judge offered each of them the opportunity to discuss their point of view individually. The 8-year-old was very talkative generally, but did not want to volunteer anything about the family situation. The 14 year old indicated that she wanted to stay overnight at her father's house but had some practical concerns about doing her homework at her father's house, in particular, not having a computer there. In reporting back to the parents on the conversation with the children, the judge was able to assist the father in understanding what her daughter needed. The judge commented:

If I'd ordered a family report in that case, the resources would have meant about two months delay and it was generally agreed that the circumstances perhaps didn't warrant that delay.

The judge indicated, however, that she believed that seeing children like this ought to be justified by the circumstances, and it was not something that she was quick to do.

Updating information on the views of the child

Another potential benefit is gaining information about the views and circumstances of a child where his or her views are likely to be very significant and the information available to the court may be out of date.[19] One Family Court judge recounted her experience of talking with a child in such a circumstance. She was completing her judgment while on leave over the Christmas break in a case involving a 15-year-old boy. He had not seen his mother for a long time and one of the issues in the case was whether the judge should make orders that would restore the boy's relationship with his mother. The judge recalled:

It came to me as I was writing the judgment that I felt really there ought to be some more updated situation about the boy's view of things. There had been a report but it had been quite old at the time and... I felt that I needed to go back to this boy, and have the mediator who did the report, talk about some things that had been discussed in the evidence

---

[19] See, for example, *ZN and YH and the Child Representative* (2002) FLC 93–101; *Gordon and Gordon* [2007] FamCA 361.

and that had not been addressed in the report...So when I came back from leave, I asked for the case to be mentioned and...lo and behold, the legal representatives told me on the mention that over the Christmas period and...through January, the boy had in fact been seeing his mother which was fresh information for me and I was quite annoyed about it because here I was ready to give judgment on the basis that the boy hadn't seen his mother for a very long time and was steadfastly refusing to see her.

The judge was told also that it was the boy who had instigated the contact. Consequently, she asked to see him. The parents and the boy consented and she spoke with him in the presence of the mediator. He wanted to continue to see his mother, but also wanted to have a say about what would happen and when. The judge's decision took account of his wishes in this regard.

As a tool for settlement

Talking to the child on the eve of the trial may also act as a tool for settlement. One Family Court judge explained his practice:

Now, I have thought that the best time to do that is on the afternoon or evening before the last court event starts. So I would give the parties every opportunity to resolve the case and quite often the family report or the expert's report will be the catalyst for a settlement. So that it's only a last resort that I'll speak to the children. So we've been through all the process—they've signed all their affidavits, we've had the family report, it's not resolved, I've allocated two days to finish the case and on the evening before I'll see the children and then report to the parties. It's another tool I felt maybe a good tool to help the parties resolve also, to be able to tell them on the morning of the first day, well I saw your children and this is what they told me.

The possible therapeutic benefits for children

Several judges referred explicitly to the possibility that talking directly to the judge could be a cathartic or therapeutic experience for a child. It was seen to be a way of showing respect for the child and allowing children to feel heard. Indeed, the experience of the judge cited earlier in relation to the child's choice being heard when it had not been on the agenda was that it was a therapeutic experience, not just for the family, but for the judge and others who were there. Seeing the positive effect of the process on the parties is not necessarily a common experience in family courts but one that is rewarding for those involved when it does occur.[20]

---

[20] Chase and Hora's survey of judges in US family law courts and drug treatment courts found that those involved in the drug treatment courts were significantly more satisfied with their work and felt they were part of a process that was more helpful than those in the family law area, consistent with therapeutic jurisprudence expectations (Chase, D J and P F Hora, 'The Implications of Therapeutic Jurisprudence for Judicial Satisfaction' (2000) 37 *Court Review* 12–19). On therapeutic jurisprudence, see Wexler, D B, 'Reflections on the Scope of Therapeutic Jurisprudence' (1995) 1 *Psychology, Public Policy, and Law* 220–236.

Judges who had not talked with children but expressed an interest in doing so all gave this as a reason for talking to children if the child wanted to do so. Even some who were opposed to doing so suggested that they were open to empirical evidence that showed some benefits for the child and to some rethinking of their role. For example:

I guess we have to start deciding about whether the courts are in the business of being therapeutic. If we are, well then maybe we have to give Johnny a place to be able to say his bit, direct to the judge. (Male federal magistrate)

Four Family Court judges, all women, expressed the view that while they would not be prepared to see children in chambers in order to assist their decision, they might be prepared to meet with children in certain circumstances, for the child's benefit. These conditions were carefully circumscribed:

If I had a child representative or a counsellor who I really trusted, and who said, 'Judge, I think you ought to see this child', and say at the end of the counselling process, the counsellor was able to say, 'Now you've told this to me, would you really like to tell that to the judge yourself?' And if I thought that was coming from the child and not the parent saying 'You should go and tell the judge' and the counsellor who had already done a vetting said that, I'd feel much more comfortable about doing that then. It would be for the child. It wouldn't be for me, it would be for the child. For the child to actually feel—I mean it must be a pretty terrible thing for a child to know that somebody, that they don't know what they look like, they have a concept about, is making this decision about their life and that they haven't really been heard. And that's why I'd do it.

There may be cases where the child, an older child insists that they want to speak to the judge, and that would be different... I think that that wish should be respected.

Another judge considered there might be value in explaining to children that it is the judge who is making the decision, not the child, so that the child's burden of responsibility is relieved. While sympathetic to the intention of such conversations, others were sceptical that any 'conversations' with a child before the judge has made a decision about the case could remain non-forensic. They doubted that children could be expected to meet the judge without wanting to have a say and influence the decision, and also whether a judge could disregard what children have said if the discussion takes place prior to the judge making a decision:

I think with the best will in the world, any decision maker would be having themselves on if they said 'I've spoken to these children but I'm going to completely disregard what they've told me in coming to a decision'. (Female Family Court judge)

How do you divide in your own mind what's influencing you? So say I say I'm not doing it for forensic purposes... because I want the child to understand that I'm the one making the decision, I want the child to feel they've participated, I can't help but be gleaning things. I won't even know how I'm using those, it might be the language the child uses about a parent, it might be the demeanour, which parent describes the demeanour that's more akin to what I've seen, it must make me think that that parent's got more insight; and yet I might have got the kid on a bad day, or a good day, or a shy day. (Female Family Court judge)

7.4 Truth, Justice and Due Process

Despite the marked reluctance of many of the judges to conduct interviews with children in chambers, there was a surprising degree of congruence in the views of judges, parents and children about the potential value—and the risks—of judicial conversations with children.

Some parents and judges, and a number of the children expressed the view that hearing what children have to say at first-hand provides a useful and often better sense of what is important to children and their experience in the family. It was particularly the children in the contested cases involving protracted disputes who expressed a desire to talk to the judge even though in most cases they had experienced being interviewed by an independent expert, and had a child representative. Like the separately represented children in a recent British study,[21] they still would like to have been heard in a more direct manner. In some cases, this was expressed as dissatisfaction with the work of a child representative or the writer of a family report. They mostly had strong opinions which they wanted to ensure were heard by the person making the decision, particularly where they had been subjected to abuse, neglect or disrespect[22] from one parent.[23] As Kelly pointed out, some children and young people have 'cogent, rational, and detailed input that they want a judge to hear because they have been rendered powerless, voiceless, and upset during the divorce process'.[24]

A number of parents, more often resident parents than non-resident parents, thought too that if children had the opportunity to talk with the judge directly, it was more likely that the truth would come out and that judges could get the 'real picture' without the distortions arising from the parents' conflict. Resident parents were more likely to express confidence in the competence and capacity of the children to know what was going on and to say what they wanted—and perhaps what the parent wanted too—rejecting the idea that children could be

[21] Douglas et al wrote: 'The children wanted the court and the judicial authorities to be "child-friendly" and work in such a way that if they wanted to put their view to the judge directly, the setting and the judge should be sufficiently approachable to enable them to do so.' (Douglas, G, M Murch, C Miles and L Scanlan, *Research into the Operation of Rule 9.5 of the Family Proceedings Rules 1991* (Report to the Department of Constitutional Affairs, 2006) p 112).

[22] As Neale comments: 'Children will clearly assert their rights to self-determination, where the family relationships are oppressive or abusive' (Neale, n 4 above, at 469). Warshak, however, takes the view that 'the child's eagerness to participate in litigation may (but certainly does not necessarily) signal the need for caution in attending to the child's voice, whereas a child who is reluctant may be the one who has the most to contribute to an optimal parenting plan' (Warshak, R A, 'Payoffs and Pitfalls of Listening to Children' (2003) 52 *Family Relations* 373–384, at 376).

[23] Smart and Neale, n 4 above; Neale, n 4 above; Tapp, P, 'Judges are Human Too: Conversation between the Judge and a Child as a Means of Giving Effect to Section 6 of the Care of Children Act 2004' (2006) *New Zealand Law Review* 35–74.

[24] Kelly, J B, 'Psychological and Legal Interventions for Parents and Children in Custody and Access Disputes: Current Research and Practice' (2002) 10 *Virginia Journal of Social Policy & Law* 129–163, at 153.

easily manipulated or citing their own experience that attempts to do so had not 'worked' in their case. The opposing model of children, and one more generally expressed by parents who were not in favour of judicial interviews (particularly non-resident parents), was that children were vulnerable to pressure and manipulation, and might also exploit the differences between their parents to get what they wanted. These were of course, the arguments against children's participation generally.[25] As Neale pointed out,[26] however:

Much of what is currently perceived almost automatically as 'manipulation' of a child's views by a parent might just as appropriately be seen in this light: as a parent consciously seeking to understand their child's point of view and actively supporting them.

There was also considerable agreement, at least between judges and parents, that the welfare professional could play a useful role, and that any conversation between the judge and the child should involve the counsellor and be an adjunct to, rather than a replacement for, the court report. Most judges and some parents were, however, concerned about the capacity of judges to make an accurate assessment of the children's views in the short time available to them, and to interpret those views properly, particularly because of their lack of experience and confidence in doing so. Judges also expressed concern about this, but their greater concern was about the risks to due process and the perceived fairness and transparency of the decision-making process.

Significantly, few of the people involved in this study had had any experience in judicial conversations with children. Only a minority of the judges had met with children in these circumstances and none of the children who were interviewed had done so although most thought they had should have the option, and most of those involved in contested matters would like to have done so. The judges who had some experience in this process were, however, positive about the benefits, and in their view, seeing the children had improved their decision-making in those cases, or at least their confidence in the outcome. None of the children and none of the parents had had any direct contact in this manner with judges so it remains an empirical question as to whether such conversations would meet their expectations and their concerns. Despite their concerns about due process, there appears to be some willingness among Australian judges to consider the potential benefits for children and for the decision-making process if their concerns can be addressed.

The due process concerns associated with children's wish to talk to the judge on a confidential basis are regarded as particularly problematic in Australia, and in many other common law jurisdictions it would be regarded as axiomatic that no one should be allowed to communicate matters to a judge of which the parties, the parents, are not aware. All the Australian judges were clear about this. The principle is one of open justice. A judge can base his or her decision only on the material, information and evidence which has been presented to the judge in

---

[25] See Chapter 4.   [26] Neale, n 4 above, at 457.

a way which all those involved have had an opportunity to respond to, comment on, contradict or correct as the case may be. For a judge to be influenced in his or her decision by a private communication, the content of which the parents are unaware, would, on this view, violate fundamental principles of due process and fairness in the adversarial process. The fact that judges have to warn children that nothing they say will be confidential significantly restricts the opportunity for children to convey their real views to the judge,[27] because they must necessarily self-censor those aspects of their story that they do not want their parents to hear.

In other jurisdictions, which do not hold so rigorously to the principle of open justice, there may not be so much concern about receiving confidential communications from children. Courts in some jurisdictions have taken the view that it is acceptable for judges to interview children in private without giving an account to the parties in the case. In *Jespersen v Jespersen*,[28] the British Columbia Court of Appeal indicated that where an interview is conducted with the consent of the parents, the judge has a discretion whether or not to reveal to the parties what the child has said.[29] Lambert JA, with whom Macdonald JA concurred, wrote:[30]

In my opinion there is no obligation on the judge who has interviewed a child in those circumstances to set out any details of the interview. The judge who conducts such an interview, by consent of counsel, without the presence of either parent, does so in the hope of obtaining a very frank statement by the child which will not cause embarrassment to the child or either parent, and it must remain the prerogative of the trial judge to decide whether anything should be said about the results of the interview and, if so, what should be said.

In *Andrusiek v Andrusiek* (2002),[31] the British Columbia Court of Appeal returned to consideration of the issue. The trial judge in this case had interviewed a 10-year-old boy who had clear views about which parent he wanted to live with, but said that he would only convey those views to the judge directly. The parents agreed that the judge should see the boy. The judge kept a record of the interview with the child but sealed its contents as the child did not want the contents disclosed. In his judgment, he indicated that the boy wanted to live with his father. This was the decision the judge reached, but he indicated that it was only one of the factors that he considered in reaching his decision. Although the appellate court noted the dangers of deciding a case on evidence about which the parties have no knowledge, and where they were unable to cross-examine, it upheld the decision of the judge, indicating that the mother could not now appeal on the basis of a process to which she had given her consent at trial.[32]

---

[27] Hunter, n 8 above.   [28] (1985) 48 RFL (2d) 193.

[29] An earlier decision of the court to the contrary was not cited: *Allan v Allan* (1958) 16 DLR (2d) 172 (information obtained by the judge should be disclosed to the parties so that they have an opportunity to controvert it). See also *Jandrisch v Jandrisch* (1980) 16 RFL (2d) 239 (Manitoba Court of Appeal).

[30] See n 28 above, at 197.   [31] (2002) 25 RFL (5th) 8.

[32] See also *Demeter v Demeter* (1996) 21 RFL (4th) 54 (Ont Gen Div).

The views of lawyers and judges in British Columbia are, however, quite varied. A number of judges indicated in a recent study that they had a practice of interviewing children with only a clerk present. In some cases an agreement was negotiated with the parties in advance that limited their right to the disclosure of what the child had said. None of the judges who responded had ever kept a record of the substance of the conversation for appeal purposes.[33]

Similarly, in a survey of 160 judges in Arizona whose responsibilities could include parenting disputes, Atwood found that of those who interviewed children regularly or at least occasionally (and this was 75% of the judges surveyed), only about half made a record of the interview.[34] One quarter of those who did make a record sealed it and made it available only in the event of an appeal.[35] Tapp's survey of New Zealand cases also indicated differences of practice, with judges 'not always' apprising the parties of the child's view.[36]

As these examples from British Columbia and Arizona indicate, there is a wide variety of practices on this issue. It seems unsatisfactory that such fundamental issues of process as to whether judges should speak with children and the process for so doing should depend on the personal preferences, values and practices of the trial judge. Of course, trial judges are given a lot of discretion and control in terms of the process of conducting a trial. However, leaving matters to the discretion of trial judges is sometimes a means by which Parliaments and appeal courts avoid hard decisions.[37]

If judges are to have conversations with children in determining parenting disputes, there ought to be agreed guidelines about when it is and is not appropriate, and agreed processes for the conduct of the meeting, the recording of its outcome, and the manner in which the substance of the conversation is conveyed to the parents. We offer some such guidelines in Chapter 8.

---

[33] Williams, S, *Through the Eyes of Young People: Meaningful Child Participation in Family Court Processes* (International Institute for Child Rights and Development, 2006) pp 43–45.

[34] Atwood, n 1 above.

[35] See also Lombard, n 9 above, and Crosby-Currie, C A, 'Children's Involvement in Contested Custody Cases: Practices and Experiences of Legal and Mental Health Professionals' (1996) 20 *Law and Human Behavior* 289–311, for similar findings for judges in Michigan and Virginia. Lombard's study, for example, found that the 26 judges in Michigan had mixed views and practice about interviews with children. Less than half made any 'stenographic record' of the interview, and of those, only four made it available to parents as well as the attorneys and appellate court. Crosby-Currie found that 'judges were somewhat likely to seal the record of their interview with the child, and not very likely to allow attorneys, present at the interview, to ask questions' (at 304).

[36] Tapp, n 23 above, at 17–18.

[37] Schneider, C, 'Discretion and Rules: A Lawyer's View' in K Hawkins (ed), *The Uses of Discretion* (Clarendon, 1992) p 47.

8

Towards a More Responsive Legal System

8.1 The Consensus on Children's Participation

Children, parents and judges were generally in agreement that it is important to hear children's views and for children to feel that they have been heard—as long as they do not feel burdened by any of the responsibility for the outcome. Their views about the positive effects of being acknowledged and having one's views heard are consistent with the relational model of procedural justice proposed by Tyler and Lind and colleagues.[1] They go beyond the focus on 'justice' or 'fairness' in the traditional or instrumental procedural justice model, featuring concern for relational aspects, and what Gilligan and Smart refer to as an an 'ethic of respect' and an 'ethic of care', in turn related to 'two of Gilligan's core elements: connect-edness and the importance of not causing harm or hurt'.[2]

Almost all the children would like the opportunity to have a say in the parenting arrangements following the separation of their mother and father, and said that from about 7 years of age onwards, they should be asked. Nonetheless, there were some differences among children in their views about participation and particularly between the children in the contested and non-contested cases. Those in the non-contested cases, which, it will be recalled, were resolved at some stage along the litigation pathway without going to a final hearing, were more concerned with 'voice' than 'choice'. They wanted a say, and often wanted to see

---

[1] Lind, E A, R Kanfer and P C Earley, 'Voice, Control, and Procedural Justice: Instrumental and Noninstrumental Concerns in Fairness Judgments' (1990) 59 *Journal of Personality and Social Psychology* 952–959. In particular, children's concern for relational aspects is consistent with Tyler and Degoey's development of the relational variant of the procedural justice model (Tyler, T R and P Degoey, 'Community, Family, and the Social Good: The Psychological Dynamics of Procedural Justice and Social Identification' in G B Melton (ed), *The Individual, the Family, and Social Good: Personal Fulfillment in Times of Change* (University of Nebraska Press, 1995) vol 42, pp 53–91).

[2] Smart et al based their analysis of children's views about their families, and in particular their views about the arrangements after their parents have separated, on the rethinking by Gilligan about questions of moral reasoning and moral development (together with that of other philosophers and sociologists). They discerned three concepts in children's reasoning: an 'ethic of fairness', an 'ethic of care' as well as an 'ethic of respect' (Smart, C, B Neale and A Wade, *The Changing Experience of Childhood: Families and Divorce* (Polity Press, 2001) pp 93–97 (ethic of care) and pp 97–100 (ethic of respect)). See also Weinstein, J, 'And Never the Twain Shall Meet: The Best Interests of Children and the Adversary System' (1997–1998) 52 *University of Miami Law Review* 79–175 for an exploration of an 'ethic of care' based on Gilligan's work.

their non-resident parent more, or wanted more flexibility in the arrangements. These children were concerned about the fairness of the arrangements, about the amount and the quality of contact they had with the non-resident parent, and the logistics of that contact, as well as allowing for greater flexibility in the arrangements as they got older. Children in contested proceedings were more concerned to have some control over the way their views were represented and were more keen to put them unfiltered to the judge as decision-maker.

The great majority of parents also said that it was appropriate for children to have a say, although some were more qualified in their support for this than others. They often articulated thoughtful opinions on why this should be so. Almost all the professionals, including the judges, shared this view as well.

Support for children's participation was not merely tokenistic. Judges, for example, emphasized how important it was to their process of decision-making to know if the children had any perspectives on the issues, whatever weight they might ultimately place on children's views. Lawyers, mediators and family report writers also emphasized the importance of children's voices.

There seems then, to be a general consensus that it is important to listen to children in family law disputes, especially as they get older. There was less consensus about the methods for hearing the voices of children, with judicial interviews being an issue where there was a lot of disagreement, but that was only to be expected. In Australia at least, there is widespread agreement on ends if not means.

8.2 The Benefits and Risks of Children's Participation

This general support for children's participation was not unqualified, and nor were children, parents or professionals unaware of the risks. How one determines what is a risk, however, depends on the purposes of listening to children's voices. The risks may also be greater or lesser, depending on how professionals engage children.

8.2.1 Why listen to children?

Five rationales emerged from the interviews with children, parents and professionals for involving children. Not all of these rationales were shared by all the groups, and the differences between these groups are significant for understanding both the justifications for children's participation and the methods of involving them.

The acknowledgement and respect rationale

Some parents and children said that children ought to have a say because this acknowledges that it was their lives about which decisions were being made. Such views were expressed without the need to offer another justification as well.

Children ought to have a say irrespective of whether this would lead to better decisions, and whether or not they were at an age and stage where they were capable of making up their own minds. There was a 'taken for granted' quality in this view of entitlement, but only a few parents and children explicitly phrased this in terms of children's right to have a say.

This justification for involving children was also expressed strongly by many counsellors. They recognized the right of children to be involved, and that right was not dependent on the children being rational in their views. The need to involve them arose from respect for their intrinsic personhood and position as primary stakeholders in the decision—the ones who had to 'live' with the arrangements. As Smart and her colleagues put it, what children seem to be looking for is 'dignity, respect, selfhood and agency' 'within a web of relationships'.[3]

The best interests or best decision rationale

Children also thought that giving them a say would lead to better decisions by parents or the courts, or put differently, that the decision-makers would be better placed to determine the best interests of children if they had the benefit of children's views and perspectives. This was endorsed also by many counsellors, who saw children's perspectives on the family situation as being a very important part of the information that they needed to gather for the family report (the 'enlightenment' theme). These perspectives could be gathered not only by talking with the children directly but also to some extent by observation of how they related to each parent when the parents and children saw the counsellor for the purpose of preparing the family report.

The best interests rationale was also strongly emphasized by parents who acknowledged that children are experts on their own family situation. They know what life is like with each parent, and what life will be like in each alternative scenario which the parents or the courts are considering. This is true, of course, only if the children's views are being sought on known alternatives. Relocation cases are particularly problematic in this regard because very often, the children will have very limited, if any, experience of life in the new situation. They might have visited on holidays or at weekends, but would not know much about what it would be like to move from the existing home, school and community on a permanent basis. Conversely, they may not have had much experience of having the other parent as their primary carer during the school and working week, if that is one of the alternative options to be considered. There might therefore be some merit in children's suggestions of being able to 'try it out' or 'reality test' the arrangements, in situations where it is practical to do so.

---

[3] Smart et al cite Minow's comment that there is 'something terribly lacking in rights for children that speak only of autonomy rather than need, especially the central need for relationships with adults who are themselves enabled to create settings where children can thrive' (Smart et al, n 2 above, p 109; Minow, M, 'Interpreting Rights: An Essay For Robert Cover' (1987) 96 *Yale Law Journal* 1860–2017, at 1910).

Lawyers, in particular, emphasized another aspect of the better decisions rationale, and that is workability. They considered, as did some parents, that if the children had very strong views, or were old enough to vote with their feet, then their views had to be taken into account in order for the parenting arrangements to work. Workability and enlightenment are two different rationales for listening to children, but they go towards the same end—making better decisions for children.

The judges who had interviewed children in their judicial capacity also thought that doing so could help them to make better decisions. Even young children, according to some judges, could provide insights into the family situation, and this was beneficial to the judge whether or not children had sufficient maturity for their 'wishes' to be taken into account.

It is not clear from this research that children who have been given a say will be happier than those who have not. Having a say did not make a difference to children's happiness, or their views about the fairness of the arrangements. The exception was in relation to contact arrangements in contested cases. Children in contested cases were more likely to say the amount of time they spent with their non-resident parent was fair if they had been given some say during the process, and mostly, these were cases where they did not want to see that parent much at all. However, with that exception, it does seem that the children adapted to their circumstances, whether or not they felt they were consulted. Two years down the track most children were generally happy with the way things had worked out, although they may not have been so happy initially and had wanted more say.

The dispute resolution rationale

A major rationale for children's participation given by mediators and counsellors was that hearing from the children could benefit the parents and thereby promote settlements. They reported that many parents don't understand how the children are feeling or what they want.[4] If they are presented with this information, then it may lead them to be willing to make compromises or to drop particular demands. On this rationale, children's voices should also be heard because they may have ideas about the middle ground that will allow for the resolution of an otherwise intractable dispute between the parents.

This is, of course, a major justification for child-inclusive mediation, and clearly this concept had a lot of support from professionals who have a great deal of

---

[4] Some of the children in the British study by Butler and his colleagues generally agreed with this proposition—about half the children indicated that their fathers knew 'very little' or 'nothing' about their feelings about the divorce; the figure for their mothers was less than half that at around 20%. Over 60% of children said that they 'never' or 'seldom' talked about their feelings about the divorce with their father that about 30% said the same in relation to their mother. Over a third of children (36%) said that they 'absolutely refused to talk to their fathers about the divorce' compared to 11% for mothers (Butler, I, L Scanlan, M Robinson, G Douglas and M Murch, *Divorcing Children: Children's Experience of their Parents' Divorce* (Jessica Kingsley, 2003) pp 39–40).

experience in family mediation. Having just two competing proposals from the parents which are irreconcilable makes gaining agreement difficult. Children's voices can therefore inject new information, or even new options, into the discussion in a way which allows for some movement and compromise.

Mediators and counsellors often qualified this by saying that whether or not they sought to include children in the mediation process (for example, by seeing the children separately themselves, or engaging a child consultant) depended on whether they thought the parents would listen to their children. If that was not likely to be the case, then the children may be worse off by having an opportunity to express a view (and then being ignored) than if they had not been given that opportunity.

The therapeutic rationale

Counsellors and parents also emphasized the potential therapeutic importance to children of having a say if they wish to do so. Empowering children gives them a greater sense of having some control over their environment, and treating children with respect can have therapeutic value for children.[5] The converse of this was that there were risks associated with not listening to children. Both counsellors and parents saw dangers in not giving children a voice in terms of problems down the track, including depression. Kaltenborn's findings provide some support for their view. In perhaps the only empirical study to date to follow-up on the long-term outcomes of arrangements made against children's preferences and attachments, Kaltenborn reported significant difficulties and 'trajectories of suffering' for the children involved.[6]

The rationale of children's emerging decision-making capacity

This rationale is that as children develop greater maturity and reasoning skills, so their views about where they want to live and when to spend time with the other parent should be given greater respect. This is a view about children's emerging decision-making capacity. It was the dominant rationale for lawyers and judges. In a situation where the parents cannot agree, then the older and more mature

---

[5] This is the crux of therapeutic jurisprudence concerning the effect of the law on people's emotional and psychological well-being. See Wexler, D B, 'Reflections on the Scope of Therapeutic Jurisprudence' (1995) 1 *Psychology, Public Policy, and Law* 220–236; Winick, B and K W Goodman, 'A Therapeutic Jurisprudence Perspective on Participation in Research by Subjects with Reduced Capacity to Consent: A Comment on Kim and Appelbaum' (2006) 24 *Behavioral Sciences and the Law* 485–494, and also Weinstein, n 2 above.

[6] See Kaltenborn K-F, 'Children's and Young People's Experiences in Various Residential Arrangements: A Longitudinal Study to Evaluate Criteria for Custody and Residence Decision-Making' (2001) 31 *British Journal of Social Work* 81–117. In addition, in relation to the 'conversational environment' for questioning children in these circumstances, Siegal pointed out that: '... to dispense with the child's wishes in the absence of what he or she perceives as an adequate justification may, at least in some cases, invite anger, cynicism, feelings and exclusion from family life, or depression' (Siegal, M, 'Concern for the Conversational Environment: Questioning Children in Custody Disputes' (1991) 22 *Professional Psychology: Research and Practice* 473–478).

the child, the greater the weight that should be placed upon those views by the alternate decision-maker, the judge, so long as those views do not seem to be the outcome of parental pressure or manipulation.

Put differently, children's voices were seen as more or less important depending on whether they could solve the problem. The problem was that the parents could not agree and so a decision had to be made. The judge may not have a very clear view about what is in the child's best interests since best interest determinations are to some extent predictions about the likely outcomes of future competing options. In some cases, the children are likely to fare alright whatever decision the judge makes, and in some cases, poorly, whatever decision the judge makes. In these situations, the child's views may offer a solution—let's do what the child wants as long as it is rational and sensible, not clearly the product of manipulation or pressure from a parent, and not obviously contrary to his or her best interests.

While lawyers and judges did not say that children should be the decision-makers, the discourse of the majority was concentrated on ascertaining where on the spectrum from total dependence to complete independence the child was, and therefore how much respect should be accorded to the child's views as a person able to make decisions for him or herself. Children's solutions to the problem therefore became a more sensible option the older and more mature they were. Judges emphasized that they looked at all the evidence concerning a child's best interests, but would place more weight on a child's views the older they were, in the absence of clear evidence that indicated a different outcome was needed.

Parents and counsellors also spoke about the age and maturity of the child as relevant issues. Age and maturity can also be relevant to the best interests rationale, since the older and more mature the child, the greater may be their insights into the family situation and their capacity to articulate their needs.

8.2.2 The risks of listening to children

There was considerable agreement between parents and professionals of the risks of involving children. The children themselves were less aware of those risks. Lawyers were the most protective professional group. They were most likely to express concerns about the risks of involving children and were less positive about the benefits, although the great majority supported children's participation.

There were two kinds of risks with which parents and professionals were concerned. The first was the risk to the decision-making process, and the second was the risk to the child.

The risk to the decision-making process

This arose from the problem of coaching, parental pressure and manipulation. There were also concerns about children expressing views based on what was fair to their parents, or to meet a parent's need, rather than what was best for themselves. There was concern too that children's views could be changeable. All of these risks contributed to the possibility that poorer decisions would be made. Judges might make decisions based upon what the child wanted, when those views of the child were the outcome of parental influence in order to win the case, or were changeable, or based upon parenting a parent.[7]

Counsellors were much less concerned about this than lawyers, first, because most of them were reasonably confident that they could discern coaching and manipulation, and secondly, because they took a much more holistic view of children's views and perspectives than the lawyers. Lawyers focused on children's 'wishes', whereas counsellors were looking for children's insights into the family situation, and information about their needs and attachments. Children's views on what the preferred decision should be were generally assessed within a much broader framework and so their wishes were recorded and assessed in the light of a great deal of other information about their needs and best interests.

The risk to children's well-being

Most professionals were concerned about placing the burden of responsibility on the child, and some were also concerned about giving the child too much power.

A particular concern, to which professionals were sensitive, was the problem of placing children in a position of divided loyalties. The children's perspectives on this issue are important. While the great majority of children thought they should have a say, they recognized that this could put them in a difficult position. Some, either speaking generally, or by specific reference to their own situations, indicated that children should not be asked to choose between their parents. They were concerned about hurting one of their parents, or being hurt by them. This was the reason why they wanted to be able to speak confidentially to the judge. Counsellors and child representatives report that many children do not in fact want to express a view when the issue is a clear choice between the competing proposals of their parents, and this right not to choose is respected.[8] However, there are many ways of having a say without being placed in a position of divided loyalties, or being forced to choose between two irreconcilable sets of proposals.

Furthermore, not all children are in positions of divided loyalty. Children in contested proceedings were particularly strong in asserting that they wanted to have a say. Many of these cases involved violence and abuse by one parent or the other. Children who had experienced violence, abuse or very high conflict were less likely to be concerned that having a say would put them in a position

---

[7] As Komulainen pointed out in relation to children's role in research, 'what is "true" and "real" about voices remains an unresolved puzzle since... "voices" are always social' (Komulainen, S, 'The Ambiguity of the Child's "Voice" in Social Research' (2007) 14 *Childhood* 11–28).

[8] Some of the children in our study and in other studies also indicated great reluctance or unwillingness to express a view in these circumstances. Some, as reported in Smart et al, sought to sidestep the issue by suggesting a 50:50 split in recognition of an ethic of fairness or suggested the 'simple expedient of talking to both of their parents', allowing everyone to be involved in the process (Smart et al, n 2 above, p 102).

of choosing between their parents. Indeed, in some of those cases, they had long since chosen. These were cases in which the relationship between the child and one of the parents had been severely, if not irreparably, damaged by past events. These children wanted the court to know their views, and in many cases, were keen to tell the judge directly.

The professionals' role in alleviating risk

The risks to children from participating in family law disputes may be exacerbated or alleviated by the manner in which professionals engage with them. This research showed some important differences between counsellors who prepare family reports. Some engaged in a collaborative approach with children, being willing to find ways to get the message across without indicating this was the child's view, and being prepared not to include material at all where necessary to protect children. Others saw their role in writing family reports as one of gathering evidence for the court. They took the view that having explained to the children that the process was not confidential and that the child should not tell the counsellor anything the child did not want the parent to know, anything the child then said could be included. Children did report repercussions from family reports, and this was a risk of which some counsellors were acutely aware.

There were risks too in the way lawyers went about ascertaining children's wishes. The direct approach, which was particularly characteristic of male lawyers, may have left them more open than the counsellors to prepared speeches, and less able to discern the influences that might have led children to express the wishes that they did. This would be of less concern where there is also an expert assessment that engages with the child's views, perspectives and experiences of family life in a holistic way; but a family report is not ordered in every case by any means, and often in making submissions at interim hearings, or assisting in negotiating settlements, lawyers do not have the benefit of any other assessment of the child's views, attachments and needs than their own understanding based upon their conversations with the child and formulaic views about what is best for children.[9] This may be one of those areas where a little knowledge of children's wishes, without being able to contextualize those wishes within a much broader assessment of children's lives and relationships, is a dangerous thing. On the other hand, lawyers were also quite suspicious about parental influence and manipulation, and less willing to believe that children's views were their own.

8.2.3 Paradoxes in views of children's participation

The views of parents and professionals therefore involved paradoxes. On the one hand, there was widespread agreement that children ought to have a say, for a variety of different reasons. On the other hand, there was widespread agreement

[9] See also Smart et al, n 2 above, p 171 for similar conclusions about court professionals.

that there were great risks involved in giving the children a say because of the difficulties this would create when their parents are unable to agree. For lawyers, the paradox was apparently resolved by saying that while parents should not talk to their children about the parenting disputes, it was alright for professionals to talk to the children. Yet most lawyers acknowledged that the great majority of parents do talk to their children about the issues in dispute and that for this reason, a child coming to talk to a professional will already have been subject to significant influence and pressure, whether that influence or pressure is applied by a parent consciously or unconsciously.

Another paradox which emerges from this research is that while professionals thought that children should have a say, certainly once they are in their primary school years, there was some scepticism about whether the authentic voice of the child could be discerned amidst the cacophony of parental voices ringing in a child's ears.

There is then a need to reconceptualize why it is that we seek the voices of children in parenting disputes, and the uses to which children's views are put. The notion that children's views should be sought out of respect for their independent citizenship and rights as individuals sits comfortably with the growing emphasis in society generally on recognizing the rights of children. However, there was a widespread consensus that children need to be protected from the adverse effects of conflict and contestation to the greatest extent possible. If this is so, then concern for children's protection must qualify the expression of their rights to have a say and govern how this is achieved.

8.3 Improving Children's Participation

How then, can legal systems around the world become more inclusive of children, gaining the benefits of their participation in terms of quality of decision-making and durability of arrangements,[10] while ensuring that they are protected from their parents' conflicts? The motto of the legal profession, like the medical profession, ought to be first, to do no harm. The cautious approach to children's participation in the past has, at least in part, been motivated by concerns about children's well-being. There has also, of course, been an under-estimation of children's capacities to make a contribution to decision-making about parenting arrangements after separation, with priority given to protection for children over their participation.[11]

A starting point in considering how to make legal systems more responsive to children's voices is to note and acknowledge the degree of consensus that already

---

[10] For a follow-up study on the longer-term outcomes of arrangements against children's wishes, see Kaltenborn, K-F, 'Children's and Young People's Experiences in Various Residential Arrangements: A Longitudinal Study to Evaluate Criteria for Custody and Residence Decision-Making' (2001) 31 *British Journal of Social Work* 81–117.

[11] Chisholm, R, 'Children's Participation in Family Court Litigation' (1999) 13 *Australian Journal of Family Law* 197–218.

exists about children's participation. In Australia, at least, there was a strong consensus of opinion between these mothers and fathers, children, mediators and family report writers, lawyers and judges that children's views are important and children should have some say in the process but that they should not carry the burden of decision-making when parents cannot agree.

There may not be the same degree of consensus between parents, children and professionals in other jurisdictions. The only way of knowing this would be to replicate our research in other countries. Nonetheless, the evidence about practice internationally suggests a broad degree of consensus about the importance of children's participation, stimulated and reinforced by Article 12 of the UN Convention on the Rights of the Child. Again, the disagreement is not about ends but means. Different views about how to involve children reflect not only individual beliefs, but also differences of history, experience, legal culture and available resources.

It is also not realistic to promote an 'optimal' way of involving children in the abstract. Reforms to the legal system, whatever they may be, need to take account of the beliefs, attitudes and training of the professionals in the system. Reforms that are introduced to a willing, or at least open, group of professionals who feel untrained for the task may well succeed with appropriate training and gradual implementation. However, reforms that are imposed on a professional group, not only against their will but against their beliefs, are bound to run into problems. This is especially so in reforms to court processes if the reforms conflict with core beliefs about procedural fairness and the judicial role.

Each jurisdiction needs to find the best way of involving children, given the history and culture of its legal system and the resources available to the court such as family report writers or independent advocates. Nonetheless, there are principles that can be utilized to guide the reform process and to promote the greater participation of children in decision-making about parenting arrangements after separation. These principles are as follows:

- distinguish between 'voice' and 'choice';
- redefine the significance of age and maturity;
- explore children's perspectives, not their 'wishes';
- distinguish between different kinds of decisions on which children's views may be invited;
- follow certain guidelines about judicial interviews;
- consider children's views with the aid of social-science expertise; and
- move beyond the focus on hearing children in trials.

8.3.1 Distinguish between voice and choice

Most children and parents, as well as most professionals, were very supportive of children's views being heard and considered as part of the decision-making process ('voice'). There was much less support for children making the decisions or their views being the determining factor ('choice') because of the risks outlined earlier and also because other people's needs have to be accommodated. Indeed, it was not what most children wanted anyway. They were generally keen to maintain relationships with their parents and wanted their views to be acknowledged and taken seriously as a sign of their parents' respect and care for them. For children in contested matters, where the decision was being made by a judge, being taken seriously also meant having control over the way their views were represented. They wanted their views to be heard unfiltered and uninterpreted directly by the decision-maker, the judge.

Being taken seriously, not making the decision, is the crux of the participation principle (Article 12) in the UN Convention on the Rights of the Child. It is a marker of respect and trust, and an acknowledgement of children as people with needs, like adults, for 'dignity, respect, selfhood and agency'. As Melton pointed out:

Nothing is more fundamental to the experience of being taken seriously than simply having a say, being heard politely, and having one's perspective considered—in effect, being part of a conversation about matters of personal significance.[12]

A *conversation* is required whenever a child is old enough to be able to express a preference—a legal rule that reflects a simple expression of courtesy, of personal respect...In that regard, the key question for policy is not the threshold for their self-determination but the means of ensuring that children perceive themselves as partners in the settings of which they are a part.[13]

It is crucial then that children know that their views will be taken seriously—but that the decisions are made based on all the relevant information and the needs of all involved. Yet, in practice, it seems that parents often have the impression that the older the child is, the more likely that their wishes will in practice be determinative. Indeed, there seems to be some continuing belief that age 12 or 14 is a 'magic age' which some parents see as giving children the right to decide where they will live for themselves.

This is another reason why the emphasis should move away from the notion that children who have reached a sufficient age and maturity should be given autonomy, and that courts should simply go along with their decisions. Courts may well go along with the decision of a mature child whose perspectives on the family situation are well thought through and whose choices coincide with the other evidence of what is likely to be best for them. A number of judges said that they would go along with the views of the child in these circumstances, but not because they were surrendering the decision to the child. In situations where

---

[12] Melton, G, 'Parents *and* Children: Legal Reform to Facilitate Children's Participation' (1999) 54 *American Psychologist* 935–944 at 936.

[13] Melton, G, 'Building Humane Communities Respectful of Children: The Significance of the Convention on the Rights of the Child' (2005) 60 *American Psychologist* 918–926 at 922.

judges concluded that there was a conflict between the wishes of children and their best interests, they would generally go against the views of the child, having weighed up the difficulties of so doing in the circumstances of the case.

Judges who have the responsibility to assess all the evidence, and to give reasons for their decisions in the light of all the evidence, would be very unlikely to base their decision purely on one part of the evidence—that is the wishes of the child. However, most cases settle without the need for a judge to determine the matter, and it is in this arena of informal justice that the greatest care must be taken to ensure that both parents and children understand that children's views will not be determinative, although their views will be heeded. If the case is settled, it is ultimately because the parents have reached agreement, not because the children had the right to choose. If the court decides the case in accordance with what the child wants, this is because, having evaluated all the circumstances, the judge, who is making the decision, considers it will be best for the child.

Paradoxically, it is precisely in giving children protection from being autonomous decision-makers, that the family law system can most readily free them to participate in the decisions that affect them with less concern about their 'competence' to do so and without being overborne by parental pressure or manipulation. The more that parents perceive that weight will be placed upon the views of a child, the more likely they are to be concerned about their choices and to subject them to significant pressure. This may be overt pressure, or the kind of subtle emotional pressure that can come when a parent conveys to the child how sad he or she will be if the decision goes against what that parent wants. While children are generally keen to be involved in the process and will often try to accommodate both parents, what they mostly need and want is to have their views taken seriously, without being responsible for the decision.

8.3.2 Redefine the significance of age and maturity

One clear implication that emerges from the paradoxical and conflicting views of all those interviewed in this study is that the rationale for listening to the voices of children cannot rest upon their age and maturity to make decisions for themselves. There was a wide recognition, of course, that it is difficult to decide parenting arrangements against the strong wishes of older teenagers; however, respect for children's autonomy did not extend as far as giving them the burden of decision-making when parents cannot agree. Decisions which may involve choosing between the positions adopted by their parents, and which place children in a conflict of loyalties, are decisions which children may not be emotionally capable of making, whatever their cognitive capacities in other respects. Indeed, some children refuse to make such choices.

Those interviewed for this study indicated that respect for children's emerging autonomy ought to be expressed in different ways than to give them responsibility for the parenting arrangements. First of all, parents need to recognize that the older the child, the more say they will want to have in the arrangements.[14] As teenagers, in particular, develop interests and social lives that reduce their availability to spend time with either parent, so their views about how much time should be spent with each parent should be taken into account and accommodated by the parents. Secondly, teenagers should be allowed to negotiate with their parents about the minutiae of the arrangements from week to week or holiday to holiday. As time with a parent conflicts with other activities in which they want to engage, so they should be encouraged to negotiate those issues with that parent. This is quite different from giving children the final say over the parenting arrangements when the parents are in dispute in court. That level of autonomy was not seen to be good for children nor fair on them when their parents are in high conflict.

If children are not to be the decision-makers in any event, it ought not to matter very much whether they are capable of logical and rational decision-making which is not influenced by pressure from either parent. The search for the rational and independent decision-maker is likely in any event to be a futile one, like chasing a mirage in a desert. There is no 'true and authentic' voice of the child that exists independently of the child's situation and family circumstances, and the context in which they are giving their views.[15] In particular, children's maturity or level of understanding is context dependent. In determining the weight to be given to children's voices therefore, concerns about cognitive capacity, maturity and contamination, ought not to be treated as of significant importance.

The age and maturity of the child may be relevant for other reasons than their capacity to exercise decision-making autonomy. As children develop and mature, they gain a greater capacity to think beyond the short term, and therefore may be more able to articulate issues that concern what is in their best interests. That is important for one aspect of determining the weight to be given to their views. If a child's views are transient, or based upon short-term issues such as a reluctance to change from an existing school, then they may be given less weight than if they are likely to have some durability. For example, where children have had

---

[14] This is a very consistent and not so surprising finding from studies in Britain, Australia and Canada (see Gollop, M, A B Smith and N J Taylor, 'Children's Involvement in Custody and Access Arrangements after Parental Separation' (2000) 12 *Child and Family Law Quarterly* 383–399; Lyon, C, 'Children's Participation in Private Law Proceedings with Particular Emphasis on the Questions of Meetings Between the Judge and the Child in Family Proceedings' in The Rt Hon Lord Justice Thorpe and E Clarke (eds), *No Fault or Flaw. The Future of the Family Law Act 1996* (Jordans, 2000) pp 67–79; Parkinson, P, J Cashmore and J Single, 'Adolescents' Views on the Fairness of Parenting and Financial Arrangements after Separation' (2005) 43 *Family Court Review* 429–444; Williams, S, *Through the Eyes of Young People: Meaningful Child Participation in Family Court Processes* (International Institute for Child Rights and Development, 2006)).

[15] James, A and A Prout, 'Strategies and Structures: Towards a New Perspective on Children's Experiences of Family Life' in J Brannen and M O'Brien (eds), *Children In Families: Research And Policy* (Falmer Press, 1996); Hunter, R, 'Close Encounters of a Judicial Kind: "Hearing" Children's "Voices" in Family Law Proceedings' (2007) 19 *Child and Family Law Quarterly* 283–303.

negative experiences of one parent, as some of the children had done in this study, their views about not wanting to live with that parent ought to carry great weight because their experiences are part of their history. Their views are not likely to be transient. They might be changed, but only in some cases by a Damascus-like transformation of the parent and his or her way of relating to the child.

Children's age and maturity are also relevant to the issue of workability. The older the child, the more difficult it will be to maintain parenting arrangements which do not accord at all with what they want. Younger children under the authority of the primary carer are much more likely to adjust and accept the situation. However, as children grow older, gain more independence and seek to assert their own positions against those of their parents, so it will be more and more difficult for a parent to maintain authority and control when the very structure of the parenting arrangements themselves is a matter in dispute between parent and child. If there is another parent who wants the child to live with him or her, and is not supportive of the existing parenting arrangements, the difficulties in maintaining parental authority and control in this situation are exacerbated.

It follows that the strength and durability of children's views are more important to decision-making in parenting disputes than their age, maturity, and freedom from parental influence. A child's views may be strongly influenced by one parent. Those views may be the product of alienation by one parent, or the need to protect a parent from the loss associated with an adverse decision. Whatever its aetiology, if the court concludes that a child's view is strong and likely to be sustained, and that consequently the child will not adapt to a decision which is contrary to what they want, the court must be concerned about whether the decision will prove to be in their best interests, however much it may appear to be in their best interests in the abstract.

Seeing the issue of children's views in that way again obviates the need to worry too much about the influences on children's wishes. If the issue is not whether the dispute should be resolved by deference to the child's choice, but rather whether the child's views are such as to make it difficult for a decision that is contrary to that choice to be workable, then the question of influence and pressure takes on a different dimension. If, for example, the child is merely echoing the words of a parent and has not internalized those views for him or herself, then those views are unlikely to be strong and durable, and the echo may fade away as the conflict recedes. In other situations, the importance of the parental influence lies in what it says about the level of responsibility of the parent and the extent to which he or she is involving the child in the hostilities. The influence thus may be a window on the capacities of each parent to promote a meaningful relationship with the other and to protect the children from conflict.

8.3.3 Explore children's perspectives, not their 'wishes'

Lawyers are used to speaking about the 'wishes' of the child. The court has to make a decision. The parents have put different proposals. What then are the views of the child on those competing proposals? What does the child want? The legal focus on a child's 'wishes' may even be applied to very young children.[16]

As some parents in this study observed, involving children in decision-making about the parenting arrangements after separation requires greater sophistication than simply asking them to express a *wish* in relation to the choices that are before the court. Asking about a child's wishes in relation to specified parenting arrangements demands that children see the issues through adult eyes and within the framework of the matters to be determined by the court. This may not be how the child perceives the issues. When the focus is on the parents' competing proposals, children are not being asked to offer their perspectives, views and experiences of the world as they see it but to express a choice about an issue as adults see it. This may mean that children's unfiltered perspectives and experiences concerning their family life and parenting arrangements cannot be heard by the court because it is seeking to explore those issues only through the lens of the matters that the court has to determine. Children's participation should not be adult-centric.

Children's perspectives are of course, only part of the picture when determining parenting arrangements, as indeed they are in relation to any family decision in both separated and non-separated families. There are long-term as well as short-term issues to be considered. Younger children in particular are unlikely to be able to assess their long-term needs. Nonetheless, their perspectives on issues at the time of the dispute are an important part of the decision-making matrix, not least because the children may be so badly affected by the disruption to their lives in the aftermath of separation, and by the conflict which has given rise to legal proceedings.

Focusing on children's perspectives rather than their 'wishes' has five advantages. First, it provides information which will help to assess how the competing proposals for parenting arrangements will impact upon the children without needing to ask them, even obliquely, to express a view about the different options and choices. As both parents and counsellors pointed out, even quite young children may have, and be able to articulate, perspectives on their needs at that particular point in time which offer decision-makers insights on how particular decisions could affect them. In particular, children's views are an important window on their attachments. Without asking a child to express a choice between the parents' different positions, it is usually possible to discern where the child's primary attachments lie. In circumstances where the child does not have a strong attachment to both parents, then this will be important to the decision

[16] In *Sahin v Germany* (Application no. 30943/96, 8 July 2003), for example, the Chamber of the European Court of Human Rights considered that the expert should have directly questioned a 3-year-old girl about whether she wanted to see her father because: 'Correct and complete information on the child's relationship to the applicant as the parent seeking access to the child is an indispensable prerequisite for establishing a child's true wishes and thereby striking a fair balance between the interests at stake' (*Sahin v Germany*, decision of the Chamber, at para 48). This position was rejected by the Grand Chamber on further review.

concerning the outcome of many parenting disputes where primary care is the major issue in contention. The risk of such indirect assessments, if not handled well, however, is that older children may feel that they have been 'tricked' into providing a preference when they did not wish to do so.[17]

Secondly, children's perspectives may assist in resolving the dispute, as the evidence about child-inclusive mediation in Australia indicates,[18] and as many counsellors and mediators in this study pointed out. For example, a child may express a strong desire to stay at her present school because of her close friendships there. Where both parents acknowledge and accept this, and it represents a viable option, then continuity of schooling may become a fixed point on the horizon that provides direction for them in working out which options are likely to be possible and which are not both in terms of the property and financial issues, and the parenting arrangements. Even if matters cannot be resolved by agreement, the perspectives children may be able to offer on what they like most to do with each parent, or about aspects of their environment, may provide information to parents in resolving disputes (particularly where they have the benefit of advice from social-science trained professionals). They may also be very helpful to judges in the small percentage of cases that go to trial.

Thirdly, focusing on children's perspectives rather than their wishes avoids the pitfalls involved in making children de facto decision-makers or placing upon them the intolerable burden of choice between their parents' proposals. Many parents in this study who were less supportive of children's participation were concerned about the loyalty conflicts for children who might be worried about disappointing one parent or the other. As has been noted, children also were worried about this, as were professionals. Exploring children's perspectives on family life, while not requiring children to take a position on the issues before the court, avoids putting them in a position of loyalty conflicts.

Fourthly, seeing the issue of participation in terms of perspectives rather than wishes allows the child's voice to be heard at whatever age and stage they may have reached without worrying about their maturity.

Finally, seeing children's participation in terms of children's views and perspectives rather than children's wishes offers a potential resolution about the role of children's legal representatives in family law proceedings. One of the problems with the 'best interests' view of advocacy on behalf of children is that the view the

---

[17] Two small studies, an earlier US PhD study by Meehan, cited by Trinder, and another more recent Australian study, both cite children who were upset by what they saw as 'trick' questions or 'subtle attempts' by custody evaluators or report writers to ascertain their preferences rather than asking them directly. See Trinder, L, 'Competing Constructions of Childhood: Children's Rights and Children's Wishes in Divorce' (1997) 19 *Journal of Social Welfare and Family Law* 291–305 and Darlington, Y, 'Experiences of Custody Evaluation: Perspectives of Young Adults Who Were the Subject of Family Court Proceedings as Children' (2006) 3 *Journal of Child Custody* 51–66.

[18] McIntosh, J, Y Wells, B Smyth and C Long, 'Child-Focused and Child-Inclusive Divorce Mediation: Comparative Outcomes from a Prospective Study of Postseparation Adjustment' (2008) 46 *Family Court Review* 105–124.

lawyer takes of the children's best interests need not be informed by children's voices at all. On the other hand, a model of advocacy for children which is based upon the child's 'instructions' assumes an adult model of representation in which lawyers are merely the agents of a principal who is directing the case to be run on his or her behalf. Applying that model to children in the family law context involves them taking a position on the issues in the litigation that may place them in the centre of their parents' conflicts and require them to take sides.

If the lawyer's role is to present the child's views and perspectives, to lead evidence in support of the positions they reflect, and to examine witnesses in the light of them, the child's voice can be heard in the proceedings, and proper weight be given to those views, without the child's lawyer taking a position in the conflict on behalf of the child that means siding with one parent against the other.

8.3.4 Distinguish between different kinds of decisions on which children's views may be invited

Sometimes, decision-making in family law involves making binary choices between irreconcilable alternatives. Once it was often so, but it is no longer, and this change in the nature of disputes about children allows much more room than a generation ago for children to participate in decision-making.

The focus on children's 'wishes' by lawyers and judges may well have its origins in a view of parenting arrangements after separation that is losing much of its currency. In the old law of custody, as it was understood and practised some 30 years ago, custody decisions involved a definitive and binary choice between one home and another.[19] Either the children should live with their mother or their father. The loser would receive the compensatory award of access.

In recent years, family law systems all over the Western world have been experiencing profound changes. One of these is that non-resident parents, mostly fathers, have been vocal in the political arena[20] about their dissatisfaction with levels of contact with their children.[21] At the same time, there is strong evidence that many children want more time with their non-resident parent,[22] as was the

---

[19] Théry, I, 'The Interest of the Child and the Regulation of the Post-Divorce Family' (1986) 14 *International Journal of the Sociology of Law* 341–358; Parkinson, P, 'Family Law and the Indissolubility of Parenthood' (2006) 40 *Family Law Quarterly* 237–280.

[20] Geldof, B, 'The Real Love that Dare not Speak its Name: A Sometimes Coherent Rant' in A Bainham, B Lindley, M Richards and L Trinder (eds), *Children and their Families: Contact, Rights and Welfare* (Hart Publishing, 2003) pp 171–200; Smith, W, 'Dads Want Their Day: Fathers Charge Legal Bias Towards Moms Hamstrings them as Full-Time Parents' (2003) 89 *ABA Journal* 38–43.

[21] Parkinson, P and B Smyth, 'Satisfaction and Dissatisfaction with Father–Child Contact Arrangements in Australia' (2004) 16 *Child and Family Law Quarterly* 289–304.

[22] A number of studies have indicated that children often want more frequent contact and more flexibility in their contact arrangements with their non-resident parent, with flexibility becoming increasingly important as children get older and their needs and interests change (Wallerstein, J S and J B Kelly, *Surviving the Break Up: How Children and Parents Cope with Divorce* (Grant

finding of this study. About a third of the children wanted more time with their non-resident parent in a cohort where just over half were in contested matters. As a result of pressures for change, laws have been amended in many jurisdictions to encourage a greater level of shared parenting,[23] and whether it is as a consequence of such changes or otherwise, a number of jurisdictions are seeing a significant growth in the proportion of shared parenting arrangements following relationship breakdown.[24]

While there are many parenting disputes which are binary in character, for example because the parents live in different cities or because the issue is whether or not the parent will be allowed any contact at all with a child, frequently disputes between parents give rise to a spectrum of possible options. In addition to the traditional custody and access arrangement in which one parent is the primary carer and the other one has weekend and holiday contact, there are many other options which can be generated, at least if the parents live within reasonable proximity of one another. There are variations on equal time arrangements, arrangements for a mixture of daytime and overnight contact during the week, options of long weekend care from Friday after school to Monday morning, and a range of other possibilities, including non-face-to-face contact, which would give to non-resident parents a substantial involvement in the lives of their children not only at weekends but also between Mondays and Fridays during term times.[25] Indeed, when the children are very young, frequent contact for shorter periods

McIntyre, 1980); Walczak, Y and S Burns, *Divorce: The Child's Point of View* (Harper & Row, 1984); Neugebauer, R, 'Divorce, Custody and Visitation: The Child's Point of View' (1989) 12 *Journal of Divorce* 153–168; McDonald, M, *Children's Perceptions of Access and their Adjustment in the Post-Separation Period* (Research report no. 9, Family Court of Australia, Office of the Chief Executive, 1990); Smith, A and M Gollop, 'Children's Perspectives on Access Visits' (June 2001) *Butterworths Family Law Journal* 259–266). As young adults, children of divorce also report a yearning to have had more time with their fathers (Fabricius, W V and J A Hall, 'Young Adults' Perspectives on Divorce: Living Arrangements' (2000) 38 *Family and Conciliation Courts Review* 446–461; Laumann-Billings, L and R Emery, 'Distress among Young Adults from Divorced Families' (2000) 14 *Journal of Family Psychology* 671–687).

[23] Rhoades, H, 'The Rise and Rise of Shared Parenting Laws' (2002) 19 *Canadian Journal of Family Law* 75–113; Parkinson, P, 'The Past Caretaking Standard in Comparative Perspective' in R Wilson (ed), *Reconceiving the Family: Critical Reflections on the American Law Institute's Principles of the Law of Family Dissolution* (Cambridge University Press, 2006) pp 446–471.

[24] Melli, M S, P R Brown and M Cancian, 'Child Custody in a Changing World: A Study of Post-Divorce Arrangements in Wisconsin' (1997) *University of Illinois Law Review* 773–800; Smyth, B and L Moloney, 'Changes in Patterns of Post-Separation Parenting over Time: A Brief Review' (2008) 14 *Journal of Family Studies* 7–22.

[25] Smyth, B, 'Parent-Child Contact in Australia: Exploring Five Different Post-Separation Patterns of Parenting' (2005) 19 *International Journal of Law, Policy and the Family* 1–22; Smyth, B, 'Time to Rethink Time? The Experience of Children After Divorce' (2005) 71 *Family Matters* 4–10; Kelly, J, 'Parenting Plan Models: Ideas and Examples' in B Smyth, N Richardson and G Soriano (eds), *Proceedings of the International Forum on Family Relationships in Transition: Legislative, Practical and Policy Responses*, Canberra 1–2 December 2005 (Australian Institute of Family Studies, 2006).

is positively encouraged by leading experts on parenting after separation though this is a contentious issue.[26]

The availability of a range of options changes the burden of choice for children in many cases. Instead of having to make a clear choice between two irreconcilable alternatives, the options of different parenting arrangements offering more or less shared parenting between two households provide multiple decisions on which children may wish to express a view and on which they ought to be able to express a view. This would make for better decisions, as the children themselves said in this study. No longer are such parenting decisions governed by the need to make a choice of custodial parent and then to fit the access of the other parent into one or other of a limited number of predefined formulae. There may well be a dispute about who should be primary carer, but more often than not the issue nowadays is not who the primary carer should be—for that continues from the pre-separation situation—but how much parenting time the other parent will have.[27] The options then range from just weekend and holiday contact through to an equal time arrangement.

When parents live within a reasonable proximity of one another, there are likely to be multiple options for sharing the parenting, to a greater or lesser extent, that could be explored. Those options will depend on the circumstances, how close the relationship is between the children and each parent, and the pattern of parents' workforce participation. Involving children in negotiating the detail of the arrangements for how their weeks will be allocated between the parents offers the possibility not only that the arrangements will work optimally for the children, but also that the children may be able to suggest options that the parents have not considered.[28]

Even if both parents want to be the primary carer, and an equal time arrangement is not practicable for various reasons including the distance between the homes, there is substantial middle ground on which the children's views may be sought. Whether they live the majority of the time with their mother or with their father, they are likely to spend some time, perhaps substantial time, with the other parent. They may well have views on how those arrangements should be structured, whether they would rather have fewer, longer visits to the other parent or more frequent, but shorter visits. They may have views about how those visits fit in with their extra-curricular activities such as weekend sport, or time with friends. They may also have views based upon their experience of the arrangements that

---

[26] Lamb, M E, R Sternberg and R A Thompson, 'The Effects of Divorce and Custody Arrangements on Children's Behavior, Development, and Adjustment' (1997) 35 *Family and Conciliation Courts Review* 393–404; Solomon, J and Z Biringen, 'The Continuing Debate about Overnight Visitation: Another Look at the Developmental Research: Commentary on Kelly and Lamb's "Using Child Development Research to Make Appropriate Custody and Access Decisions for Young Children"' (2001) 39 *Family and Conciliation Courts Review* 355–364.

[27] Rešetar, B and R Emery, 'Children's Rights in European Legal Proceedings: Why Are Family Practices So Different from Legal Theories?' (2008) 46 *Family Court Review* 65–77, at 65.

[28] Chisholm, n 11 above, at 218.

are currently in place. They can be asked about the arrangements that they would prefer without asking them to make a choice about which parent they should primarily live with. The focus that lawyers in particular, seemed to have on children's views concerning the parents' competing proposals, risks missing the rich information that might be gathered from children about what will work best for them in terms of the details of the parenting arrangements.

Beyond issues of time with each parent, children may also have a view on the circumstances of the living arrangements with each parent. These issues might be relatively straightforward, concerning the lack of activities or toys at one home, for example, or they might be more difficult, involving children's resentment or unhappiness about the intrusion of their parent's new partner. Either way, these issues are more likely to be resolved if children's views and perspectives are brought into the picture.

It follows that whether and how children are given an opportunity to participate in expressing a choice about the parenting arrangements ought to depend, inter alia, on the kinds of choices that are before the court. Children should be protected from loyalty conflicts. The concerns about a tug-of-war arise when the issues are presented as an either/or choice between two parents who are both loved. We cannot assume, of course, that a close attachment to both parents exists. In this study, there had been an irretrievable breakdown in the relationship between a number of the children and one of their parents, mainly in circumstances of violence and abuse. In such circumstances, the children did not feel safe and cared for and there was little loyalty conflict; the depths of children's feelings need to be heard. In other situations, however, the dangers of a loyalty conflict are very real.

Children's participation ought to be the greatest when there is substantial middle ground that can be explored, for the child is not being asked to choose necessarily either the mother's ground or the father's. It may well be that in exploring that middle ground it becomes clear that there are no options for compromise that are going to be suitable options for the child, in which case there may have to be a choice between the alternative positions of the mother and father. However, exploring the compromise options need not be confronting, nor need it place children in a position of loyalty conflicts. It can be a discussion about practicalities rather than loyalties.

There is, of course, a danger that in trying to be fair to both parents, the children will come up with a compromise that involves them in bearing the burden of satisfying the competing demands. As counsellors noted in this study, many children and young people feel a need to be fair to both parents.[29] However, this does not mean that the solution they come up with is not the best one in the circumstances. Children's views may be motivated, at least in part, by the desire to be fair to both parents. However, they are not the less real and deeply held for

---

[29] See also Parkinson et al, n 14 above.

that. Children are not autonomous individuals whose ideas and opinions can be isolated from their family circumstances.[30]

Conversely, in disputes in which the parents' proposals are mutually exclusive, and there is a very narrow range of options, considerable caution needs to be exercised before involving children in offering choices. In a case, for example, where the children's primary carer wants to move with the children to another continent, and both parents have hitherto been actively involved in the children's lives, there may be no middle ground between allowing the relocation and refusing permission. In such circumstances, the parents may be presenting to the court a stark either/or choice, and if children are asked which option they would prefer, they may well feel they are being asked to choose between their parents. Even more poignant are those relocation cases in which one parent makes it clear that she or he will be going with or without the child. Asking children in this circumstance to choose between two stark choices, each of which is deeply painful, is to invite them to make a choice that they should never be asked to make, akin to asking them which of two legs they would rather lose.

The more that conversations with children about parenting disputes focus on the issues in dispute between the parents, and the competing proposals of the parents, the more danger there is that children will be placed in a tug-of-war situation. Children may unwittingly be dragged into the conflict, with each parent trying to persuade them to their point of view, when what is best for them is to be shielded, as far as possible, from the parents' conflict. Such participation is unlikely to be in the best interests of the child concerned. There is a danger that conversations with children will focus on the competing proposals of the parents as a consequence of child representation if lawyers selected for this role are poorly chosen or inadequately trained.

Furthermore, where the choice is presented as one between the competing proposals of the parents, there is the greatest risk of undue influence and manipulation by the parents.[31] Even if this is not really so in a given case, the perception of one parent that the child is being pressured or manipulated by the other parent is itself damaging to that parent's confidence in the process of resolving the dispute. A number of the non-resident parents in this study who had concerns about children's participation in court proceedings expressed their fears about manipulation by the resident parent, either with reference to their own case, or more generally. The perception of procedural fairness is as important as the reality of it. When the legal system invites children to express a choice between their parents' competing proposals, and a parent has concerns about undue influence

---

[30] Smart et al, n 2 above, p 109:

... what children seem to want is social recognition, respect and inclusion rather than simply legal rights. They do not appear to want to be free, autonomous individuals but persons in their own right in the context of a web of relationships.

[31] Warshak, R A, 'Payoffs and Pitfalls of Listening to Children' (2003) 52 *Family Relations* 373–384.

or pressure by the other parent, the result may be a lack of faith in the justice system itself.

8.3.5 Follow certain guidelines about judicial interviews

There is a great diversity of international practice on the issue of judicial conversations with children in the course of deciding parenting disputes, both on whether judges should talk with the children concerned in parenting disputes, and if so, how this should be done.[32]

The majority of Australian judges interviewed for this study were against the practice and indicated that they would rarely or never talk directly with a child.[33] A minority of judges strongly supported the practice. Similarly, the majority of lawyers and counsellors were opposed to judges talking with children, largely because they believed that judges were mostly ill-equipped to do so or out of concerns for procedural justice. That division of opinion has been observed also in some other jurisdictions. However, in other jurisdictions, such as Scotland,[34] Germany[35] and New Zealand,[36] the practice is much more widely accepted.

Whether or not it is desirable for judges to talk with children directly may depend, at least in part, on what other options are available for hearing children's voices. In jurisdictions where there is not a well-established and funded system for having reports from social-science trained professionals who can talk with children as part of the process of evaluating the family circumstances, having the judge talk with the children is likely to be much better than not having the children's voices heard at all.[37]

The largest group of parents in this study considered that children should talk to counsellors or some other independent person of that kind. The next largest group of parents indicated that the judge, either alone or together with a counsellor, would be the best option. It is clear from the interviews with the children in this study that while most think that children should have the option of talking

---

[32] See, for example, Atwood, B, 'The Child's Voice in Custody Litigation: An Empirical Survey and Suggestions for Reform' (2003) 45 *Arizona Law Review* 629–690; Williams, n 14 above.

[33] See Chapter 7.

[34] Raitt, F, 'Hearing Children in Family Law Proceedings: Can Judges Make a Difference?' (2007) 19 *Child and Family Law Quarterly* 204–224.

[35] Carl, E, *Giving Children their own Voice in Family Court Proceedings: A German Perspective* (4th World Congress on Family Law and Children's Rights, Cape Town, South Africa, 20–23 March 2005).

[36] Boshier, P, 'Involving Children in Decision-Making: Lessons from New Zealand' (2006) 20 *Australian Journal of Family Law* 145–153; Tapp, P, 'Judges are Human Too: Conversation Between the Judge and a Child as a Means of Giving Effect to Section 6 of the Care of Children Act 2004' (2006) *New Zealand Law Review* 35–74.

[37] For a discussion of the relative benefits of expert and judicial interviews in the US context, see Crosby-Currie, C A, 'Children's Involvement in Contested Custody Cases: Practices and Experiences of Legal and Mental Health Professionals' (1996) 20 *Law and Human Behavior* 289–311.

to the judge, some would have found it intimidating for themselves and preferred talking to a counsellor or to keep it within the family. Many of the counsellors, lawyers and judges who were interviewed also expressed concerns about an interview with the judge being intimidating for the child.

However, it was apparent from the interviews with the judges who had talked with children in the course of deciding cases that this could sometimes be a very useful strategy in addition to the information provided in the family report. In some cases, the advantage of speaking with the children directly was to persuade the judge of the strength of the children's views, reinforcing what the family report had already indicated. In other situations, a family report was not available or not up to date, or the matter was urgent, and talking with the children directly was the best way to resolve the issues.

Judges reported that children's perspectives could be important in determining how the child might react to different decisions that the court might make. For example, a pre-adolescent child may have expressed a very clear view on future parenting arrangements, while an expert, for sound reasons, proposes a resolution of the matter which goes against the strongly held views of that child. In such situations, participation may involve exploring with the child how they would respond if another decision was taken which did not correspond with their preferences.[38]

Judges who spoke in favour of talking with children in this study did not want this to replace the normal system of hearing children's voices through family reports and having counsel for children. They saw it as an additional method of gaining information about the case in certain circumstances.

On an issue where views among judges diverge so widely, there is value in guidelines that will not only provide a model of best practice to those judges who do want to meet with children,[39] and in jurisdictions where it is required or expected, but will also provide reassurance to other judges, and indeed lawyers, who have grave reservations about the matter. In the light of the interviews conducted for this study, the following guidelines are suggested.

There is a recommendation from the family report writer or the counsel for the child to do so or circumstances of urgency make it the optimal course

The professionals who have had most to do with the child are in the best position to know whether it would be helpful to the child to talk with the judge. There will

---

[38] In *R and R* (2000) 155 FLR 29, the Full Court of the Family Court of Australia indicated that family report writers should routinely talk to children about how they would feel if the decision went against the children's wishes so that the judge can be aware of how children might react to such a decision.

[39] For earlier guidelines drawn up by three Canadian judges, see Abella, R S, C L' Heureux-Dubé and M L Rothman, 'A Code of Recommended Procedures in the Resolution of Family Law Disputes' in R S Abella and C L' Heureux-Dubé (eds), *Family Law: Dimensions of Justice* (Butterworths, 1983) pp 321–330, at 329.

be situations where it is contra-indicated. In a situation where the report writer or counsel for the child considers there has been coaching or manipulation, then there may well be nothing to gain from another discussion with the judge and some detriment from so doing. In a situation where a child has been put under a lot of pressure from one or both parents to make a particular choice, or is feeling an acute loyalty conflict, then having a conversation with the judge may actually be damaging.

The welfare professionals involved with the child are in the best position to decide whether it would be helpful to give the children an opportunity to talk with the judge either before or after the judge reaches a decision. Since judges vary so much in their willingness to talk with children, the onus is probably on the judge in the first instance to raise with the counsel for the child or welfare professional the option of talking to the child if the judge thinks it may be appropriate. One reason why it may be appropriate is to make sure the child is feeling heard through the counsel for the child and family report writer and not, for example, being misinterpreted, according to the child. Another reason is to help the young person to accept the decision. If the child has confidence in the decision-maker, the decision is more likely to be accepted and 'work'.[40]

There are of course situations of urgency where it is not possible to rely on the advice of a welfare professional who has seen the child. This is also likely to be the case in interim matters where there has been a limited involvement of welfare professionals with the family at that point in time. Such decisions really have to be made on a case-by-case basis, taking account of the exigencies of the moment. The principle ought to be, however, that the judge should seek the view of a welfare professional who has had the opportunity of talking with the children, or at least the parents, if it is at all possible to do so.

The parties agree or the judge is satisfied that it is in the best interests of the child to meet even without a parent's agreement

Many of the risks of perceived unfairness expressed by Australian parents and judges in this study can be alleviated if the parties agree to the process and how it will be done. If the parents have agreed, and agree also on the details of how the conversation will be recorded and reported back, then the grounds for complaint about the process on an appeal are strictly circumscribed.[41]

This study indicates that many non-resident parents in particular have concerns about judicial interviews. If there is a parental objection, then it would risk the perceived integrity of the process for the judge to talk to the children.

However, there may be circumstances where the court-appointed welfare professional advises that a judge should see a child even though one party objects or

---

[40] This is one of the principles and findings of procedural justice research. See also Lind et al, n 1 above; Chisholm, n 11 above; Gollop et al, n 14 above.

[41] See, for example, *Andrusiek v Andrusiek* (2002) 25 RFL (5th) 8 (British Columbia).

has reservations. Such situations are most likely to arise where it is perceived that there will be a therapeutic benefit to the child to be able to talk directly to the judge about his or her situation. As the views of a parent and the needs of a child may be in conflict, the judge ought to have a discretion to talk with a child notwithstanding the objection of a parent.[42] The principles for so doing have been well articulated by Martinson J in a decision in British Columbia:[43]

[T]he court has jurisdiction to interview the children, even in the absence of the consent of both parents…A judge must consider, on a case by case basis, whether conducting such an interview is in the best interests of the child in question…

In doing so, the judge can consider the general purposes of such an interview, and the general benefits of and concerns relating to the judge interview process. In addition, the judge can consider case specific factors by looking at the relevance of the information that would be obtained to the issues that have to be decided, the reliability of the information, and the necessity of conducting the interview rather than obtaining the information in another way.

The question of whether a parent consents to an interview is not irrelevant. While a parent cannot simply veto an interview, a parent's specific reasons for withholding consent may be important to a determination of relevance, reliability, and necessity.

The child has either requested to talk with the judge or has agreed to do so

If a major purpose of judicial interviews is to help the child to feel heard, and therefore to be more accepting of the decision, then it follows that judicial interviews should occur only at the request of or with the consent of the child. This ought to be the case whether the conversation occurs before or after decision.

There is at least an audiotape of the discussion and report available on the record to indicate what was said

In case issues are raised about what was said, a visual or audio recording should be made. This ought to be made available to the parties on request. A visual recording is preferable if the facilities available allow for this. However, such equipment should be as unobtrusive as possible, and this may in practice mean that only an audio recording is feasible.

A welfare professional should be present and should report back in open court

A welfare professional, preferably the family report writer, should be present at all such meetings except where, in exceptional circumstances, no one is available. If a welfare professional is not available, then someone else such as the judge's

---

[42] This is also the position that has been taken in Canada (*Hamilton v Hamilton* (1989) 20 RFL (3d) 152 (Sask CA); *Jandrisch v Jandrisch* (1980) 16 RFL (2d) 239 (Man CA)).

[43] *G (LE) v G (A)* 2002 CarswellBC 2643 (BCSC) at paras 3, 5–6.

associate or a counsel for the child should be present. The welfare professional may conduct some or all of the conversation and write it up. These are matters that could be discussed with the parties and counsel for the child. Even if the judge prefers to talk with the child directly, the welfare professional should not merely be seen as a witness and record-keeper of the meeting. In particular where the welfare professional knows the child, he or she may play a useful role in facilitating the conversation and ensuring that the child gets across what he or she wants to say to the judge.

In our view, it is insufficient that only the counsel for the child is there, at least in jurisdictions where a welfare professional employed by the court or with a role of assisting the court, is readily available to the judge.[44] The counsel for the child is an advocate, not a witness, and the report back to the court should take the form of evidence. This does not mean that the welfare professional should be able to be cross-examined on what questions the judge asked. If there are issues about that, then the appropriate course would probably be to adjourn the matter and to give the side contesting the child's views an opportunity to call evidence from a social scientist who has seen the videotape or heard the audiotape. However, the parties need to be given an opportunity to ask the welfare professional questions about his or her observations of the child's demeanour and other such matters.

The child should be told, whether and to what extent discussions with the judge are confidential

Many children in our study saw one advantage of talking with the judge was that they could say things without their parents knowing in order to avoid hurting them or being punished.

There was a universal view expressed by judges in this study that the judge cannot receive confidential communications. The parties to any dispute must know the evidence on which the judge relies, have an opportunity to test that evidence, and be able to make submissions in relation to that evidence. The counsel for the child is the one to whom the child ought to be able to speak confidentially.

Not every jurisdiction takes the same view. In some, confidential communications with a judge are accepted. Whatever the position may be, the issue of confidentiality needs to be clear. The child may otherwise have a different understanding from the judge about whether his or her views will be reported back to their parents.

---

[44] Contrast the view of Bala et al, writing in relation to Canada who argue that the counsel for the child should always be present (Bala, N, V Talwar and J Harris, 'The Voice of the Child in Canadian Family Law Cases' (2005) 24 *Canadian Family Law Quarterly* 221–274, at 250). The justification given by Bala et al for having the counsel for the child present is that he or she can ensure that the child's position is clearly communicated to the judge, and may also facilitate communication between the child and the judge.

8.3.6 Consider children's views with the aid of social-science expertise

One of the concerns expressed about judicial interviews, particularly by the professionals in the system (including the judges themselves), was that judges do not have the training or skills to assess what the children are saying to them and to discern the influences there may have been upon the formation of the children's views. Some parents were also concerned about the issue of manipulation and whether judges would be able to discern and take account of this when it occurred. Lawyers also, who represent children, may not have those skills.

This is one of the most difficult issues in relation to children's participation. The cases that go to trial in the family law jurisdiction are usually the most intractable, with high levels of conflict and much at stake. In these cases, either there are significant safety concerns, or there is very little room for compromise or one or both parents find it too difficult to make concessions in order to resolve the dispute. Whatever view may be taken about children as social actors in the general population, it must be recognized that the cases that go to trial are of unusual difficulty.

The role of the social-science trained professional is critical in providing some understanding of the context of children's views. Those views are formed within the context in which children live, and particularly the nature of their relationships with other family members. As counsellors noted in this study, it is vital that when children's views are considered, they are appropriately contextualized and considered in the light of all the other information that can be provided about the family circumstances and relationships. This is a role that a custody evaluator or other such social-science trained professional is best qualifed to play. One of their tasks is to try to discern when children's voices have, in Warshak's words, been 'dubbed with the words of the parent who exercises the most influence over him or her'[45] and whether those views have been internalized by the child. They should also be able to provide other information about the child's relationship with each parent and what significance ought to be given to the child's view in the circumstances.

The risk for children is that their views are discounted because of the perceived influence, pressure or manipulation of one or both parents. Certainly some children in our study and in others indicated their unhappiness about having their views filtered or misinterpreted by counsellors without recourse to any means of correcting it. They were also upset by unexpected reporting of their views to their parents in breach of what they thought were confidential conversations. Counsellors therefore need to address children's concern for transparency especially about the information that will be revealed to their parents. One way to do that is to check with children what they are willing to reveal to their parents and

---

[45] Warshak, n 31 above, at 375.

to ask children for their reactions to the possible options and ways to express their views.

When social-science trained experts report on the voices of children and assess them in the context of the family relationships and other circumstances of the child's life, that report is admitted into evidence. Since judges must determine the case on the basis of evidence, giving reasons for placing greater or less reliance on such evidence, the judge must consider carefully not only what the child has said but also any interpretation of those views and perspectives that are offered by the family report writer. That discipline of evaluation of the evidence, and the requirement to give reasons for the conclusions derived from the evidence, ensures both that children's voices are heard and that the judge has the benefit of expert opinion on how to contextualize and understand those views in the light of all the other evidence. This is preferable to a situation where the judge only has the benefit of talking to the child without that assistance in contextualization and evaluation.

8.3.7 Move beyond the focus on hearing children in trials

Much work has been done on methods of discerning children's views in the context of trials. Indeed, this has tended to be the primary focus of lawyers in giving effect to Article 12 of the UN Convention on the Rights of the Child. Judges in particular, are trial-oriented, for this is their core business. Lawyers too have a tendency to see the issue of children's participation in terms of how to get evidence of children's wishes into court in the context of a trial.

It is understandable that lawyers and judges should concentrate on ways to hear children in the context of court proceedings, for this is the focus of legal processes. Cases are prepared for trial unless, along the way, they can be resolved by settlement. This use of the court process as a strategy for promoting settlement has been termed 'litigotiation'.[46]

However, a focus on hearing children in trials is a focus on a small minority of families. The great majority of family law issues in Western countries are resolved without the need for a judge to make the final decisions. The evidence from the UK is that only about 10% of separated parents have court orders at all.[47] In Australia, only about 6% of cases filed in the Family Court are resolved by a judge following a trial.[48] The remainder are settled. In the litigotiation process, children may or may not be heard, depending on the jurisdiction and

---

[46] Galanter, M, 'Worlds of Deals: Using Negotiation to Teach about Legal Process' (1984) 34 *J Legal Education* 268–276.

[47] Hunt, J and C Roberts, *Child Contact with Non-Resident Parents* (Family Policy Briefing 3, Department of Social Policy and Social Work, University of Oxford, 2004).

[48] House of Representatives, Standing Committee on Family and Community Affairs, *Every Picture Tells a Story: Report of the Inquiry into Child Custody Arrangements in the Event of Family Separation* (Parliament of Australia, 2003), pp 6–7.

how far along the litigation pathway the case travels. Children's voices may, for example, be heard through professionals who are appointed in order to assist the court in resolving the matter. These include social scientists, who prepare family reports, and child representatives. Even if one includes cases that settle after an opportunity has been given for the child's voice to be heard in the course of legal proceedings either through a report writer or child representative, it is still a small minority of children who benefit from the processes of hearing children's voices which dominate discussion of the issue in legal circles.

For these reasons, it is important to think about children's participation outside of the legal paradigm as well. The fact that parents resolve the parenting arrangements without requiring a judge to make a decision does not necessarily mean that the issues were resolved either amicably or well. Acquiescence, abandonment and self-help are all means by which disputes are brought to an end without reaching an agreement. Nor is there any reason to believe that arrangements made outside of a legal process are more likely to be sensitive to children's perspectives.[49]

Child-inclusive mediation, discussed in Chapter 3, offers one way to include children's voices in the processes for resolving disputes without the necessity for court proceedings, and this kind of process was supported by lawyers who favoured greater involvement of children in resolving parenting disputes. Lawyers and counsellors may also be able to help parents to listen sensitively to their children in the course of working through the most appropriate parenting arrangements for that point in time. In our research, there was a disconnect between what parents believed about the importance of children having a say and the experience of the children themselves. While the idea of giving children a say was endorsed by 87% of parents, only 60% of children reported that they actually had a say. This was only partially related to age. Four out of 23 children aged 12 and over reported having no say in the parenting arrangements, as did 12 out of 20 of the under 12 year olds.

Children's experiences were discordant from their views. Nine out of ten children said that they should be heard in the process of decision-making, even though most recognized that their views should just be a factor, rather than being determinative. They expressed such views even though 70% recognized that it might well put them in a difficult position.

One way in which families going through separation may be assisted in the process of organizing the parenting arrangements would be to give them help and advice on how and how not to talk with children about the issues. Such advice needs to be provided outside of the legal system and away from it. Because parenting after separation has been categorized historically as a legal issue, the

---

[49] Douglas, G, M Murch, L Scanlan and A Perry, 'Safeguarding Children's Welfare in Non-Contentious Divorce: Towards a New Conception of the Legal Process' (2000) 63 *Modern Law Review* 177–196.

tendency remains to see the provision of advice as something to be channelled through lawyers[50] or by making information available in court buildings. A variety of information and support services are needed by families after separation[51] and advice on post-separation parenting may best be channelled through community networks.[52]

A further reason for thinking about children's participation outside the legal paradigm is that the legal process, for most separating families, only occurs at one stage of their post-separation lives. Families are dynamic. Court orders are not. They are made at a certain point in time and reflect the circumstances of that time—the ages of the children, their needs at that time and, in terms of the arrangements for contact with the non-resident parent, the practicalities of enabling the parent to spend time with the children given the constraints of the distance between homes, children's schooling and their other activities. Yet the needs of a child at the age of 3 may be quite different from his or her needs at age 10, and in the intervening years many changes are likely to occur in the circumstances of the parents such as moving house, repartnering and changing jobs.

The focus on hearing the voice of the child in judicial proceedings can distract attention from the importance of involving children in decision-making about how to adjust the parenting arrangements in the light of changing circumstances and needs. Sometimes, the children themselves may want arrangements to change. A pattern of parenting that works at one time, for example that the children visit their father every alternate weekend from Friday to Sunday, may become problematic if the child starts playing a competitive sport and would let the team down if he or she could not play every other Saturday morning. A teenager who was happy with a shared care arrangement in primary school may decide that he or she does not want the constant changes of home any more.

As children get older, their capacity and willingness to articulate what they want change. Lawyers and counsellors can help parents to understand that parenting arrangements, even those made after a trial, may need to be adjusted in the light of changing circumstances in future years and that children's voices should be heard in that process, the more so as they grow older and are better able to articulate what they want.

---

[50] In England and Wales, Family Advice and Information Networks (FAInS), were established by the Legal Services Commission using lawyers as the means of information and referral (Walker, J, 'FAInS—A New Approach for Family Lawyers?' (2004) 34 *Family Law* 436–441).

[51] Douglas, G and R Moorhead, 'Providing Advice for Lone Parents: From Parent to Citizen' (2005) 17 *Child and Family Law Quarterly* 55–74; Parkinson, P, 'Keeping in Contact: The Role of Family Relationship Centres in Australia' (2006) 18 *Child and Family Law Quarterly* 157–174.

[52] In Australia, the Child Support Agency fulfils an important informational role. It reaches the great majority of parents because most use its services for assessment and updating of child support obligations, if not for collection. It has produced a number of helpful booklets on coping with separation and parenting after separation which are in wide circulation, not only through the Agency itself but other avenues such as child care services.

8.4 Conclusion

In thinking about the whole landscape of children's participation, and the variety of issues on which their input may be sought, there is no more difficult issue than working out how to give them a say in parenting disputes. The protective approach to the involvement of children in such disputes has a sound basis. Yet the rationale for involving them more in decision-making also has a sound basis. Reconciling these conflicting positions, and those who advocate for them, is a complex problem.

The way forward is to abandon the idea that children's best interests can be served by protection from participation, and to find ways of protecting them in participation. By reframing also why it is that we want to hear the voices of children, and the issues on which children's views will most readily be sought, we can avoid the problem of placing them in the midst of loyalty conflicts and subjecting them to parental pressure and manipulation.

All of this, however, depends on the commitment of governments to resource the family law system appropriately. Australia has the advantage over some other jurisdictions that it has long had a tradition of public funding for family reports and for independent children's lawyers. The parents, children, counsellors, lawyers and judges who were interviewed for the purposes of this study had experience of numerous different ways in which children's voices could be heard. More recently, child-inclusive mediation has emerged as another important way to hear the voices of children.

Other jurisdictions do not have the same history, traditions or resources made available to give children a voice. However, the principles suggested in this chapter are capable of application in a variety of different legal traditions and with different approaches to hearing the voice of the child. The UN Convention on the Rights of the Child is expressed in terms of principles, not specific processes. In such a complex area as hearing children's voices in parenting disputes, it is by reflection on those principles in the light of the history, experience and resources of each jurisdiction, that a way forward can best be found.

References

Abella, R S, C L' Heureux-Dubé and M L Rothman, 'A Code of Recommended Procedures in the Resolution of Family Law Disputes' in R S Abella and C L' Heureux-Dubé (eds), *Family Law: Dimensions of Justice* (Butterworths, 1983) pp 321–330.

Ackerman, J, M C Ackerman, L L Steffen and S Kelley-Poulos, 'Psychologists' Practices Compared to the Expectations of Family Law Judges and Attorneys in Child Custody Cases' (2004) 1 *Journal of Child Custody* 41–60.

Ackers, L, 'From "Best Interests" to Participatory Rights: Children's Involvement in Family Migration Decisions' (Working Paper 18, Centre for Research on Family, Kinship and Childhood, University of Leeds, 2000).

Alderson, P and V Morrow, *Ethics, Social Research and Consulting with Children and Young People* (Barnardos, 2004).

Aldgate, J and J Statham, *The Children Act Now: Messages from Research* (The Stationery Office, 2001).

Allen, J, 'Child Custody—Some Aspects of the Problem' in P E Nygh (ed), *Seminar on the Problems of Child Custody* (Sydney University Law Graduates Association Family Law Committee, 1972).

Amato, P, 'The Consequences of Divorce for Adults and Children' (2000) 62 *Journal of Marriage and Family* 1269–1287.

——'Children of Divorce in the 1990s: An Update of the Amato and Keith (1991) Meta-Analysis' (2001) 15 *Journal of Family Psychology* 355–370.

Amato, P R and J M Sobolewski, 'The Effects of Divorce and Marital Discord on Adult Children's Psychological Well-Being' (2001) 66 *American Sociological Review* 900–921.

Aquilino, W S, 'Two Views of One Relationship: Comparing Parents' and Young Adult Children's Reports of the Quality of Intergenerational Relations' (1999) 61 *Journal of Marriage and the Family* 858–870.

Atkinson, A, S McKay and N Dominy, *Future Policy Options For Child Support: The Views of Parents* (Department for Work and Pensions Research Report no. 380, 2006).

Atwood, B, 'The Child's Voice in Custody Litigation: An Empirical Survey and Suggestions for Reform' (2003) 45 *Arizona Law Review* 629–690. Available at: http://www.spig.clara.net/hunt.htm.

Australian Law Reform Commission and the Human Rights and Equal Opportunity Commission, *Seen and Heard: Priority for Children in the Legal Process* (ALRC Report 84) (1997) ch 13. Available at: http://www.austlii.edu.au/au/other/alrc/publications/reports/84/13.html (accessed 10 June 2008).

Bala, N, 'Assessments for Postseparation Parenting Disputes in Canada' (2004) 42 *Family Court Review* 485–506.

Bala, N, V Talwar and J Harris, 'The Voice of the Child in Canadian Family Law Cases' (2005) 24 *Canadian Family Law Quarterly* 221–274.

Baumrind, D, 'Child Care Practices Anteceding Three Patterns of Preschool Behavior' (1967) 75 *Genetic Psychology Monographs* 43–88.

——'Authoritarian v Authoritative Control' (1968) 3 *Adolescence* 255–272.

——'Effective Parenting During the Early Adolescent Transition' in P A Cowan and E M Hetherington (eds), *Advances in Family Research* (Erlbaum, 1991) vol 2, pp 111–163.

Bellamy, C and G Lord, 'Reflections on Family Proceedings Rule 9.5' (2003) 33 *Family Law* 265–269.

Bernard, J, *The Future of Marriage* (Bantam Books, 1972).

Bersoff, D, 'Representation of Children in Custody Decisions: All That Glitters is Not *Gault*' (1979) 15 *Journal of Family Law* 27–49.

Bessner, R, *The Voice of the Child in Divorce, Custody and Access Proceedings* (Family, Children and Youth Section, Department of Justice, 2002).

Bienenfeld, F, 'The Power of Child Custody Mediation' (1985) 9 *Mediation Quarterly* 35–47.

Blackman, L, *Representing Children and Young People: A Lawyers' Practice Guide* (Victoria Law Foundation, 2002).

Blaine, G B, 'The Effect of Divorce Upon the Personality Development of Children and Youth' in E A Grollman (ed), *Explaining Divorce to Children* (Beacon, 1969).

Boshier, P, 'Involving Children in Decision-Making: Lessons from New Zealand' (2006) 20 *Australian Journal of Family Law* 145–153.

Boshier, Hon P and D Steel-Baker, 'Invisible Parties: Listening to Children' (2007) 45 *Family Court Review* 548–559.

Bretherton, H, ' "Because it's me the Decisions are About"—Children's Experiences of Private Law Proceedings' [2002] 32 *Family Law* 450–457.

Bronfenbrenner, U, *The Ecology of Human Development: Experiments by Nature and Design* (Harvard University Press, 1979).

Bryant, D, 'The Role of the Family Court in Promoting Child-Centred Practice' (2006) 20 *Australian Journal of Family Law* 127–144.

Buchanan, A, J Hunt, H Bretherton and V Bream, *Families in Conflict: The Perspectives of Children and Parents on the Family Court Welfare Service* (The Policy Press, 2001).

Butler, I, L Scanlan, M Robinson, G Douglas and M Murch, 'Children's Involvement in their Parents' Divorce: Implications for Practice' (2002) 16 *Children and Society* 89–102.

——*Divorcing Children: Children's Experience of their Parents' Divorce* (Jessica Kingsley, 2003).

Cantwell, B and S Scott, 'Children's Wishes, Children's Burdens' (1995) 17 *Journal of Social Welfare and Family Law* 337–354.

Carl, E, *Giving Children their own Voice in Family Court Proceedings: A German Perspective* (Paper presented at 4th World Congress on Family Law and Children's Rights, Cape Town, South Africa, 20–23 March 2005). Available at: http://www.childjustice.org/docs/carl2005.pdf.

Carmody, T, 'Child Relocation: An Intractable International Family Law Problem' (2007) 45 *Family Court Review* 214–246.

Cashmore, J, 'Invited Commentary: Ethical Issues Concerning Consent in Obtaining Children's Reports on their Experience of Violence: Commentary on Carroll-Lind, Chapman, Gregory and Maxwell' (2006) 30 *Child Abuse and Neglect: The International Journal* 969–977.

Cashmore, J, 'Children's Participation in Family Law Matters' in C Hallett and A Prout (eds) *Hearing the Voices of Children: Social Policy for a New Century* (Routledge Falmer, 2003) pp 158–176.

Cashmore, J and K Bussey, 'Perceptions of Children and Lawyers in Care and Protection Proceedings' (1994) 8 *International Journal of Law and the Family* 319–336.

Cashmore, J and J Goodnow, 'Agreement between Generations: A Two-Process Approach' (1985) 56 *Child Development* 493–501.

Cashmore, J and P Parkinson, 'Children's and Parents' Perceptions of Children's Participation in Decision-Making after Parental Separation and Divorce' (2008) 46 *Family Court Review* 91–104.

——'Hearing the Voices of Children: The Responsibility of Courts in Relation to Criminal and Family Law' (2007) 15 *International Journal of Children's Rights* 43–60.

Ceci, S and M Bruck, 'Suggestibility of the Child Witness: A Historical Review and Synthesis' (1993) 113 *Psychological Bulletin* 403–439.

Chan, Y, R Chun, G Lam and S Lam, 'The Development of Family Mediation Services in Hong Kong: Review of an Evaluation Study' (2007) 29 *Journal of Social Welfare & Family Law* 3–16.

Chase, D J and P F Hora, 'The Implications of Therapeutic Jurisprudence for Judicial Satisfaction' (2000) 37 *Court Review* 12–19.

Chisholm, R, 'Children's Participation in Family Court Litigation' (1999) 13 *Australian Journal of Family Law* 197–218.

——'The Family Law Amendment (Shared Parental Responsibility) Bill 2006: Putting Children at Centre Stage?' paper at the *Contact and Relocation—Focusing on the Children Conference* (Byron Bay, Australia, May 2006).

Clark, B K, 'Acting in the Best Interest of the Child: Essential Components of the Child Custody Evaluation' (1995) 29 *Family Law Quarterly* 19–38.

Cook, W L and M J Goldstein, 'Multiple Perspectives on Family Relationships: A Latent Variables Model' (1993) 64 *Child Development* 1377–1388.

Cooper, D, 'More Law and More Rights: Will Children Benefit?' (1998) 3 *Child and Family Social Work* 77–86.

Crichton, N, 'Listening to Children' (2006) 36 *Family Law* 849–854.

Crosby-Currie, C A, 'Children's Involvement in Contested Custody Cases: Practices and Experiences of Legal and Mental Health Professionals' (1996) 20 *Law and Human Behavior* 289–311.

Cummings, E M and A C Schermerhorn, 'A Developmental Perspective on Children as Agents in the Family' in L Kuczynski (ed), *Handbook of Dynamics in Parent-Child Relations* (Sage Publications, 2003) pp 91–108.

Darlington, Y, 'Experiences of Custody Evaluation: Perspectives of Young Adults Who Were the Subject of Family Court Proceedings as Children' (2006) 3 *Journal of Child Custody* 51–66.

Davies, C, 'Access to Justice for Children: The Voice of the Child in Custody and Access' (2004) 22 *Canadian Family Law Quarterly* 153–175.

Day Sclater, S and C Piper, 'Social Exclusion and the Welfare of the Child' (2001) 28 *Journal of Law and Society* 409–429.

Derdyn, A P, 'Child Custody Consultation' (1975) 45 *American Journal of Ortho-psychiatry* 791–801.

Douglas, G and R Moorhead, 'Providing Advice for Lone Parents: From Parent to Citizen' (2005) 17 *Child and Family Law Quarterly* 55–74.

Douglas, G and M Murch, 'Taking Account of Children's Needs in Divorce—A Study of Family Solicitors' Responses to New Policy and Practice Initiatives' (2002) 14 *Child and Family Law Quarterly* 57–75.

Douglas, G, M Murch, C Miles and L Scanlan, *Research into the Operation of Rule 9.5 of the Family Proceedings Rules 1991* (Report to the Department of Constitutional Affairs, 2006). Available at: http://www.dca.gov.uk/family/familyprocrules_research.pdf.

Douglas, G, M Murch and A Perry, 'Supporting Children When Parents Separate—A Neglected Family Justice or Mental Health Issue?' (1996) 8 *Child and Family Law Quarterly* 121–135.

Douglas, G, M Murch, L Scanlan and A Perry, 'Safeguarding Children's Welfare in Non-Contentious Divorce: Towards a New Conception of the Legal Process' (2000) 63 *Modern Law Review* 177–196.

Duggan, D, 'Rock-Paper-Scissors: Playing the Odds with the Law of Child Relocation' (2007) 45 *Family Court Review* 193–213.

Dunn, J, 'Contact and Children's Perspectives on Parental Relationships' in A Bainham, M Lindley, M Richards and L Trinder (eds), *Children and Their Families: Contact, Rights and Welfare* (Hart Publishing, 2003) pp 15–32.

Dunn, J and K Deater-Deckard, *Children's Views of Their Changing Families* (Joseph Rowntree Foundation, 2001).

Durkheim, E, *Durkheim: Essays on Morals and Education* (Routledge and Kegan Paul, 1979).

Emery, R E, 'Children's Voices: Listening—and Deciding—is an Adult Responsibility' (2003) 45 *Arizona Law Review* 621–627.

Fabricius, W V and J A Hall, 'Young Adults' Perspectives on Divorce: Living Arrangements' (2000) 38 *Family and Conciliation Courts Review* 446–461.

Family Court of Australia, *Children's Cases Program News & Reviews* (Issue 2, 2005). Available at: http://www.familycourt.gov.au/wps/wcm/resources/file/ebc5e804ce98d04/CCPnewsletter_02-2005.pdf.

Family Law Council, *Pathways for Children: A Review of Children's Representation in Family Law* (2004), Australian Government: Attorney-General's Department. Available at: http://www.ag.gov.au/www/agd/agd.nsf/Page/FamilyLawCouncil_Publications_ReportstotheAttorney-General_PathwaysforChildren-Areviewofchildrensrepresentationinfamilylaw.

Felner, R D, L Terre, S Farber, J Primavera and T A Bishop, 'Child Custody: Practices and Perspectives of Legal Professionals' (1985) 14 *Journal of Clinical Child Psychology* 27–34.

Felner, R D, L Terre, A Goldfarb, S Farber, J Primavera, T A Bishop and M S Aber, 'Party Status of Children during Marital Dissolution: Child Preference and Legal Representation in Custody Decisions' (1985) 14 *Journal of Clinical Child Psychology* 42–48.

Fisher, C B, 'Integrating Science and Ethics in Research with High-risk Children and Youth' (1993) 7 *SRCD Social Policy Report* (no. 4) 1–27.

Fondacaro, M R, E M Brank, J Stuart, S Villanueva-Abraham, J Luescher and P S McNatt, 'Identity Orientation, Voice, and Judgments of Procedural Justice During Late Adolescence' (2006) 35 *Journal of Youth and Adolescence* 987–997.

Fondacaro, M R, S L Jackson and J Luescher, 'Toward the Assessment of Procedural and Distributive Justice in Resolving Family Disputes' (2002) 15 *Social Justice Research* 341–371.

Fortin, J, *Children's Rights and the Developing Law* (Lexis Nexis, 2003; 2nd ed).

Foster, H H and D J Freed, 'Child Custody (Part One)' (1964) 39 *New York University Law Review* 423–443.

Fox Harding, L, *Perspectives in Child Care Policy* (Longman, 1997; 2nd ed).

Frankel, S, 'Researching Children's Morality: Developing Research Methods that Allow Children's Involvement in Discourses Relevant to their Everyday Lives' (2007) Available at: http://www.childhoodstoday.org/download.php?id=8 (accessed 26 August 2008).

Fretchling, J, L Sharp and Westat Inc (eds), *User Friendly Handbook for Mixed Method Evaluations* (Directorate for Education and Human Resources, August 1997). Available at: http://www.nsf.gov/pubs/1997/nsf97153/start.htm (accessed 10 October 2007).

Frost, L, 'Children's Rights to be Heard about Family Life and Privacy—When the Family Falls Apart' in N Lowe and G Douglas, *Families Across Frontiers* (Martinus Nijhoff, 1996) pp 165–178.

Funder, K, *Remaking Families: Adaptation of Parents and Children to Divorce* (Australian Institute of Family Studies, 1996).

Galanter, M, 'Worlds of Deals: Using Negotiation to Teach about Legal Process' (1984) 34 *Journal of Legal Education* 268–276.

Garrison, E G, 'Children's Competence to Participate in Divorce Custody Decision-Making' (1991) 20 *Journal of Clinical Child Psychology* 78–87.

Garwood, F, 'Children in Conciliation—The Experience of Involving Children in Conciliation' (1990) 28 *Family and Conciliation Courts Review* 43–51.

Geldof, B, 'The Real Love that Dare not Speak its Name: A Sometimes Coherent Rant' in A Bainham, B Lindley, M Richards and L Trinder (eds), *Children and their Families: Contact, Rights and Welfare* (Hart Publishing, 2003) pp 171–200.

Gollop, M, A B Smith and N J Taylor, 'Children's Involvement in Custody and Access Arrangements after Parental Separation' (2000) 12 *Child and Family Law Quarterly* 383–399.

Goodnow, J J, 'Parenting and the "Transmission" and "Internalization" of Values: From Social-Cultural Perspectives to Within-Family Analyses' in J E Grusec and L Kuczynski (eds), *Handbook of Parenting and the Transmission of Values* (Wiley, 1997) pp 333–361.

Graham, A and R Fitzgerald, 'Taking Account of the "To and Fro" of Children's Experiences in Family Law' (2006) 31 *Children Australia* 30–36.

Gray, A and P Martin, *The Role of Counsel for the Child: Research Report* (Department for Courts, Wellington, 1998).

Greene, S, 'Child Development: Old Themes, New Directions' in M Woodhead, D Faulkner and K Littleton (eds), *Making Sense of Social Development* (Routledge and Open University Press, 1999) pp 250–268.

Greene, S and D Hogan (eds), *Researching Children's Experience: Approaches and Methods* (Sage, 2005).

Grimes, A and J McIntosh, 'Emerging Practice in Child-Inclusive Divorce Mediation' (2004) 10 *Journal of Family Studies* 113–120.

Guggenheim, M, *What's Wrong with Children's Rights?* (Harvard University Press, 2005).

Hale, B, 'Children's Participation in Family Law Decision-Making: Lessons from Abroad' (2006) 20 *Australian Journal of Family Law* 119–126.

Halse, C and A Honey, 'Unraveling Ethics: Illuminating the Moral Dilemmas of Research Ethics' (2005) 30 *Signs: Journal of Women in Culture and Society* 2141–2162.

Harman, H, 'Listening to Children: In Open and Accountable Family Courts' speech at *Care and Health/CAFCASS Conference 'Opening Up the Family Courts: An Open or Closed Case?'* (Millennium Mayfair Hotel, London, 30 October 2006). Available at: http://www.dca.gov.uk/speeches/2006/sp061030b.htm.

Harrison, M, *A Better Way* (Family Court of Australia, 2007).

Hetherington, M E, 'Should we Stay Together for the Sake of the Children?' in M E Hetherington (ed), *Coping with Divorce, Single Parenting and Remarriage: A Risk and Resiliency Perspective* (Lawrence Erlbaum, 1999) pp 93–116.

Hetherington, M E and J Kelly, *For Better or for Worse: Divorce Reconsidered* (W W Norton & Company, 2002).

Hewlett, W, 'Accessing the Parental Mind through the Heart: A Case Study in Child-Inclusive Mediation' (2007) 13 *Journal of Family Studies* 94–103.

Hicks, A J and J A Lawrence, 'Children's Criteria for Procedural Justice: Developing a Young People's Procedural Justice Scale' (1993) 6 *Social Justice Research* 163–182.

Hogan, D, 'Researching "The Child" in Developmental Psychology' in S Greene and D Hogan (eds), *Researching Children's Experience: Approaches and Methods* (Sage, 2005; 2ⁿᵈ ed) pp 22–41.

Hogan, D M, D Halpenny and S Greene, 'Change and Continuity after Parental Separation: Children's Experiences of Family Transitions in Ireland' (2003) 10 *Childhood* 163–180.

Holmes, J G and G Levinger, 'Paradoxical Effects of Closeness in Relationships on Perceptions of Justice: An Interdependence-Theory Perspective' in M J Lerner and G Mikula (eds), *Entitlement and the Affectional Bond: Justice in Close Relationships,* (Plenum Press, 1994) pp 149–173.

House of Representatives, Standing Committee on Family and Community Affairs, *Every Picture Tells a Story: Report of the Inquiry into Child Custody Arrangements in the Event of Family Separation* (Parliament of Australia, 2003).

Hunt, J and C Roberts, *Child Contact with Non-Resident Parents* (Family Policy Briefing 3, Department of Social Policy and Social Work, University of Oxford, 2004).

Hunter, R, 'Child-Related Proceedings under Pt VII Div 12A of the Family Law Act: What the Children's Cases Pilot Program Can and Can't Tell Us' (2006) 20 *Australian Journal of Family Law* 227–248.

—— 'Close Encounters of a Judicial Kind: "Hearing" Children's "Voices" in Family Law Proceedings' (2007) 19 *Child and Family Law Quarterly* 283–303.

James, A L and A James, 'Pump Up the Volume: Listening to Children in Separation and Divorce' (1999) 6 *Childhood* 189–206.

James, A and A Prout (eds), *Constructing and Reconstructing Childhood: Contemporary Issues in the Sociological Study of Childhood* (Falmer Press, 1997; 2ⁿᵈ ed).

James, A and A Prout, 'Strategies and Structures: Towards a New Perspective on Children's Experiences of Family Life' in J Brannen and M O Brien (eds), *Children In Families: Research And Policy* (Falmer Press, 1996).

Jans, M, 'Children as Citizens: Towards a Contemporary Notion of Child Participation' (2004) 11 *Childhood* 27–44.

Jenkins, R L, 'Maxims in Child Custody Cases' (1977) 26 *The Family Coordinator* 385–389.

Jessop, D J, 'Family Relationships as Viewed by Parents and Adolescents: A Specification' (1981) 43 *Journal of Marriage and the Family* 95–107.

Johansson, K and T Palm, 'Children in Trouble with the Law: Child Justice in Sweden and South Africa' (2003) 17 *International Journal of Law, Policy and the Family* 308–337.

Jones, J C, 'Judicial Questioning of Children in Custody and Visitation Proceedings' (1984) 18 *Family Law Quarterly* 43–91.

Jones, E and P Parkinson, 'Child Sexual Abuse, Access and the Wishes of Children' (1995) 9 *International Journal of Law and the Family* 54–85.

Joyal, R and A Queniart, 'Enhancing the Child's Point of View in Custody and Access Cases in Quebec: Preliminary Results of a Study Conducted in Quebec' (2002) 19 *Canadian Journal of Family Law* 173–192.

Kaltenborn, K-F, 'Children's and Young People's Experiences in Various Residential Arrangements: A Longitudinal Study to Evaluate Criteria for Custody and Residence Decision-Making' (2001) 31 *British Journal of Social Work* 81–17.

——'Individualization, Family Transitions and Children's Agency' (2001) 8 *Childhood* 463–498.

Kaslow, F and L Schwarz, *The Dynamics of Divorce: A Life Cycle Perspective* (Brunner/Mazel, 1987).

Kay, E, M Tisdall, R Bray, K Marshall and A Cleland, 'Children's Participation in Family Law Proceedings: A Step too Far or a Step Too Small?' (2004) 26 *Journal of Social Welfare and Family Law* 17–33.

Kelly, J B, 'Psychological and Legal Interventions for Parents and Children in Custody and Access Disputes: Current Research and Practice' (2002) 10 *Virginia Journal of Social Policy & Law* 129–163.

——'Parenting Plan Models: Ideas and Examples' in B Smyth, N Richardson and G Soriano (eds), *Proceedings of the International Forum on Family Relationships in Transition: Legislative, Practical and Policy Responses*, Canberra 1–2 December 2005 (Australian Institute of Family Studies, 2006).

Kelly, J B and R E Emery, 'Children's Adjustment Following Divorce: Risk and Resilience Perspectives' (2003) 52 *Family Relations* 352–362.

Keough, W, *Child Representation in Family Law* (Law Book Company, 2000).

Kilkelly, U, 'Operationalising Children's Rights: Lessons from Research' (2006) 1 *Journal of Children's Services* 35–45.

King, M, 'The Sociology of Childhood as Scientific Communication: Observations from a Social Systems Perspective' (2007) 14 *Childhood* 193–213.

King, M and C Piper, *How the Law Thinks about Children* (Ashgate, 1995).

Kitzmann, K M and R E Emery, 'Procedural Justice and Parents' Satisfaction in a Field Study of Child Custody Dispute Resolution' (1993) 17 *Law and Human Behavior* 554–567.

Komulainen, S, 'The Ambiguity of the Child's "Voice" in Social Research' (2007) 14 *Childhood* 11–28.

Kroll, B, 'Working with Children' in F Kaganas, M King and C Piper (eds), *Legislating for Harmony: Partnership under the Children Act 1989* (Jessica Kingsley, 1995) pp 89–101.

Kronborg, A and I L Svendsen, 'Children's Right to be Heard: The Interplay between Human Rights and National Law' in P LØdrup and E Modvar (eds), *Family Life and Human Rights*, (Gyldendal Akademisk, 2004) pp 405–416.

Kuczynski, L, 'Beyond Bidirectionality: Bilateral Conceptual Frameworks for Understanding Dynamics in Parent-Child Relations' in L Kuczynski (ed), *Handbook of Dynamics in Parent-Child Relations* (Sage Publications, 2003) pp 3–24.

Kunin, C, E Ebbesen and V Konecni, 'Archival Study of Decision-making in Child Custody Disputes' (1992) 48 *Journal of Clinical Psychology* 564–573.

Lamb, M E, R Sternberg and R A Thompson, 'The Effects of Divorce and Custody Arrangements on Children's Behavior, Development, and Adjustment' (1997) 35 *Family and Conciliation Courts Review* 393–404.

Lansdown, G, 'Children's Rights to Participation and Protection: A Critique' in C Cloke and M Davies (eds), *Participation and Empowerment in Child Protection* (Wiley, 1995) pp 19–38.

Lansdown, G, *Taking Part: Children's Participation in Decision-Making* (Institute of Public Policy Research, London, 1995).

Landsman, K J and M L Minow, 'Lawyering for the Child: Principles of Representation in Custody and Visitation Disputes Arising from Divorce' (1978) 87 *Yale Law Review* 1126–1190.

Larson, R and M Richards, *Divergent Realities* (Basic Books, 1994).

Laumann-Billings, L and R Emery, 'Distress among Young Adults from Divorced Families' (2000) 14 *Journal of Family Psychology* 671–687.

Law Society of New South Wales, *Representation Principles—A Guide for Children's Lawyers, 2000.*

Lawrence, J, 'The Developing Child and the Law' in G Monahan and L Young (eds), *Children and the Law in Australia* (Lexis Nexis, 2008) pp 83–104.

Lempp, R, 'Child Welfare and the Law: A Medical and Psychiatric Viewpoint' in F Bates (ed), *The Child and the Law: The Proceedings of the First World Conference of the International Society on Family Law, Berlin, 1975* (Dobbs Ferry, 1976) vol 1, cited by A Lutzyk, 'Investigation of Children's Custodial Wishes' (1979) 14 *Australian Journal of Social Issues* 218–229, at 219.

L'Heureux-Dubé, C, 'A Response to Remarks by Dr. Judith Wallerstein on the Long-term Impact of Divorce on Children' (1998) 36 *Family and Conciliation Courts Review* 384–391.

Lin, I-F and S S McLanahan, 'Parental Beliefs About Nonresident Fathers' Obligations and Rights' (2007) 69 *Journal of Marriage and Family* 382–398.

Lind, E A, R Kanfer and P C Earley, 'Voice, Control, and Procedural Justice: Instrumental and Noninstrumental Concerns in Fairness Judgments' (1990) 59 *Journal of Personality and Social Psychology* 952–959.

Lind, E A and T R Tyler, *The Social Psychology of Procedural Justice* (Plenum Press, 1988).

Lister, R, 'Why Citizenship: Where, When and How Children?' (2007) 8 *Theoretical Inquiries in Law* 693–718. Available at: http://www.bepress.com/til/default/vol8/iss2/art13 (accessed November 2007).

Littner, N, 'The Effects on Child of Family Disruption and Separation from One or Both Parents' (1973) 11 *Reports of Family Law* 1–15.

Lombard, F, 'Judicial Interviewing of Children in Custody Cases: An Empirical and Analytical Study' (1984) 17 *UC Davis Law Review* 807–851.

Lowe, N and M Murch, 'Children's Participation in the Family Justice System—Translating Principles into Practice' (2001) 13 *Child and Family Law Quarterly* 137–158.

Lutzyk, A, 'Investigation of Children's Custodial Wishes' (1979) 14 *Australian Journal of Social Issues* 218–229.

Lyon, C, 'Children's Participation in Private Law Proceedings with Particular Emphasis on the Questions of Meetings Between the Judge and the Child in Family Proceedings' in The Rt Hon Lord Justice Thorpe and E Clarke (eds), *No Fault or Flaw. The Future of the Family Law Act 1996* (Jordans, 2000) pp 67–79.

Lyon, C, E Surrey and J E Timms, 'Effective Support Services for Children and Young People when Parental Relationships Breakdown—A Child-Centred Approach' (Calouste Gulbenkian Foundation, 1999).

Maccoby, E E and R H Mnookin, *Dividing the Child: Social and Legal Terms of Custody* (Harvard University Press, 1992).

Mantle, G, J Leslie, S Parsons and R Shaffer, 'Establishing Children's Wishes and Feelings for Family Court Reports: The Significance Attached to the Age of the Child (2006) 13 *Childhood* 499–518.

Mantle, G, T Moules, K Johnson, J Leslie, S Parsons and R Shaffer, 'Establishing Children's Wishes and Feelings for Family Court Reports' (2007) 37 *British Journal of Social Work* 785–805.

Marchant, R and P Kirby, 'The Participation of Young Children: Communication, Consultation and Involvement' in B Neale (ed), *Young Children's Citizenship: Ideas into Practice* (Joseph Rowntree Foundation, 2004) pp 92–163.

Marquard, E, *Between Two Worlds: The Inner Lives of Children of Divorce* (Three Rivers Press, 2005).

Marshall, K, *Children's Rights in the Balance: The Participation-Protection Debate* (The Stationery Office, 1997).

Masson, J, 'Paternalism, Participation and Placation: Young People's Experiences of Representation in Child Protection Proceedings in England and Wales' in J Dewar and S Parker (eds), *Family Law: Processes, Practices, Pressures* (Hart Publishing, 2003) pp 79–98.

Matthews, S H, 'Window on the "New" Sociology of Childhood' (2007) 1 *Sociology Compass* 322–334.

May, V and C Smart, 'Silence in Court?: Hearing Children in Residence and Contact Disputes' (2004) 16 *Child and Family Law Quarterly* 305–316.

Mayall, B (ed), *Children's Childhoods: Observed and Experienced* (Falmer Press, 1994).

McDonald, M, *Children's Perceptions of Access and their Adjustment in the Post-Separation Period* (Research report no. 9, Family Court of Australia, Office of the Chief Executive, 1990).

McIntosh, J, 'Child-Inclusive Divorce Mediation: Report on a Qualitative Research Study' (2000) 18 *Mediation Quarterly* 55–69.

——'Enduring Conflict in Parental Separation: Pathways of Impact on Child Development' (2003) 9 *Journal of Family Studies* 63–80.

——*The Children's Cases Pilot Project: An Exploratory Study of Impacts on Parenting Capacity and Child Well-Being* (Family Transitions, 2006).

——*Child Inclusion as a Principle and as Evidence-Based Practice: Applications to Family Law Services and Related Sectors* (AFRC Issues no 1, Australian Family Relationships Clearinghouse, 2007).

McIntosh, J, D Bryant and K Murray, 'Evidence of a Different Nature: The Child-Responsive and Less Adversarial Initiatives of the Family Court of Australia' (2008) 46 *Family Court Review* 125–136.

McIntosh, J and C Long, *Children Beyond Dispute: A Prospective Study Of Outcomes from Child Focused and Child Inclusive Post-Separation Family Dispute Resolution* (Final Report to the Attorney-General's Department, 2006). Available at: http://www.ag.gov.au/www/agd/agd.nsf/Page/Publications_ChildrenBeyondDispute-October2006.

McIntosh, J, Y Wells, B Smyth and C Long, 'Child-Focused and Child-Inclusive Divorce Mediation: Comparative Outcomes from a Prospective Study of Postseparation Adjustment' (2008) 46 *Family Court Review* 105–124.

McNamee, S, A L James and A James, 'Can Children's Voices be Heard in Family Law Proceedings? Family Law and the Construction of Childhood in England and Wales' (2003) 16 *Representing Children* 168–178.

Meggs, G, 'Issues in Divorce Mediation Methodology and Ethics' (1993) 4 *Australian Dispute Resolution Journal* 198–209.

Melli, M S, P R Brown and M Cancian, 'Child Custody in a Changing World: A Study of Post-Divorce Arrangements in Wisconsin' (1997) *University of Illinois Law Review* 773–800.

Ministry of Justice, *Separate Representation of Children: Summary of Responses to a Consultation Paper* (London, 2007). Available at: http://www.justice.gov.uk/docs/cp2006-responses.pdf.

Minow, M, 'Interpreting Rights: An Essay For Robert Cover' (1987) 96 *Yale Law Journal* 1860–2017.

Mitchell, A, *Children in the Middle: Living Through Divorce* (Tavistock Publications, 1985).

Mnookin, R H, 'Child-Custody Adjudication: Judicial Functions in the Face of Indeterminacy' (1975) 39 *Law & Contemporary Problems* 226–293.

Moloney, L and J McIntosh, 'Child-Responsive Practices in Australian Family Law: Past Problems and Future Directions' (2004) 10 *Journal of Family Studies* 71–86.

Morrow, V, *Understanding Families: Children's Perspectives* (National Children's Bureau, 1998).

—— 'Perspectives on Children's Agency Within Families' in L Kuczynski (ed), *Handbook of Dynamics in Parent-Child Relations* (Sage Publications, 2003) pp 109–129.

Morrow, V, 'Dilemmas in Children's Participation in England' in A Invernizzi and J Williams (eds), *Children and Citizenship* (Sage Publications, 2007) pp 120–130.

Moylan, A, 'Children's Participation in Proceedings—The View from Europe' in M Thorpe and J Cadbury (eds), *Hearing the Children* (Family Law, 2004) pp 171–185.

Murch, M, G Douglas, L Scanlan, A Perry, C Lisles, K Bader and M Borkowski, *Safeguarding Children's Welfare in Uncontentious Divorce: A Study of S41 of the Matrimonial Causes Act* (Lord Chancellor's Department, Research Series 7/99).

Neale, B, 'Dialogues with Children: Children, Divorce and Citizenship' (2002) 9 *Childhood* 455–475.

Neale, B and J Flowerdew, 'Time, Texture and Childhood: The Contours of Longitudinal Qualitative Research' (2003) 6 *International Journal of Social Research Methodology* 189–199.

—— 'New Structures, New Agency: The Dynamics of Child-Parent Relationships after Divorce' (2007) 15 *International Journal of Children's Rights* 25–42.

230   *References*

Neale, B and C Smart, 'Agents or Dependants? Struggling to Listen to Children in Family Law and Family Research' (Working Paper 3, Centre for Research on Family, Kinship and Childhood, University of Leeds, 1998).

——*Good to Talk: Conversations with Children after Divorce* (Report for the Nuffield Foundation, 2001).

Neugebauer, R, 'Divorce, Custody and Visitation: The Child's Point of View' (1989) 12 *Journal of Divorce* 153–168.

Nicholson, A, (Chief Justice, Family Court of Australia), *Children and Young People—the Law and Human Rights* (Sir Richard Blackburn Lecture 14 May 2002, Canberra). Available at: http://www.familycourt.gov.au/wps/wcm/connect/FCOA/home/publications/papers_and_reports/archived_papers/FCOA_pr_Children_Young_People.

O'Quigley, A, *Listening to Children's Views: The Findings and Recommendations of Recent Research* (Joseph Rowntree Foundation, 2000).

Oakley, A, 'People's Ways of Knowing: Gender and Methodology' in S Hood, B Mayall and S Oliver (eds), *Critical Issues in Social Research: Power and Prejudice* (Oxford University Press, 1999).

Pahl, J, *Money and Marriage* (Palgrave Macmillan, 1989).

Paquin, G, 'Protecting the Interests of Children in Divorce Mediation' (1987–88) 26 *Journal of Family Law* 279–315.

——'The Child's Input in the Mediation Process: Promoting the Best Interests of the Child' (1988) 22 *Mediation Quarterly* 69–81.

Parkinson, P, 'The Child Participation Principle in Child Protection Law in New South Wales' (2001) 9 *International Journal of Children's Rights* 259–272.

——'Research and Promises of Confidentiality to Children' (2002) 16 *Australian Journal of Family Law* 2–4.

——'Family Law and the Indissolubility of Parenthood' (2006) 40 *Family Law Quarterly* 237–280.

——'Keeping in Contact: The Role of Family Relationship Centres in Australia' (2006) 18 *Child and Family Law Quarterly* 157–174.

——'The Realities of Relocation: Messages from Judicial Decisions' (2008) 22 *Australian Journal of Family Law* 35–55.

——'The Past Caretaking Standard in Comparative Perspective' in R Wilson (ed), *Reconceiving the Family: Critical Reflections on the American Law Institute's Principles of the Law of Family Dissolution* (Cambridge University Press, 2006) pp 446–471.

Parkinson, P and J Cashmore, 'Judicial Conversations with Children in Parenting Disputes: The Views of Australian Judges' (2007) 21 *International Journal of Law, Policy and the Family* 160–189.

Parkinson, P, J Cashmore and J Single, 'Adolescents' Views on the Fairness of Parenting and Financial Arrangements after Separation' (2005) 43 *Family Court Review* 429–444.

——'Parents' and Children's Views on Talking to Judges in Parenting Disputes in Australia' (2007) 21 *International Journal of Law, Policy and the Family* 84–107.

Parkinson, P and B Smyth, 'Satisfaction and Dissatisfaction with Father–Child Contact Arrangements in Australia' (2004) 16 *Child and Family Law Quarterly* 289–304.

Perlesz, A and J Lindsay, 'Methodological Triangulation in Researching Families: Making Sense of Dissonant Data' (2003) 6 *International Journal of Social Research Methodology* 25–40.

Piper, C, 'Ascertaining the Wishes and Feelings of the Child' (1997) *Family Law* 796–800.

——'Assumptions about Children's Best Interests' (2000) 22 *Journal of Social Welfare and Family Law* 261–276.

——'The Wishes and Feelings of the Child' in S Sclater and C Piper (eds), *Undercurrents of Divorce* (Ashgate, 1999).

Potter, M, 'The Family in the 21st Century' paper at *17th World Congress of the International Association of Youth and Family Judges and Magistrates* (Belfast, 28 August 2006). Available at: http://www.judiciary.gov.uk/publications_media/speeches/2006/sp280806.htm.

Pryor, J and R Emery, 'Children of Divorce' in P Pufall and R Unsworth (eds), *Rethinking Childhood* (Rutgers University Press, 2004).

Pryor, J and B Rodgers, *Children in Changing Families: Life after Parental Separation* (Blackwell, 2001).

Raitt, F E, 'Judicial Discretion and Methods of Ascertaining the Views of a Child' (2004) 16 *Child and Family Law Quarterly* 151–164.

——'Hearing Children in Family Law Proceedings: Can Judges Make a Difference?' (2007) 19 *Child and Family Law Quarterly* 204–224.

Rešetar, B and R Emery, 'Children's Rights in European Legal Proceedings: Why Are Family Practices So Different from Legal Theories?' (2008) 46 *Family Court Review* 65–77.

Rhoades, H, 'The Rise and Rise of Shared Parenting Laws' (2002) 19 *Canadian Journal of Family Law* 75–113.

Ribbens McCarthy, J, J Holland and V Gillies, 'Multiple Perspectives on the "Family" Lives of Young People: Methodological and Theoretical Issues in Case Study Research' (2003) 6 *International Journal of Social Research Methodology* 1–23.

Richards, M, 'But What about the Children? Some Reflections on the Divorce White Paper' (1995) 7 *Child and Family Law Quarterly* 223–227.

Roche, J, 'Children: Rights, Participation and Citizenship' (1999) 6 *Childhood* 475.

Rodgers, B and J Pryor, *Divorce and Separation: The Outcomes for Children* (Joseph Rowntree Foundation, 1998).

Ruschena, E, M Prior, A Sanson and D Smart, 'A Longitudinal Study of Adolescent Adjustment Following Family Transitions' (2005) 46 *Journal of Child Psychology and Psychiatry* 353–363.

Ryrstedt, E and T Mattsson, 'Children's Rights to Representation: A Comparison between Sweden and England' (2008) 22 *International Journal of Law, Policy and the Family* 135–147.

Sameroff, A, 'Transactional Models in Early Social Relations' (1975) 18 *Human Development* 65–79.

——'The Social Context of Development' in M Woodhead, R Carr and P Light (eds), *Becoming a Person: Child Development in Social Context* (Taylor & Francis/Routledge, 1991) vol 1, pp 167–189.

Sandbaek, M, 'Adult Images of Childhood and Research on Client Children' (1999) 2 *International Journal of Social Research Methodology* 191–202.

Sandor, D, 'A More Future-Focused Approach to Children's Hearings in the Family Court' (2004) 18 *Australian Journal of Family Law* 5–12.

Sawyer, C, 'The Competence of Children to Participate in Family Proceedings' (1995) 7 *Child and Family Law Quarterly* 180–195.

Sawyer, C, 'One Step Forward, Two Steps Back—The European Convention on the Exercise of Children's Rights' (1999) 11 *Child and Family Law Quarterly* 151–170.

——'Ascertaining the Child's Wishes and Feelings' (2000) 30 *Family Law* 170–174.

——'Applications by Children: Still Seen But Not Heard?' (2001) 117 *Law Quarterly Review* 203–207.

Schepard, A, *Children, Courts and Custody* (Cambridge University Press, 2004).

Schick, A, 'Behavioral and Emotional Differences between Children of Divorce and Children from Intact Families: Clinical Significance and Mediating Processes' (2002) 61 *Swiss Journal of Psychology* 5–14.

Schneider, C, 'Discretion and Rules: A Lawyer's View' in K Hawkins (ed), *The Uses of Discretion* (Clarendon, 1992).

Schofield, G, 'Making Sense of the Ascertainable Wishes and Feelings of Insecurely Attached Children (1998) 10 *Child and Family Law Quarterly* 363–375.

Scott, E S, N D Reppucci and M Aber, 'Children's Preferences in Adjudicated Custody Decisions' (1988) 22 *Georgia Law Review* 1035–1078.

Siegal, M, 'Concern for the Conversational Environment: Questioning Children in Custody Disputes' (1991) 22 *Professional Psychology: Research And Practice* 473–478.

Siegel, D M and S Hurley, 'The Role of the Child's Preference in Custody Proceedings' (1977) 11 *Family Law Quarterly* 1–58.

Simons, R L, L B Whitbeck, J Beaman and R D Conger, 'The Impact of Mother's Parenting, Involvement by Nonresidential Fathers, and Parental Conflict on the Adjustment of Adolescent Children' (1994) 56 *Journal of Marriage and Family* 356–374.

Smart, C, 'Divorce in England 1950–2000: A Moral Tale. CAVA Workshop Paper 2' prepared for *Workshop One: Frameworks for Understanding Policy Change and Culture* (1999).

——'Changing Family Relationships' keynote address presented at *Law Conference* (Christchurch, New Zealand, 4–8 October 2001).

——'Children's Voices' plenary address given at the *25th Anniversary Conference, Justice, Courts & Community: The Continuing Challenge, Family Courts of Australia* (Sydney, Australia, Thursday 26–Sunday 29 July 2001).

Smart, C and B Neale, ' "It's My Life Too"—Children's Perspectives on Post-Divorce Parenting' (2000) 30 *Family Law* 163–169.

——*Family Fragments?* (Polity Press, 1999).

Smart, C, B Neale and A Wade, *The Changing Experience of Childhood: Families and Divorce* (Polity Press, 2001).

Smart, C, A Wade and B Neale, ' "Objects of Concern"?—Children and Divorce' (1999) 11 *Child and Family Law Quarterly* 365–376.

Smith, W, 'Dads Want Their Day: Fathers Charge Legal Bias Towards Moms Hamstrings them as Full-Time Parents' (2003) 89 *ABA Journal* 38–43.

Smith, A and M Gollop, 'Children's Perspectives on Access Visits' (June 2001) *Butterworths Family Law Journal* 259–266.

Smith, A B, N Taylor and P Tapp, 'Rethinking Children's Involvement in Decision-Making after Parental Separation' (2003) 10 *Childhood* 203–218.

Smyth, B, 'Parent-Child Contact in Australia: Exploring Five Different Post-Separation Patterns of Parenting' (2005) 19 *International Journal of Law, Policy and the Family* 1–22.

——'Time to Rethink Time? The Experience of Children After Divorce' (2005) 71 *Family Matters* 4–10.

Smyth, B and L Moloney, 'Changes in Patterns of Post-Separation Parenting over Time: A Brief Review' (2008) 14 *Journal of Family Studies* 7–22.

Smyth, B and R Weston, *A Snapshot of Contemporary Attitudes to Child Support* (Research report no. 13, Australian Institute of Family Studies, 2005).

Sobolewski, J M and V King, 'The Importance of the Coparental Relationship for Non-Resident Fathers' Ties to Children' (2005) 67 *Journal of Marriage and Family* 1196–1212.

Solomon, J and Z Biringen, 'The Continuing Debate about Overnight Visitation: Another Look at the Developmental Research: Commentary on Kelly and Lamb's "Using Child Development Research to Make Appropriate Custody and Access Decisions for Young Children"' (2001) 39 *Family and Conciliation Courts Review* 355–364.

Sorenson, E, J Goldman, L Sheeber, I Albanese, M Ward, L Williamson and C McDanal, 'Judges' Reliance on Psychological, Sociological, and Legal Variables in Contested Custody Decisions' (1997) 27 *Journal of Divorce & Remarriage* 1–24.

Spencer, J R and R H Flin, *The Evidence of Children: The Law and the Psychology* (Blackstone, 1993; 2nd ed).

Stamps, L E, S Kunen and R Lawyer, 'Judicial Attitudes Regarding Custody and Visitation Issues' (1996) 25 *Journal of Divorce & Remarriage* 23–37.

Starnes, C, 'Swords in the Hands of Babes: Rethinking Custody Interviews after Troxel' (2003) *Wisconsin Law Review* 115–169.

Starr, L, *Counsel of Perfection* (Oxford University Press, 1996).

Steinberg, L, 'We Know Some Things: Parent-Adolescent Relationships in Retrospect and Prospect' (2001) 11 *Journal of Research on Adolescence* 1–19.

Sternlight, J R and J K Robbennolt, 'Good Lawyers Should Be Good Psychologists: Insights for Interviewing and Counseling Clients' (2008) 23 *Ohio State Journal on Dispute Resolution* 437–548.

Tapp, P, 'Judges are Human Too: Conversation between the Judge and a Child as a Means of Giving Effect to Section 6 of the Care of Children Act 2004' (2006) *New Zealand Law Review* 35–74.

Taylor, N, 'What do We Know about Involving Children and Young People in Family Law Decision Making? A Research Update' (2006) 20 *Australian Journal of Family Law* 154–178.

Taylor, N J, M Gollop and A B Smith, 'Children and Young People's Perspectives on their Legal Representation' in A B Smith, N J Taylor and M Gollop (eds), *Children's Voices: Research, Policy and Practice* (2000, Pearson Education) pp 110–133.

Taylor, N J, M Gollop, A B Smith and P F Tapp, *The Role of Counsel for the Child—Perspectives of Children, Young People and their Lawyers: Research Report* (Department for Courts, Wellington, 1999).

Taylor, N, P Tapp and M Henaghan 'Respecting Children's Participation in Family Law Proceedings' (2007) 15 *International Journal of Children's Rights* 61–82.

Tein, J-Y, M Roosa and M Michaels, 'Agreement between Parent and Child Reports on Parental Behaviors' (1994) 56 *Journal of Marriage and the Family* 341–355.

Théry, I, '"The Interest of the Child" and the Regulation of the Post-Divorce Family' (1986) 14 *International Journal of the Sociology of Law* 341–358.

Thibaut, J and L Walker, *Procedural Justice: A Psychological Analysis* (Erlbaum, 1975).

Thomas, I and T Pietropiccolo, 'Children's Wishes and Legal Outcomes: Is there a Relationship?' in *Proceedings First Australian Family Research Conference* (Institute of Family Studies, 1984) vol 2, pp 333–385.

Treseder, P, 'Involving and Empowering Children and Young People: Overcoming the Barriers' in C Cloke and M Davies (eds), *Participation and Empowerment in Child Protection* (Wiley, 1995) pp 207–231.

Trinder, L, 'Competing Constructions of Childhood: Children's Rights and Children's Wishes in Divorce' (1997) 19 *Journal of Social Welfare and Family Law* 291–305.

Tyler, T R and P Degoey, 'Community, Family, and the Social Good: The Psychological Dynamics of Procedural Justice and Social Identification' in G B Melton (ed), *The Individual, the Family, and Social Good: Personal Fulfillment in Times of Change* (University of Nebraska Press, 1995) vol 42, pp 53–91.

Tyler, T R and E A Lind, 'A Relational Model of Authority in Groups' in M Zanna (ed), *Advances in Experimental Social Psychology* (Academic Press, 1992) vol 25, pp 115–191.

United Nations Committee on the Rights of the Child, *General Guidelines Regarding the Form and Content of Initial Reports to be Submitted by States Parties Under Article 44, Paragraph 1(a), of the Convention: CRC/C/5* (Committee on the Rights of the Child, 1991). Available at: http://www.unhchr.ch/tbs/doc.nsf/(Symbol)/CRC.C.5.En?Opendocument

Van den Bos, K, H Wilke and E A Lind 'Evaluating Outcomes by Means of the Fair Process Effect: Evidence for Different Processes in Fairness and Satisfaction Judgments' (1998) 74 *Journal of Personality and Social Psychology* 1493–1503.

van der Veer, R and J Valsiner, *Understanding Vygotsky: A Quest for Synthesis* (Blackwell Publishers, 1991).

Van Krieken, R, 'The "Best Interests of the Child" and Parental Separation: on the "Civilizing of Parents"' (2005) 68 *The Modern Law Review* 25–48.

Vygotsky, L S, 'Mastery of Memory and Thinking' in M Cole, V John-Steiner, S Scribner and E Souberman (eds), *Mind in Society: The Development of Higher Psychological Processes* (Harvard University Press, 1978) pp 38–51.

—— *Thought and Language* (MIT Press, 1986; 7th printing ed).

Walczak, Y and S Burns, *Divorce: The Child's Point of View* (Harper & Row, 1984).

Walker, J, 'FAInS—A New Approach for Family Lawyers?' (2004) 34 *Family Law* 436–441.

Waller, E M and A E Daniel, 'Purpose and Utility of Child Custody Evaluations: From the Perspective of Judges' (2004) 32 *Journal of Psychiatry and Law* 5–27.

Wallerstein, J S and J B Kelly, *Surviving the Break Up: How Children and Parents Cope with Divorce* (Grant McIntyre, 1980).

Warin, J, Y Solomon and C Lewis, 'Swapping Stories: Comparing Plots: Triangulating Individual Narratives within Families' (2007) 10 *International Journal of Social Research Methodology* 121–134.

Warshak, R A, 'Payoffs and Pitfalls of Listening to Children' (2003) 52 *Family Relations* 373–384.

Weinstein, J, 'And Never the Twain Shall Meet: The Best Interests of Children and the Adversary System' (1997–1998) 52 *University of Miami Law Review* 79–175.

Wexler, D B, 'Reflections on the Scope of Therapeutic Jurisprudence' (1995) 1 *Psychology, Public Policy, and Law* 220–236.

Wiles, R, S Heath, G Crow and V Charles, *Informed Consent in Social Research: A Literature Review* (Methods Paper Series) (ESRC National Centre for Research Methods, undated). Available at: www.ncrm.ac.uk/research/outputs/publications/methodsreview/MethodsReviewPaperNCRM-001.pdf.

Williams, S, *Through the Eyes of Young People: Meaningful Child Participation in Family Court Processes* (International Institute for Child Rights and Development, 2008).

Woodhouse, B, 'Re-Visioning Rights for Children' in P Pufall and R Unsworth (eds), *Rethinking Childhood* (Rutgers University Press, 2004) pp 229–243.

Index